Balderdash &

Poppycock

How to Crash an Economy

A Chronological Field Guide to the Financial Crisis and Beyond

1791 to 2008

With a Brief Aftermath and Pondering Points

By

Michael Long

(A cantankerous, grumpy, politically incorrect, old cur; that had to know how we got into this mess and was just derelict enough to take the time to check it out)

"The happiest thing that can be said about democracy... is that it is one of the few systems that has been willing to risk a long period of confusion and mixed purposes for the sake of giving man a chance to grow up in mind and responsibility." **H.A. Overstreet**

Table of Contents

Preface

This was of curiosity born, obsession pursued and panic completed.

A simple asking of what I thought was a straightforward question of, how did we get into this mess? By mess I mean the huge national debt, recession and banking fiasco. I soon learned it was, on one hand, anything but straightforward and on the other simple nearly beyond comprehension. *Was that an oxymoron?* This originally was for my benefit simply because I did not know the answer and realized I had never had any idea what was going on and wanted to understand. Everything I'd heard was wrong. Everything I'd learned was incomplete. Everything I'd been taught was biased. Whether it was from the political left or right it just didn't add up. So, what did happen?

How could any of us everyday sort of folks have seen this coming? Certainly it is so complicated we cannot understand it. Our leaders don't or don't seem to. True enough about understanding the intricacies involved. What I am referring to are the simple and easy for anybody to see sort of things. All it takes is a little time and you'll get the picture and have what you need to call out the morons and make them see daylight. After all, the morons spend most of their time in a place referred to as 'the beltway' and everybody knows where your head is when it is under your belt. *Bad dog. Bad, bad dog.*

They, the greedy huskers (sp.) on Wall Street, in banking and the miscreants we elected to Washington brought this mess about and so did we. I have been corrupted by the spins and lies because I wanted to believe our elected officials were trying to act in our best interest and just didn't take the time to find out what was what for myself. Likely you were in the same boat trying to keep the family fed, sheltered and clothed. Even if I did figure it out what could I have done? A good start would have been to quit using my head for something besides a hat rack or as my father was fond of saying, *"Son you can't go through life like those rocks in the field".*

This has all happened before and it will happen again (*Didn't that start a story about flying kids?*), and again unless we make provisions elsewise. It has happened many times before and our elected representatives should have known better because the information was there and knowledgeable people were telling them not to allow the camels' nose beneath the tent. (*Camels are well known for following their noses. It is also well known, among those with camels, that the last thing you want in your tent is a smelly camel and his thousand fleas.*) The founders of this republic were aware of the dangers of banks and the nature of money and how some would manipulate things to their personal advantage to the detriment of others. It is after all part of the nature of mankind and has happened before throughout history since the ice melted and probably before.

When I say the information was there I mean historically. Not just in the United States but Europe, India, China, ancient Egypt and Rome. This writing will concentrate on the United States with a couple of references to like historical events that the founders of this country were aware.

My hope is anyone reading this will look up the events herein referred to. My explanations are inadequate in providing a profound understanding of anything presented. I believe the main and germane points are accurately set down. Also you will find errors here. Some are debatable and others will be just plain wrong. Nothing will be in error to purposely skew the information or data.

This writing is biased as all things written by a human being are biased. This writing is also not objective as it is incomplete and done by a human being. All errors are mine.

There is no pretense to scholarly work here. It is just information in the common body of knowledge and observations of a mean cantankerous old cur. There are no profound answers either although there certainly needs to be.

I thought about presenting this as I came upon the information and presenting my own illumination as it came, too darn confusing. So what you are about to read is a chronology of events and circumstances with several crass comments interspersed, crass, because the editor vetoed the more colorful/profane/anatomically correct/crude/ lewd ones. As you journey thru this history you may have some of those kinds of comments, I hope so.

To start I set up a database in excel and started looking around for information as to what the National DEBT has been since the United States began and tried to understand our depressed economic times both as a nation and for individuals. From here it snow balled quickly.

The players are the Supreme Court, the House of Representatives and the Senate, Laws (when they passed or didn't pass), civil unrest, civil issues, recessions and depressions, wars, labor conflicts, political parties and other events that may have been important to the evolution of the financial issue or contributed to the culture of the time or provided illumination as to the state of things in general at the time. The financial issue is the point of this effort but cannot stand alone as an issue because everything is inter-related as we engage in life and government as "We the People". I found it unsettling to learn that the Declaration of Independence is not a legal document in the sense that it makes any of the laws by which we are governed. The Republic is truly the first of its kind. Surely it has evolved as painfully as any endeavor of mankind, but it has evolved and tests our ability to govern ourselves.

The yearly history notes are here so you might gain a sense of what was going on at the time and see that the world was a very busy place as the financial part of society evolved. I found this helpful in understanding the dynamics of each era. I also came to understand that the only things that have changed are the tools we use and the toys we play with. Boys still chase girls until the girls catch them, wives are always right (*bad dog*) and slow horses loose races. That is just the ways it is.

My take on all this is in the comments throughout and the conclusions section and will likely tick some people off. In fact I sincerely hope anybody who reads this finds something to tick them off, if not in the information then with me. That works too. Those who have read and commented on this work while it was being developed expressed enjoyment at having been reminded of events they'd forgotten and learning about events they'd not heard of before and looking them up. I hope you look up many events and find much more than what is presented.

Something else to consider as you trudge thru this historical chronology is perspective. 1776 approximates the generally accepted beginning of the Industrial Revolution. Why bring up the Industrial Revolution? Western standards of living would not have come about without the associated efficiencies of the Industrial Revolution.

Hope you have a good time.

Mike.

Introduction
The world changes each moment.

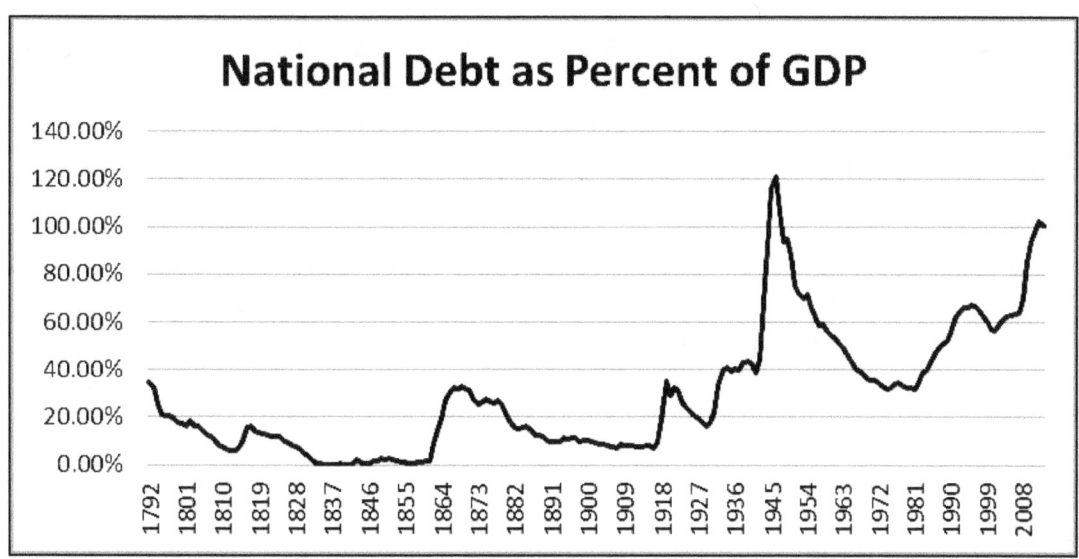

This research began with gathering information and putting it in a database. The first question, what was the National Debt for the country from 1791 (the Constitution) to present. I didn't know! In looking for debt information the topic of Gross Domestic Product kept popping up so I found that and entered it, then population, inflation and on and on. The data has been taken from official government sources and various others with all being found in at least three locations. This took a lot of time but led me to new and enlightening information. I found Wikipedia to be generally a good starting point but not complete or always accurate. If you use any search engine on the internet some the best and most informative sites will be several pages back and I mean easily as many as 50 or more. Some of the numerical data has been averaged rather than relying on a single data source. As an instance the national debt or allusions to its reduction will depend on if you count intra-governmental debt, per example Social Security is required to buy government bonds with whatever it has left over each year. The information is meant as an overview. Rather than getting bogged down in the minutia the big picture is interesting and informative enough.

The National Debt as Percent of Gross Domestic Product chart shown above was initially generated early on. As the research continued I referred back to this chart frequently to gain perspective on the information I was reading. What became apparent was wars typically caused the sharp rises seen in the chart. The most notable exceptions were the 'Great Depression', 1980 and 2008. So what happened in 1980 to start the climb we see in the chart? There was no 'depression' and there was no war. There was 'oil'. But that can't have been the entire reason. Could it? To be candid there was a recession brought on by several factors and there was a war of sorts in 1980 to be discussed during that era.

To appreciate the forthcoming chronology I believe it best to hold several concepts in mind.

Concept 1

'There is nothing new under the sun'... *I believe it.*

We did this to ourselves because we, including me, did not learn from the past. Because we did not learn from the past we were unable to protect ourselves from our own greed and ignorance and the greed and ignorance of others! When we did learn from the past we did too little. Perhaps we had become too polarized in our two party, us or them, political system or perhaps....well I just don't know.

The development of the recent financial affair has been a long time coming. So long that it has happened before many times and will happen again many times unless we learn that history is our friend and keep it close to our hearts and minds.

Really, you say.

Truly, I say.

Concept 2

BOOM and BUST Cycle

The BOOM and BUST Cycle is rather new to mankind as an economic event.

Money is created by the Federal government to be placed into an economy that fundamentally requires GROWTH. That GROWTH is financed by DEBT. The economy is CYCLIC, the BOOM or BUST philosophy. The necessity for GROWTH may be a little hard to wrap one's mind around. *Lord it took me ages.*

When money is loaned, creating DEBT that has interest to be paid against that debt, there must be GROWTH to pay back the money borrowed and the interest attached to that money. GROWTH is essential! Without GROWTH there is no economy because those that lend the money will not get any interest on their money. Beans, they probably would not even get a reasonable portion of the money they loaned back. So why would they loan out money if they cannot get it back with interest. After all it is the interest that they live off of.

When DEBT is created the person or entity in DEBT has to get more money to pay back the money borrowed and the interest against that money. If they don't meet their obligation to return the borrowed money with interest they become an undesirable risk. Who wants to lend money when those asking for it have a record of not repaying their DEBTs? After all, the lender has to make a living from the interest on that money.

CYCLIC is the best part of this whole mess. Without CYCLIC we would have either less of a mess or no mess at all. 'BOOM OR BUST', gotta love it. Goes up ... BOOM. Goes down ... BUST. That is the cycle. The DEBT finances the BOOM and the interest on that DEBT has to be realized before the BUST or it all 'goes to hell in a hand basket' as Granny was fond of saying.

8

(Granny lived through the "Great Depression"; it seems she knew what she was talking about.) Unless there is sufficient money to finance the BOOM then it is a little BOOM and where is the fun in that! So why not borrow lots of money to make a really big BOOM. (Everybody likes big BOOMS....well, guys seem to more than gals .... and it is lots of fun.)

What is the problem with all that? It has always been this way. Everybody knows this. So, what is the problem?

Concept 3

Nobody has a darn clue about Economics. It is all just theory that occasionally works out or in the words of John Kenneth Galbraith **"…the only function of economic forecasting is to make astrology look respectable."**

So maybe it isn't about Economics either. Well, it is about Economics or rather the use of economics in the social political environment.

Concept 4

Democracy as a viable political concept is relatively new to mankind and democracy in the hands of the populace was unheard of before the United States. *I had come to think of England's electorate as being widely Democratic at the time of the revolution but this was untrue as it was limited to the Aristocracy until 1832. Greek and Roman democracy was limited and short lived also. Some will argue this but I really don't care.*

Part of the problem

That a National Bank was not mentioned in the Constitution does not mean it was not a point under discussion before and during the Constitutional Convention. Similarly having all people free in this 'bastion of freedom' was discussed but was such a fiercely contested political issue it was decided remedying it at the time was impossible and would prevent preserving the union of states. So possibly was the issue of a National or Central Bank.

The very early years of the Republic found a national bank being formed and much controversy was generated by the chartering of the first **Bank of the United States**. Much of this controversy consisted of fears of a too strong central government directly controlling banking that would be corruptive and deprive the states of their place in the nation and impinge upon the freedoms so recently won. Another concern was the centralization of wealth and that the National or Central Bank would favor the eastern business concern over the rest of the country should that central bank be privately owned and operated by the same Eastern Business concerns/Bankers. After all history to this point had this to be the case almost universally that central banking created a corrupt centralization of wealth that dominated governments and deprived 'the people'. *Seems our forefathers didn't cotton to the idea of fighting and dying so some folks could get rich off their toil and sacrifice.*

Another important aspect of Democracy is that the voters are a bunch of individuals each with their own idea of what is important and what will best serve their interests. There is nothing really wrong with that. I mean we mostly descended from those crazy folks who started all this and they accomplished something rather remarkable.

9

Concept 5

The Industrial Revolution 1776 falls within the generally accepted dates of the beginning of the industrial revolution as does 1791. Why so wide a range of dates? The dates range in the literature is even wider than 1776 to 1791. It seems the experts all have different ideas as to what constitutes the beginning of the Industrial Revolution just as economists have different ideas about what constitutes a working model for an economy. What is generally agreed upon is that without the change from an agricultural economy to an industrial economy our current standard of living would not be much better than it was 250 years ago. Just keep this in mind as a complete look would take several tens of thousands of pages.

In the beginning - Life with The Articles of Confederation and Perpetual Union & Making a Constitution

There were a bunch of disenfranchised, disillusioned, disenchanted, uppity malcontents who got together and had themselves a revolution. These revolutionaries were also educated and thoughtful folks who had a great notion about a better world where a man's destiny was his own to determine free of governmental control or interference, which some of them called the New World Order. No, this not going to be about Masons or any other sort of like notion! Somewhere along the way they got the crazy idea that the 'people' could govern themselves (this is the New World Order). Because there were thirteen regional governments already in place in the land of these now free crazy people they settled on a Confederation of Perpetual Union and wrote up some Articles of such and proceeded to have a nation, sort of.

Turned out the **Confederation** wasn't working so well, the government of this Perpetual Union was always broke because the 'sovereign states' didn't do so well in paying their allotted share of the National Debt from the Revolution and the central government of the Confederation had no viable means of raising money, so some of the boys got together and decided to have a Constitutional Convention were they'd try again to make a viable new nation.

Some people figured they'd better get at this Constitutional Convention thing because there had been trouble brewing in them thar' hills.

Shays' Rebellion 1786 and 1787

Conditions for rebellion in the states had been developing since during the Revolutionary War. Congress had issued large amounts of paper currency creating inflation in a time when many war supplies had to be purchased from abroad. Such supplies had to be purchased with hard currency, gold or silver, or on credit from those countries that backed the new United States in its battle against Britain.

During the war those who served were either paid little or not at all. The consequence of which was they were unable to pay their bills and taxes. Many returning home during the war came home to find they had no home because creditors had gone to court seeking relief for past due credit or the state or local governments had proceeded against the land owners for back overdue taxes.

The conclusion of the Revolutionary War brought the return of all those who had fought only to find similar circumstances with the additional condition that even four years and more later seemingly most soldiers had not been paid even with the paper money from the Continental Congress, 'script' referred to as 'Continentals'.

After the war importing and manufacturing businesses that relied on materials and goods from abroad found their suppliers demanding payment, upon order, in hard currency which they in turn had, in the course of business, demanded payment from their customers in hard currency and these local merchants were then forced to demand payment in hard currency from their customers and pertinent here, the rural populations of the states had the least access to hard currency, hard currency being gold or silver.

While Shays Rebellion occurred in Massachusetts many of the states suffered similar conditions with their rural citizenry protesting seeking relief from this harsh burden that is more than adequately expressed by Plough Jogger.

> "I have been greatly abused, have been obliged to do more than my part in the war, been loaded with class rates, town rates, province rates, Continental rates and all rates ... been pulled and hauled by sheriffs, constables and collectors, and had my cattle sold for less than they were worth ... The great men are going to get all we have and I think it is time for us to rise and put a stop to it, and have no more courts, nor sheriffs, nor collectors nor lawyers."

Other states had dealt quickly and harshly with such protestors but Massachusetts' governor, John Hancock, took a deliberately patient stance in collection of delinquent taxes and declined to pursue any protestors. This patience while being considerate of the plight of the rural citizens also gave them opportunity to become organized to the extent where armed clashes resulted in death and injury to citizens and members of the states militia.

John Hancock resigned and his successor took a deliberately strong stand against the Rebels with two being hung.

This armed rebellion likely had a significant influence on the upcoming Constitutional Convention.

As an aside Rhode Island also suffered from the same economic conditions but the rural citizenry won elections, took over the government and enacted laws relieving the burdens they had been suffering. A more lengthy examination of Shays Rebellion would be interesting and informative.

This making of a new government wasn't such an easy thing as there wasn't any reference material around about how to make a new nation, let alone a modern democracy with thirteen stiff necked governmental participants and their obviously well-armed and overburdened citizens. Besides, the effort hadn't worked out so well the first time. Anyway, they came up with something but it still had to be ratified. Ratification was not guaranteed just because each of the states had representatives at the Convention. In fact this Constitutional Convention was contentious and heated.

The following quote from Benjamin Franklin addressing the assembled delegates to the Constitutional Convention in 1787 eloquently demonstrates the fallibility of men in the writing of this Constitution and the hope it might endure.

> I CONFESS that I do not entirely approve of this Constitution at present; but, sir, I am not sure I shall never approve of it, for, having lived long, I have experienced many instances of being obliged, by better information or fuller consideration, to change

opinions even on important subjects, which I once thought right, but found to be otherwise. It is therefore that, the older I grow, the more apt I am to doubt my own judgment of others. Most men, indeed, as well as most sects in religion, think themselves in possession of all truth, and that wherever others differ from them, it is so far error. Steele, a Protestant, in a dedication, tells the pope that the only difference between our two churches in their opinions of the certainty of their doctrine is, the Romish Church is infallible, and the Church of England is never in the wrong. But, tho many private persons think almost as highly of their own infallibility as of that of their sect, few express it so naturally as a certain French lady, who, in a little dispute with her sister said: "But I meet with nobody but myself that is always in the right."

In these sentiments, sir, I agree to this Constitution with all its faults—if they are such—because I think a general government necessary for us, and there is no form of government but what may be a blessing to the people if well administered; and I believe, further, that this is likely to be well administered for a course of years, and can only end in despotism, as other forms have done before it, when the people shall become so corrupted as to need despotic government, being incapable of any other. I doubt, too, whether any other convention we can obtain may be able to make a better Constitution; for, when you assemble a number of men, to have the advantage of their joint wisdom, you inevitably assemble with those men all their prejudices, their passions, their errors of opinion, their local interests, and their selfish views. From such an assembly can a perfect production be expected?

It therefore astonishes me, sir, to find this system approaching so near to perfection as it does; and I think it will astonish our enemies, who are waiting with confidence to hear that our counsels are confounded like those of the builders of Babel, and that our States are on the point of separation, only to meet hereafter for the purpose of cutting one another's throats. Thus I consent, sir, to this Constitution, because I expect no better, and because I am not sure that it is not the best. The opinions I have had of its errors I sacrifice to the public good. I have never whispered a syllable of them abroad. Within these walls they were born, and here they shall die. If every one of us, in returning to our constituents, were to report the objections he has had to it, and endeavor to gain partizans in support of them, we might prevent its being generally received, and thereby lose all the salutary effects and great advantages resulting naturally in our favor among foreign nations, as well as among ourselves, from our real or apparent unanimity. Much of the strength and efficiency of any government, in procuring and securing happiness to the people, depends on opinion, on the general opinion of the goodness of that government, as well as of the wisdom and integrity of its governors. I hope, therefore, for our own sakes, as a part of the people, and for the sake of our posterity, that we shall act heartily and unanimously in recommending this Constitution wherever our influence may extend, and turn our future thoughts and endeavors to the means of having it well administered.

On the whole, sir, I cannot help expressing a wish that every member of the convention who may still have objections to it, would, with me, on this occasion, doubt a little of his own infallibility, and, to make manifest our unanimity, put his name to this instrument.

This idea of 'Federalism' was not well favored by all of the citizens so a few fellows got together and wrote a mess of papers commonly referred to as the **Federalist Papers** to plead the case of a stronger federal government under the Constitution. A mess of the other folks were not particularly enamored with this 'Federalism' idea so they wrote a mess of papers commonly referred to as the **Anti-Federalist Papers** to plead their case against a stronger federal government.

The Federalists prevailed and to paraphrase Mister Franklin again, we got us a "Republic, if we can hold it." *Keep this in mind as you follow the chronology. While I had studied 'Political Science' in college I had not understood the full ramifications of the 'Republic'.*

There you go we got us a Democratic Republic, of sovereign states, guided by a Constitution (a **Constitutional Democratic Republic**) and we were off and running. *This might also have something to do with the Anti-Federalist Papers not being nearly as widely read as the Federalist Papers.*

Alas, this Constitution made not provision for many issues of the time, banking and slavery among lots of other issues both of the time and others unimaginable. That the Constitution failed to establish any 'national banking' guidelines causes in these times uncertainty as to the security of any banking philosophies and subjects us to the efforts of special interest groups and their agendas more readily to changes laws which are far easier to change than the constitution itself.

"Why has government been instituted at all, because the passions of men will not conform to the dictates of reason and justice, without constraint?" **Alexander Hamilton**

1791 to 1836 First Bank Bail-Out, Westward the Tide & Debt Free
President: George Washington 1789 to 1797, Federalist

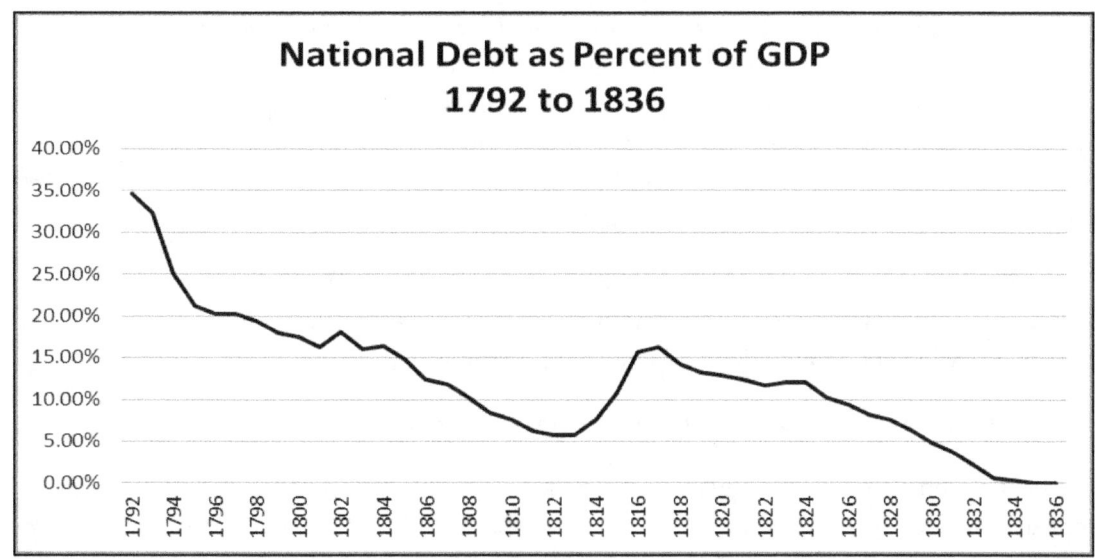

Today the National Debt is about 100% of the Gross Domestic Product. As you can you see the National Debt was 0% of the Gross Domestic Product in 1836 meaning there was no National DEBT. National Debt is what the government owes. The Gross Domestic Product is the value of what was produced in a given year in the nation.

> *West lies the 'Promised Land'. Before Europeans began to populate the 'New World' they were looking East which turned out to be West. After they arrived it was ever west to the 'promised land' until the continent was populated under two governments.*

The United States was about Seventy-five million dollars in DEBT in 1791. This was for a country with a population of a little over three million nine hundred thousand people. That's men, women and children and they had lots of kids in those days. I bring this up because we currently have a larger percentage of the population in the taxable age range.

> *In 1791 the infant mortality rate in the United States was twenty to thirty percent. (Pointed history)*

The Constitution had just come into effect with George Washington as President and Alexander Hamilton, Secretary of the Treasury, supporting the **Federalist** idea of a strong central government with a national bank to support merchants and financiers in building the industrial base of the country. The **Democratic –Republicans**, who used to be the **Anti-Federalists**, supported by Thomas Jefferson (Secretary of State) and James Madison favored an agrarian society with people determining their own destiny by their labors on land they owned (*yeoman farmers*) and did not like the idea of a national bank as it would favor the wealthy and hinder the advancement of the agrarian individual. *Both were blessed with far sight.*

The first **Bank of the United States**

The first **Bank of the United States** was created; *the National Bank or Central Bank was argued as a Constitutional issue at the time,* as the national government assumed the revolutionary debt of the states, established tariffs and taxes to pay that debt. This plan encouraged the states and the wealthy to support the National government. Some states owed more than others. Specifically southern states had already retired much of their debt. *Let's see, the industrial/merchant north owes more money than the agrarian south. There might be something to this!*

Hamilton's goals were to establish financial order, clarity, and credit (internally and externally) and figure out how to resolve the issue of the 'Continental' , the aforementioned 'script' (the 'fiat currency') issued by the country during the Revolutionary war.

The functions of the first Bank of the United States were…

Control the money supply by regulating the currency state banks could issue. *This was largely accomplished by determining a discount rate for the state bank notes. This rate could vary from 0% discount to, well, a lot depending on the relationship between the notes in circulation and hard money reserves of the individual banks. As you can imagine this could create some friction between the state banks and the central bank that was making the rules and competing with the state banks at the same time.*

Function as the Depository of the money of the Treasury.

It also would transfer deposits to different areas banks. This could also cause some friction because who ever had those funds could make some money off them.

> *There were 4 banks besides the Bank of the United States initially with many more on the way.*

The organization of the first Bank of the United States was

Supervised by the Secretary of the Treasury who could inspect the transactions of the bank, not individuals, and demand an audit any darn time he felt like it.

Capitalized by $10 million in stock at a par value of $400 each with 25,000 total shares and at least 25% had to be paid in hard currency.

80% or so sold to investors 20% retained by the government with no individual being able to own over 30 shares.

The bank could not buy government bonds and could not issue notes (currency) or incur debts beyond its actual capitalization. Directors had to be changed periodically.

> *Foreigners could own stock but would have no voting power. As a privately owned enterprise it competed for customers, for deposits and for loans against the state chartered banks.*

An aside: an excise tax was to be placed on imported and domestically made whiskey. This would cause problems in the near future.

Federal income at this time was from; tariffs, excise taxes and sale of land.

The inflation rate was about three point eight percent. The French Revolution was underway, the precursor to the New York Stock Exchange is operating in New York City under the Buttonwood Agreement and baseball (or something very like it) was banded within 80 yards of the Pittsfield, Mass, meeting hall (*might have had something to do with windows which were rather expensive in those days*). The rest of the world was doing what our world seems to enjoy nearly as much as procreation, fighting over territory and materials and trying to make the other person see it 'our way'.

Overall things went along pretty well for the next few years while the nation got itself organized or as organized as it would until after...I was going to say the Civil War....hum....anyway...

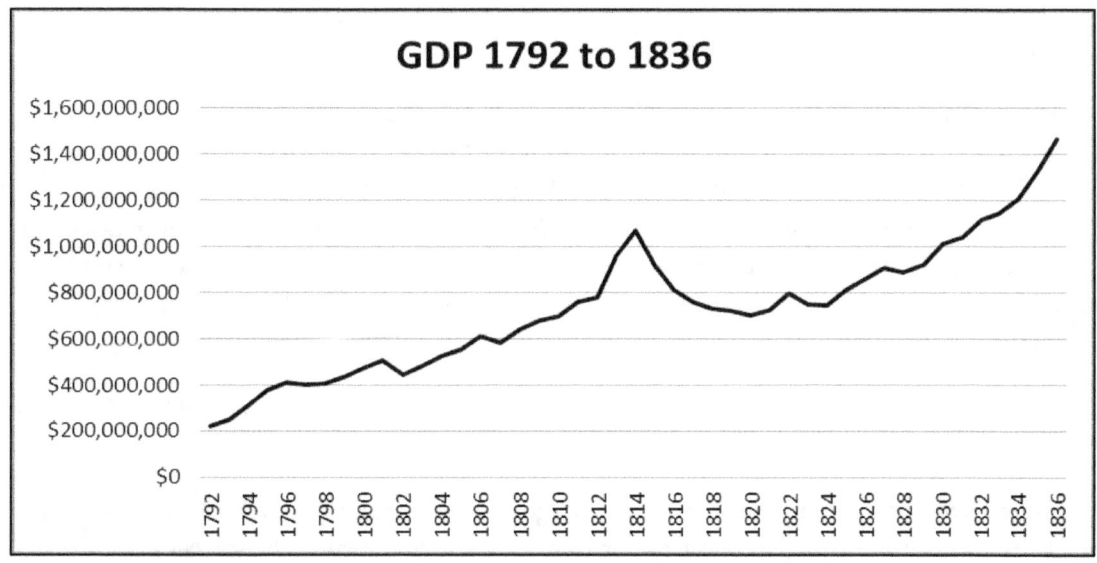

The Gross Domestic Product grew about seven fold from 1791 to 1836. *That isn't bad!*

The graph shows the Gross Domestic Products growth from 1791 to 1836, when the National Debt reached zero. The GDP doubled from 1791 to 1800, again in 1813. Shown on future charts it doubles again in 1845, 1855, 1864 (Civil War), 1900, 1915, 1919, 1942 (WWII), 1982, 1993, 2006 and has remained rather level since.

"Government is not reason; it is not eloquence; it is force! Like fire, it is a dangerous servant and a fearful master." **George Washington**

1792

The Coinage Act of 1792 a.k.a. Mint Act Officially - *An act establishing a mint, and regulating the Coins of the United States.* The act established the silver dollar as the official currency and legal tender of the United States. Makes sense and sounds fine. *Wait until 1806 or so!*

An Act to Provide for a Copper Coinage was also passed in 1792.

The two Acts established the money of the United States. $10 Gold Eagle, $5 gold Half Eagle, $2.50 Quarter Eagle, $1 Silver Dollar, $0.50 Silver Half Dollar, $0.25 Silver Quarter Dollar, $0.10 Silver Dime, $0.05 Silver Half Dime, $0.01 Copper Cent, and $0.005 Copper Half Cent. That is the 'hard currency' of the United States.

Alexander Hamilton, in his report concerning the mint

> To annul the use of either of the metals, gold or silver, as money is to abridge the quantity of circulating medium, and is liable to all the objections which arise from a comparison of the benefits of a fall with the evils of a scanty circulation.

> *The more money in circulation the more business that can be transacted and it made it easier for folks to pay taxes and debts as governments and creditors tend to be displeased with an offer of carrots or young pigs as payment.*

Panic of 1792 and the First Bank Bailout

Alexander Hamilton, Secretary of the Treasury, starts buying back government issued bonds and the price rises. A guy, Duer, gets together with some of 'the boys' and they figure to grab up the stock of the Bank of New York and the Bank of the United States because, well, those bonds may have been a better investment than was figured. Duer gets way out on a limb by over extending his leverage position on the aforementioned stocks. People start asking for their money and Duer has to liquidate and the stock prices crash taking the reputation of the Bank of New York with him down the tubes.

> *That has got to sound awfully danged familiar! This is essentially what happened to the Big Five Wall Street banks in 2008.*

Alexander Hamilton sees the crashing values and goes to the Bank of New York and guarantees the prices of bonds to be used as collateral for loans. This bailout insures the solvency of the bank and makes Hamilton and his policy look good. In fact it was well done and averted what could have caused lots of folks' pain and suffering.

I do not believe Duer got any hard, prison, time for his actions.

Even as Napoleon is signing peace treaties in Italy, on behalf of the French Revolutionary government, he is, in letters to Talleyrand the French Foreign Minister, speaking of opening trade with the east and the need to overthrow the English Monarchy.

Kentucky Statehood

1793

"Freedom is government divided into small fragments." **Thomas Hobbes** *He wrote a great book,* **Leviathan,** *which takes a very long time to get through. Senator E. Dirksen might have been a descendent.*

France is deeply engulfed in revolution and war with most of Europe. France, all filled with righteousness, calls upon its revolutionary friend the Unites States to come to their aid under the auspicious of its 1778 alliance with the United States. Alas for France the United States has a policy of neutrality that was well supported, but not totally supported as the Democratic-Republicans favored France and its revolutionary ways.

Later in the year Britain starts seizing the United States' merchant shipping as well as impressing the crews. This makes the Federalists look stupid as they supported neutrality wanting to maintain trading relations with the British, *their biggest client*. Follow the money honey. The Democratic-Republicans are up in the air screaming look, look, we told you not to trust the darn British, *hoping they can still come to the aid of France. If you think the nation is fractionalized now read some of the stuff printed during this period and that nothing new under sun bit sounds about right.*

1794

The **Britain/France** question was somewhat answered when the United States made a deal with the British, the **Jay Treaty**, where the British would remove troops from the frontier forts and the United States would stop selling to France, let alone aid them. The treaty still needed to be ratified.

George Rogers Clark *(yes related to that other famous Clark of American lore)* is involved in a couple of conspiracies to open the Mississippi river to American navigation and thus open western lands. Conspiracies because he acted without the knowledge or consent of the Federal Government and tried to engaged the assistance of other nations. *Governments tend to like to handle their affairs themselves and take exception to 'private' persons causing or waging wars or making deals with other governments. As to that last point realize this was before multinational corporations became well developed.*

> The population grew, the DEBT grew and fell, inflation was high, we had what is called the Whiskey Rebellion over a really unfair tax on whiskey production, the Russian-Ottoman Empire war ends, the Postal Service is started, a flushing toilet is patented *(I really like that one)*, Hope Diamond is Stolen *(great fun that)*, Europe is in conflict *(financially good for us)*, possibly the first caesarian section is performed, a democratic revolution in Amsterdam, Beethoven is doing his thing, the **Rothschild family begins banking throughout Europe**, Napoleon gets the ball rolling, and on and on. Things are typical for the activities of mankind, the nation is growing, and Europe is consuming itself in war. Oh! An iron plow was patented in 1797 but did not sell well because the farmers were concerned about what the iron might do to the soil. All is goodish with the exception of various epidemics in Pennsylvania and Virginia.

"Give me control of a nation's money and I care not who makes its laws." **Mayer Amschel Bauer Rothschild**

Concern over this notion will be repeated often in this chronology as it arises in our history.

The **Whiskey Rebellion** was about an excise tax on whiskey production. The tax could be paid as a flat rate or by the gallon. I believe the flat rate was $25.00 and per gallon was $0.50 each.

Because people on the frontier made significantly smaller amounts than the big producers in the East the frontier people paid a higher rate per gallon. On the frontier cash was scarce and the whiskey was often used en lieu of cash. The feeling was that Eastern big business was being given an advantage over the poor small farmers of the rural frontier area. *Hum, something familiar about that.*

George Washington invokes the Militia Law of 1792 and raises and army of over 10,000 men. Off they march, with Washington at the head, to put down the rebellion in the Monongahela Valley. The poor frontiersmen upon seeing the 'Father of the Country" or maybe the 10,000 armed men behind him gave it up and went home.

Aside: Revenuers are still unpopular in some areas where whiskey is distilled privately.

1795

The **Jay Treaty ratification** turned into a nasty bit of discussion and name calling until the 'Father of the Country' stepped in and told the boys to take a time out and figure out a way to be nice and let the Republican form of government work its magic. During this deliberation the French really stepped on their appendage with the Reign of Terror and the Jacobin anti-religious stuff. Jefferson, perhaps feeling his faith in the French had been betrayed, resigned as Secretary of State.

The **Jay Treaty** gets signed and the French get all upset about it and tell the United States to go make like a Wyoming sheep herders because now France is going to intercept American shipping going to Britain. This goes along for a while with the internal factions of the United States still very much actively split about France and England.

> First state university in U.S. opens, University of North Carolina, 1st state appropriation of money for road building, Kentucky and Pinckney's Treaty between Spain and U.S. is signed, establishing southern boundary of U.S. and giving Americans right to send goods down the Mississippi river.

"Few men have virtue to withstand the highest bidder." **George Washington**

Alexander Hamilton leaves the Treasury position. Shortly afterward the United States stocks in the Bank are sold. *I personally think this was a very bad move.*

1796

Right about here United States politics is dominated by the Federalists, Alexander Hamilton and George Washington and the Democratic-Republicans, Thomas Jefferson and James Madison. The two party political systems of the United States is not yet entrenched as the political philosophy of the country leaves republican ideals for a polarizing and contentious two party system.

Land Act of 1796 allowed the purchase of public lands at $2.00 per acre in tracts of 640 acres. That is $1,280 cash up front. This situation made it possible for land speculators to buy land far more readily than people who wanted to homestead.

Freedom of worship established in France under constitution, fire destroys 1/3 of Copenhagen; 18,000 injured, US pays $800,000 & a frigate as tribute to Algiers & Tunis.

Then we have the Panic of 1796-1797 which was the result of a constriction of credit by the Bank of England because people were pulling out money (*bank run*) over fear of a French invasion (*which did happen*) and the bursting of a *land speculation bubble* in the United States that resulted in several prominent business men in the northeast going broke including Robert Morris, whose financial aid was critical during the revolution. (*Where have I heard that 'Bubble' thing before?*) Lots of credit until somebody starts pulling their funding and things go south. Or more to the point folks go broke because England is pulling money home and somebody else ends up owning the land. *I'll be a blue nosed gopher' that sounds almighty familiar too.* The legal result was the **Bankruptcy Act of 1800,** to help people thru this tough time, which expired three years later! *Sounds like a temporary fix.*

> *Also during this period Philadelphia is hit by severe 'Yellow Fever' epidemics in 1793, 1796, 1797 and 1798. Look up epidemics in the US and in general. Ghastly stuff! You might notice that the Epidemics were generally concentrated in the cities. Good reasons for that!*

Things roll along recessiony for a couple of years and start to look good while the war between France and England drives commodity prices up, people are making lots of money. Then the dangdist thing happens. France and England get together and have a peace, *sort of*, causing the recession of 1802. Commodity prices fall and pirates are making a grand mess of things. The United States has the Barbary War (*look it up - Really! Look it up*) ending several years of paying tribute of one million dollars annually to the Barbary States, the deficit starts to fall significantly and the United States has another rebellion (*yeah*).

Tennessee Statehood

1797

John Adams becomes President March 4 1797 to March 4 1801, the last Federalist to serve in the office.

"A pen is certainly an excellent instrument to fix a man's attention and to inflame his ambition." **John Adams**

France has taken over 250 ships and won't talk to the United States at all.

> Earthquake in Quito, Ecuador kills 41,000, 1st U.S. frigate, the "United States," is launched in Philadelphia, U.S. frigate Constitution (Old Ironsides) launched in Boston, British naval forces defeat Dutch off Camperdown, Netherlands and Andre-Jacques Garnerin makes 1st parachute jump from balloon (Paris).

1798

The Federalists held the governmental reins and passed four important Acts with John Adams as President.

The opposition to the *Federalists* was the *Democratic-Republicans*. The Federalists supported a strong central government and the National Bank. The Democratic-Republicans favored a lesser strength in the federal government and were generally opposed to the notion of a National Bank because they had seen the power banks had exerted historically. *This is an over simplified assessment! Like duh.*

The **Naturalization Act**, amended the same act of 1795 (it extended the residence requirement from five years to fourteen years), The **Alien Act**, the president could deport any resident alien felt to be a threat to the 'peace and safety' of the United States (a two year expiration date), the **Alien Enemies Act** , the President could arrest and deport resident aliens if the United States was at war with those resident aliens home countries, (is still on the books), the **Sedition Act** , it was now a crime to publish false, scandalous and malicious writing against the government and certain officials, expired March 3 1801. John Adams' (a Federalist) term ended March 4, 1801. *Sounds familiar again! Also might have had to do with the rebellion thing.*

These were likely passed because the Quasi War with France looked like it was going to escalate and many people were on the side of France, some notably in the leadership of the Democratic-Republicans. *Isn't a two party system fun? This all sounds rather familiar too.*

> **Democratic Republic** *That is; each member of the republic that constitutes the United States is a member of the Republic and operates under a democratic system. This democratic system is exercised in each member of the Republic and the democratically elected representatives of the member States of the Republic constitute the elected members of the Federal Government. Personally I like a Republic...should keep mob mentality to a minimum and we will see much later how maintaining the Republic would have helped us now.*

Congress expands the Army and Navy because when John Adams sent some guys to try to talk to the French about the situation they were not nice and even demanded bribes. To pay for these military expansions the **Direct House Tax** is imposed on real estate and slaves to raise the two million dollars needed and portioned among the states as required by the constitution.

> An Irish Rebellion begins, Kentucky nullifies an act of Congress (*is there an elephant in the room*), U. S. Signatory of the Constitution, Senator William Blount impeachment trial begins (*we're having fun now*), 11th Amendment ratified, Territory of Mississippi formed, Napoleon in Egypt, British Honduras beats Spain at battle of Saint George and a nut and bolt machine is patented (*industrialization really moving along*).

Moses and Gerson Warburg start the M. M. Warburg & Co. a bank that still exists today in Germany. *The Warburg's wouldn't be in this at all if I hadn't fallen over the Jekyll Island event.*

Quasi War with France amounted to several naval battles: but things are looking like a major conflict will develop.

1799

President Adams says what the heck let's try to talk with those crazy French one more time. This time Napoleon is in charge and things go better.

Jenner's small pox vaccine introduced, US Patent for a seed machine, Massachusetts passes a law regulating insurance *(this is a really big deal)*, slavery abolished in New York state *(this is too)*, Napoleon calls for establishing Jerusalem for Jews, Bank of Manhattan Company opens in New York *(forerunner of Chase Manhattan)*, George Washington dies and we have Fries' Rebellion, the Harpes serial killers on the frontier and the Cave-in-Rock River Pirates.

The Bank of the Manhattan Company established by Aaron Burr, *he was pretty slick the way he did it too.*

Fries' Rebellion was a reaction to the **Direct House Tax** and was concentrated among the Pennsylvania Dutch. The method of determining the tax on houses in Pennsylvania was by counting the size and number of windows. Fries and the boys figured that the tax was unconstitutional because it was not being levied in proportion to population. Many of the people involved had been members of the Continental Army and couldn't see their way clear to pay an unconstitutional tax. So a urinating contest gets going. Shots fired all around and more great fun is had. Short version is that a couple of dozen or so folks get put on trial with Fries and a couple of others convicted of treason. With the **Federalists** all furrowing brows and gnashing their teeth the boys were sentenced to hang. John Adams pardoned them all and blamed the whole incident on the opposition, **Democratic-Republicans**, as, paraphrase here, 'they obviously stirred up the population and after all, the rebels were nothing more than ignorant dupes and couldn't be hanged as such'. *Bad precedent, that notion. I mean really these are citizens and veterans and the hanging part was just a stupid idea.*

"Democracy is two wolves and a lamb deciding what to have for dinner. Liberty is a well-armed lamb." Some attribute this to Benjamin Franklin.

1800

The **Convention of 1800** releases the US from the **1778 Alliance** with France and peace is all in the air. There was a minor exception; France refused to pay restitution for the ships it had seized to the tune of $20 million. *That could have left a bad taste in the mouths of the ship owners and merchants who'd lost their property, probably from Boston and New York mostly.*

There are about **29 banks** in the United States including the 'Bank of the United States" which was chartered by the Federal Government. There were just **4 banks** in the United States in **1790**. *Looks to me like the Banking business must be good even with the Bank of the United States competing in the market place.*

A little something about the chartering of State Banks during this period, to start a state bank a Charter from the state assembly was required. *Consider that for a moment and you may come to the conclusion that favors and money might have traded hands in that process.*

The world population was nearly a billion, Volta invents chemical battery, slave rebellion in Virginia (Gabriel Prosser), and Washington D.C. becomes the US capitol and the **Harrison Land Act of 1800**. From this point on the Federalists are on their way out because they were dominated by big money concentrated in New England, the major commercial, banking and trading area of the country, and the expanding country was mostly rural and identified with Jeffersonian ideals of an agrarian nation of independent people enjoying the bounty of their labor on their own land.

From 1800 to 1900 represents the greatest change in living standards and products than any other 100 year period before and 1800 standards were little changed from 1000CE (AD).

Dutch East Indies Company dissolves, Wild Boy of Aveyron discovered in southern France, James Ross discovers North Magnetic pole, Library of Congress established with $5,000 allocation and White House completed and President and Mrs. John Adams move in, and Mount Vernon Gardens becomes site of 1st summer theater in U.S.

The **Harrison Land Act of 1800** superseded the Land Act of 1796. $1,280.00 in 1800 was generally beyond the means of most people willing to brave the frontier so many simply squatted on the land. The Harrison Act allowed the minimum sized tract reduced to 320 acres and further made CREDIT available in the form of 25% down and the balance in equal installments over four years. Let us cipher this out, $640.00 total purchase price with $160.00 down and $120.00 per year for four years. There was a grace year to make up arrears. As the average income in 1800 was about $16.50 per week this made it far easier for the less financially endowed, just easier but still made it more likely that the more financially endowed would make the investment as speculation. *This looks good until you consider that most of this land was in areas that had little law enforcement, angry Indian tribes and loss of crops from bad weather, the bane of all farmers and the BOOM/BUST cycle.*

The Land Acts encouraged settlement of the western lands expanding the rural population and popularity of the Jeffersonian ideals supported by the Democratic-Republicans pushing the Federalists, as a political party, into oblivion. Not exactly oblivion as much of their ideals and causes are taken up by future political parties as the country develops and political issues realign.

1801

Thomas Jefferson becomes President 1801 to 1809, a Democratic-Republican

"The price of freedom is eternal vigilance." Thomas Jefferson

John Marshall (*a Federalist*) is appointed Chief Justice of the United States Supreme Court (*this is like a really super big deal*), Piazzi discovers asteroid, David Emanuel of Georgia becomes first Jewish Governor of a state, Tripoli declares war on US for refusing to pay the expected tribute (*think Marines here*), Kentucky outlaws dueling, John Adams gets the Judiciary Act of 1801 passed and loads up the new federal circuit courts with Federalists before Jefferson enters office, presidential election is tied in the Electoral College and congress puts Jefferson, a Democratic-Republican, in as president and Aaron Burr as Vice President.

John Marshall being of a Federalist nature was critical in developing the central nature of the Federal Government by his interpretations of the Constitution. This is also a great example of how the membership of the Supreme Court

can affect the nation as a Federalist made the appointment as a Democratic-Republican was about to enter office.. It was Marshall who put credence to the notion of a National Bank.

1802

Thomas Jefferson in a letter to **John Adams** points out the friction concerning the issuance of notes by state banks and the use of notes by the Bank of the United States.

"I believe that banking institutions are more dangerous to our liberties than standing armies. Already they have raised up a monied aristocracy that has set the government at defiance. The issuing power should be taken away from the banks and restored to the people to whom it properly belongs."

> The population is now five million six hundred thousand or so, inflation is a bit over three percent, GDP drops over twelve percent (*folks are making lots less and folks are buying less, unemployment etc.*) and the deficit drops two million bucks. Jefferson and the Democratic – Republicans undo the Judiciary Act of 1800 and are supported by the <u>Stuart v. Laird</u> case, West Point is established, Gia Long captures Hanoi unifying Vietnam (*more about Vietnam later, duh!*), war ends between Sweden and Tripoli, Suriname is purchased by the Dutch from England, Napoleon keeps it up (*didn't mean it that way*), the Wasp is published (*first comic book*). The recession lasts into 1804 and then we get the Depression of 1807.

Barings, a bank in England, buys over 2000 shares of the 'Bank of the United States'.

1803

Marbury v Madison the Supreme Court under John Marshall establishes that the Supreme Court is able to review and overturn legislation passed by Congress. *Jefferson is PO'd and goes hunting Justices he believes abusive of their power. See 1806.*

This year provides one of the great lessons on bankers. ***Like ever!*** Great Britain and France are at war. Napoleon is in need of money to continue the war so he offers the Louisiana Purchase to the United States. But lo, the United States had not the money! So how does the United States get the money? Not from taxes. Not from tariffs. They get it from banks in England and Holland. **That's right**. Barings (the United States government made them the official banking agent in London earlier in the year), a major bank in England and Hope & Company (from Amsterdam), arrange for England's' enemy to finance a war against their own country and ally! Lord love a duck, international banking at its' savage best. *Note: Nobody got hung for this, dang it, might have set a good precedent.*

> Apple parer patented by Moses Coats, Downington, Pennsylvania, 1,800 sovereign German states unite into 60 states, Great fire in Bombay, India, 1st performance of Beethoven's 2nd Symphony in D, Meteorites fall in L'Aigle, France, John Hawkins and Richard French patent the Reaping Machine, and Battle of Vertieres, in which Haitians defeat French Dessalines and Christophe declare St. Domingue (Haiti) independent.

The **Louisiana Purchase** cost fifteen million dollars, cancellation of three point seven five million in DEBTs, three million in gold (from the reserves) and the US Government issued bonds for the balance. The National Debt takes a big jump. *Yuh think!*

Things have been BOOMing and more DEBT. Sell more land! Raise tariffs!

Ohio Statehood

1804

Aaron Burr kills Alexander Hamilton *(the guy on the ten dollar bill))* in a duel. *Some are of the opinion that Burrs' likeness should be on a coin. Yes, really! I have spoken to them.*

> The National DEBT jumps twelve percent but starts getting paid down again nicely over the next several years. Population growth has been a little over three percent and the GDP has been growing from five to nine percent or so annually. Lewis & Clark set out, Haiti becomes independent of France, and New Jersey is last Northern state to abolish slavery and the Twelfth Amendment to United States Constitution.

The Land Act of 1804 reduced the minimum tract size to 160 acres and continued the loan and credit features of the Harrison Land Act of 1800. Reduction of tract size makes the land more available for settlement.

Things have been BOOMing and more people are buying land on credit, familiar?

1805

"One man with courage is a majority." **Thomas Jefferson**

The British defeating of the French and Spanish fleet at the **Battle of Trafalgar** made them masters of the high seas and did they ever make the best of it, seizing American ships and forcing their crews to ships of the Royal Navy.

> Supreme Court Justice Samuel Pace acquitted of impeachment charges *(more rollicking good fun that as Jefferson's hunting expedition found a target for his wrath)*, Thomas Jefferson takes office, 2nd term, as President, United States Marines and Berbers attack Derna, a Tripolitan city *(The Shores of Tripoli)*, Detroit burns to the ground *(there wasn't even a cow to blame)*, and Horatio Nelson dies.

1806

Thomas Jefferson stops the minting of silver coins because the darn things keep disappearing as people are taking them places where they are worth more than what the US values them at (start thinking 1971 here) and the silver was used to pay foreign debts. *When the weights of gold and silver coinage were initially set up silver was a little heavy and therefore it presented an opportunity for profit so people took them overseas.*

Dutch surrender to British at Cape of Good Hope, **National Road is authorized**, Pike Expedition begins (*Pike's Peak*), Holy Roman Empire ends after nearly a thousand years, Webster's Dictionary published, Elizabeth Barrett Browning born, carbon paper invented (this was important until the advent of computers), **Aaron Burr**, former Vice President of the United States is arrested, with others, for treason and a few other things. *Burr basically gets off.*

Things have been BOOMing, look out!

The **National Bank** charter expires in 1811 and is reinstated in 1816 and expires again in 1836 and the notion of a National Bank does not return until the Civil War. More depressions and recessions, the Supreme Court gets into the banking issue some more, several epidemics and the south is further distanced from the Union.

During this period the United States Military is involved in the following areas in varying capacities. Gulf of Mexico concerning pirates, West Florida (frequently), Amelia Island, War of 1812, Spanish Florida, Caribbean, Algiers, Seminole War, German Coast Uprising (slave revolt), Africa - US Naval Forces raid African slave traffic Pursuant to the 1819 Act of Congress, Cuba (frequently), Puerto Rico, Greece, Sumatra, Falkland Islands, Nat Turner's Slave Rebellion, Argentina, Peru and Mexico.

1807

The **Embargo Act of 1807** prevented all American ships from sailing to a foreign port. The British were dependent on American goods to the point that Jefferson thought they would settle. For about fifteen months New York, Boston and nearby export businesses suffered enough to bring a depression to the North East United States. Evading the Embargo was rather too easy to avoid, but still put a major crimp in business, and the effects had enlivened the Federalists party. Madison became president and the Embargo was dropped. Madison had the great idea of offering to support either England or France if they stopped their offensive practices. Napoleon agreed and America turned its' wrath on England in 1812. *Not quite this simple but you get the general idea.*

The national DEBT had been falling and is now down to around sixty-nine million dollars after peaking at around eighty-six million dollars. Most of the income for the national government is still from tariffs, excise taxes and land sales. Population is about six point six million and the GDP drops only about four point six percent then begins to rise nicely again in 1808.

> London's Pall Mall is 1st street lit by gaslight, Townsend Speakman 1st sells fruit-flavored carbonated drinks in Philadelphia and Robert Fulton's steamboat Clermont begins 1st trip up Hudson River.

People start losing their land.

Depression of 1807 Big BUST! The Embargo Act of 1807 caused restricted trade and prices fell. As with any depression there was much unemployment and a lack of money running around because those that had money were inclined to hold on to it, especially as there was no new money coming in, and folks had it bad. There was some loss of land for those who turned out to have insufficient markets for their crops and couldn't make their payments. It generally screwed things up all around.

1808

"The Central Bank is an institution of the most deadly hostility existing against the principles and form of our Constitution...if the American people allow private banks to control the issuance of their currency, first by inflation and then by deflation, the banks and corporations that will grow up around them will deprive the people of all their property until their children will wake up homeless on the continent their fathers conquered." **Thomas Jefferson**

Virtually all of Europe is in turmoil! James Madison wins Presidential Election. Part 1 of Goethe's Faust is published. Did I mention Europe is in turmoil? *This is like a really big deal.* Napoleon is causing such a mess that many of the European countries are bleeding money and people. John Jacob Astor gets the American Fur Company going. *(Poor Muskrats, where's the Love?)* Anthracite coal 1st burned as fuel, experimentally, Wilkes-Barre, PA.

1809

James Madison becomes President 1809 to 1817 Democratic-Republican

"History records that the money changers have used every form of abuse, intrigue, deceit, and violent means possible to maintain their control over governments by controlling money and its issuance." **James Madison**

State banks start issuing more paper money because hard money, silver and gold, is in short supply and holding up business as there is not enough cash to make transactions. The banks issue the paper money against the assets of the bank. *Unless you want to start using whiskey and get into that mess again.* A State taxes the National Bank and sort of gets away with it. *A jolly old time is had by all.*

Robert Fulton patents steamboat, Mary Kies is 1st woman issued a U.S. patent (weaving straw), 1st U.S. steamboat to a make an ocean voyage leaves New York for Philadelphia, 1st practical U.S. railroad track (wooden, for horse-drawn cars), Philadelphia, Peregrine Williamson of Baltimore patents a steel pen and wearing masks at balls forbidden in Boston.

Ohio issues warrants of five, ten & twenty dollars, to be used in Ohio, because of the shortage of coinage that resulted from Jefferson halting the minting of silver coins. *This is another big deal. Warrants are like paper money or credit drafts against the specie assets of the bank.*

The **Non-Intercourse Act** *replaced the Embargo Act of 1807 opening American shipping to all nations except France and England.*

"... The modern theory of the perpetuation of debt has drenched the earth with blood, and crushed its inhabitants under burdens ever accumulating." **Thomas Jefferson**

The **Supreme Court** enters the fray with <u>**United States v. Deveaux.**</u>

Georgia, not being fond of the Bank of the United States, as many States were not fond of the Bank of the United States, enacted a tax on the Georgia branch of said bank in the year 1805. *Bad dog or good dog?* The Georgia branch of the Bank of the United States gets all uppity and refuses to pay the tax. Georgia, all filled with ire and indignation, seizes the deposits of said bank to satisfy the tax debt. The Supreme Court of the United States ruled that citizens of Pennsylvania could sue in Federal Court to recover their deposits from the State of Georgia as Georgia had no right to tax the bank. *Oh yeah, good luck with that suing business. The ruling lays the foundation for future considerations.*

Spain's American colonies began to revolt causing a vast reduction of precious metals going to Europe. This loss of gold and silver significantly lowered the amount of money circulating causing slowdowns in European commerce. Without the additional funds to stimulate business the Europeans suffered financially, especially the lower classes as prices fell.

1810

"I believe there are more instances of the abridgement of the freedom of the people by gradual and silent encroachments of those in power than by violent and sudden usurpations." **James Madison**

> 1st Insurance Co. managed by blacks, American Insurance Company of Philadelphia, John Jacob Astor organizes Pacific Fur Co and 1st Irish magazine in U.S., Shamrock, is published.

1811

"The truth is that all men having power ought to be mistrusted." **James Madison**

State banks continue to issue warrants and the National Bank charter expires and is not renewed until 1816. In 1811 construction of the National Road begins the building of national infrastructure. The National DEBT continues to fall and GDP grows at a rate greater than the population growth. This is a good thing! There is not much going on in the way of epidemics.

Financial Panic in England

> Louisiana slave revolt by Charles Deslondes at German Coast, Russian settlers establish Ft Ross trading post, north of San Francisco, Austria declares bankruptcy, 1st US colonists on Pacific coast arrive at Cape Disappointment, Washington, Paraguay gains independence from Spain, Venezuela gains independence from Spain, Italian scientist Amedeo Avogadro publishes his memoir about molecular content of gases and Father Miguel Hidalgo y Costilla, leader of the Mexican insurgency, is executed by the Spanish in Chihuahua, Mexico.

New Madrid earthquake, considered the largest earthquake in the United States, is felt hundreds of miles away and changes the course of a river. This was in the greater Mississippi River Valley.

Demise of the first Bank of the United States   As the Bank of the United States had some $5 million in notes circulating as a strong and stable currency and it was discounting notes from some state banks that probably had over issued those notes against their reserves, the Constitutional question was not yet settled and the issue of foreign ownership was a real thorn in its side the banks' charter was not renewed.   The foreign owner ship was over 65% and was receiving a dividend of over 8% of specie; gold and silver, the leaving the country could well have cemented the question.

Stephen Girard buys almost all of the stock and property of the Bank of the United States and opens his own bank as a sole proprietor thereby avoiding having to get a state charter. *Slick move.*

A result of the Bank of the United States demise was *unregulated state banks running amuck.*   Banks sprang up just about everywhere and issued huge amounts of notes creating inflation and uncertainty as to the value of the notes, especially as the war of 1812 came along.

So far lots of stuff happening again

1812

The War of 1812, a.k.a. **Mister Madison's War**, comes along because the British won't leave our ships alone and they keep snagging our sailors away on the high seas and the slightly smooth ride of the last few years is shot right in the anterior posterior. From 1812 to 1816 the National DEBT jumps from around forty-five million to over one hundred twenty-seven million dollars as the government borrows to pay for the war. GDP also jumps as orders for the war fuel the economy. 1815 has GDP dropping fourteen percent and 1816 it drops eleven percent and continues to drop at a lower rate for the next few years until the Panic of 1819. 1st cargo arrives in New Orleans by steam, from Natchez, Massachusetts Governor Elbridge Gerry signs a redistricting bill - 1st "gerrymander", earthquake destroys 90% of Caracas Venezuela; about 20,000 die, US passes 1st foreign aid bill (Venezuela earthquake victims), Prime Minister Spencer Perceval is assassinated by John Bellingham in the lobby of the House of Commons, US warship Constitution defeats British warship Guerriere, US frigate United States captures British vessel Macedonian and the USS Constitution under the command of Captain William Bainbridge, captures the HMS Java off the coast of Brazil after a three hour battle.

Demand for war supplies causes orders to increase from manufacturing and agricultural sectors causing a dramatic rise in the GDP and inflation as banks issue more notes all the way through the war until 1815. International trade slipped off ticking off New England interests and reducing the inflow of gold and silver.

The Hartford Convention was a result of New England Federalists seeing their influence in the Federal government eroding and their loss of income since the Embargo Act of 1807. They acted on making a separate peace with England during the War of 1812 but it fizzled when Andrew Jackson defeated the British at New Orleans. Bet you never heard about this one before! Also no treason charges were made. Maybe that had something to do with these guys having control over so much of the money and the manufacturing base. This would be shades of 2013 when HSBC got off so easy. Am I being a 'But Head' here or what?

During the War of 1812 Girard's Bank provided the financial support needed by the Federal government. When the second Bank of the United States was chartered he became a major stockholder and a director. *Stephen Girard is a person worth looking up especially as he is virtually unknown in American historical lore. He really was quiet a guy and has made my top fifty Americans list.*

City Bank of New York opens and will become Citibank.

Louisiana Statehood

1813 The American victory at the **Battle of Lake Erie** cut off British support of the tribes of the Northwest Territories. US National Debt is at $ 55,962,828

> Pineapple introduced to Hawaii, Pride and Prejudice is first published, David Melville, Newport, RI, patents apparatus for making coal gas, Rubber is patented, Pacific Fur Company trading post in Astoria, Oregon is turned over to the rival British North West Company, Tax revolt in Amsterdam and Ludwig von Beethoven's 7th Symphony in A, premieres.

OOPS!

1814

The British burn Washington in August

US National Debt is at $ 81,487,846

Amidst all this the **United States government stops paying its'** DEBTs in hard currency, specie, (gold and silver) except to foreign DEBT holders, as they accept payments only in hard currency. Foreign DEBT holders are getting to be a real pain in the tooth because it looks like those DEBTs are going to mess up the financial dealings of America and incurring foreign DEBT for the war automatically means less hard money in America.

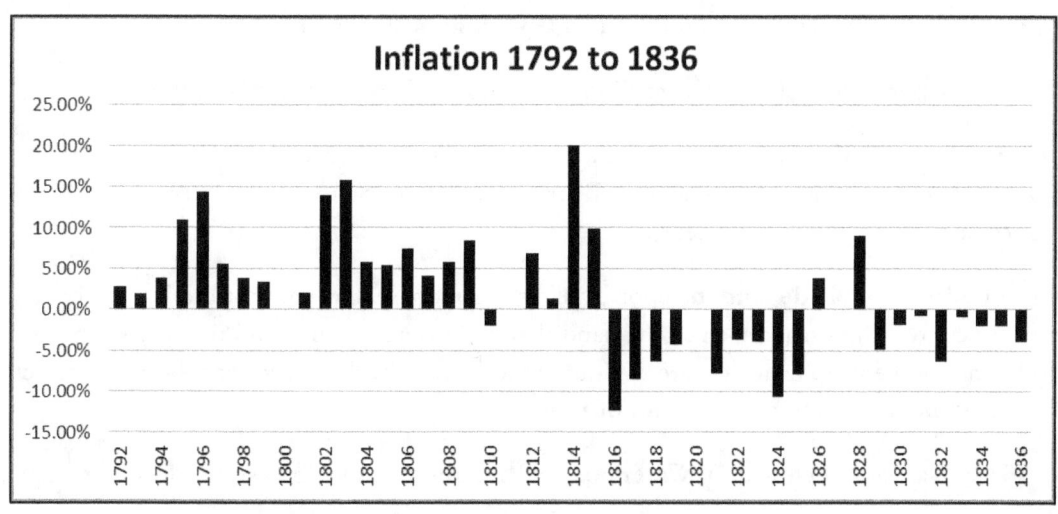

31

Battle at Horseshoe Bend: General Andrew Jackson defeats the Red Sticks, part of the Creek Indian tribe near Dadeville, Alabama, George Stephenson introduced the 1st steam locomotive, Pope Pius VII reinstates Jesuits, Francis Scott Key inspired to write "Star-Spangled Banner" published as a poem, London Beer Flood occurs in London killing nine and the Times in London is for the first time printed by automatic, steam powered presses built by the German inventors Friedrich Koenig and Andreas Friedrich Bauer.

Banks are issuing warrants and the Feds are issuing paper money. Inflation jumps then falls, becoming deflation much like a yo-yo and 'specie payments' are suspended in some areas of the country.

1815

US National Debt is at $ 99,833,660

War of 1812 ends with the Treaty of Ghent shortly before the **Andrew Jackson** defeats the British at the **Battle of New Orleans.** With the end of the War of 1812 the Native Americans loose British support. The **Federalist Party** lost its support because of its opposition to a popular war with a popular victory and its seeming elitist ideas in a land where the common man was beginning to gain political power. The victory bolstered national honor and **Andrew Jackson became the 'National Hero'.**

Burned Library of Congress reestablished with Jefferson's 6500 volumes, New Jersey issues 1st US railroad charter (John Stevens), 1st natural gas well in US is discovered, Sir Humphrey Davy of London patents miner's safety lamp and **Eruption of Tambora volcano (Sumbawa Java).**

News Flash Napoleon escapes Elba and is accompanied by 1,200 loyal followers. Fears are he will try a re-conquest of France. **Market price of Gold jumps 25 percent.**

Americans have purchased roughly **one million acres** of land from the federal government.

The Depression of 1815 was a post war reaction as orders crashed causing GDP to plummet from the year before numbers. The second Bank of the Unites States was chartered in 1816 to help the country recover from the recent war.

"When a government is dependent upon bankers for money, they and not the leaders of the government control the situation, since the hand that gives is above the hand that takes…below. Money has no motherland; financiers are without patriotism and without decency; their sole object is gain." **Napoleon Bonaparte, Emperor of France**

News Flash Napoleon defeated at **Waterloo,** gold returns to pre Elba escape prices or there about.

1816

US National Debt is at $ 127,334,934

The second **Bank of the United States** starts up with the same powers of the first Bank of the United States and promptly begins **inflationary** policies by **pushing more paper money** into the **economy than it has gold reserves to cover**. Then all of a sudden the Bank starts with the discounting policy of state bank notes again thus torqueing off the state banks and the associated political powers. Further the Bank was associated with fraud and management problems making it a real mess until 1823.

Everybody and his third cousin has opened a bank and is making paper money and putting into circulation further creating inflation, that is if the everybody and his third cousins' paper money is worth a darn or wasn't counterfeit.

England makes law to go to a gold standard as the gold sovereign coin is produced by the Royal Mint at Tower Hill.

> France decrees Bonaparte family excluded from the country forever, 1st savings bank in US opens (Philadelphia Savings Fund Society) and 1st double decked steamboat the Washington arrives in New Orleans making an icon of American lore.

June 10" snowfall in New England, July frost in Waltham, MA, **"year without a summer"** caused by the Mount Tambora eruption in 1815. Reports indicate that harvests in much of northern and central United States were extremely low contributing to a decline in agricultural income and low supplies to other areas of the country let alone near starvation in some of the Northern states. *This also contributed to westward migration as folks looked for better opportunity in the Ohio Valley and beyond. Imagine what would happen in the world should a year without a summer should occur today.*

Indiana Statehood

> Indiana has in its constitution provision for the legislature to establish a system of free education for its citizens.

1817

James Monroe Becomes President 1817 to 1825 Democratic-Republican

"National honor is a national property of the highest value." **James Monroe**

US National Debt is at $ 123,491,965

Construction was started on the **Erie Canal** building more infrastructures. Lyrics; *Low bridge everybody down, low bridge fore we're comin' to a town, you'll always know your neighbor, you'll always know your pal if you've ever navigated on the Erie Canal. My apologies to Mrs. Wagoner if I got the lyrics wrong, it has been 45 years.*

Rossini's opera "La Cenerentola" premieres in Rome, 1st US gas company is incorporated, Baltimore (coal gas for street lights), 1st US city lit by gas (Baltimore) and 1st coffee planted in Hawaii (Kona).

Mississippi Statehood

1818

Things bounce around and begin to rise until 1819 when the feces encounter the bladed mechanism after the second **Bank of the United States reverses monetary policy to curb inflation** in 1818.

The second Bank of the United States starts **calling loans from state banks** refusing any currency as **payment demanding specie (gold and silver)** to pay the 'foreign debts' because those nasty foreigners can't see their way clear to take paper money. The state banks are having the arm put on them as the gold and silver backing up their currency heads to the second Bank of the United States making their money loose value so the **state banks start calling** in loans from their customers (*the people*) demanding specie. Times are getting darn hard for folk especially as specie is rather hard to come by these days.

> **Calling Loans** – Say you're a farmer and borrowed some money to purchase the land and some more for seeds and are counting on making the planned payments. One day Mr. Banker drops by and tells you that deal for three years to pay back the money doesn't mean anything and he wants the money now or he's going to take the property. You are now on the road without even the money you put up in the first place and Mr. Banker has your land. Most times Mr. Banker would rather have the money but not always.

Maryland, Ohio and other states start placing taxes on the second Bank of the United States figuring those taxes could be used to help alleviate the money problems of their citizenry by making loans to those that couldn't make their payments. Ohio and Maryland come to the forefront via the Supreme Court soon.

> Official reopening of the White House, Keats writes his poem "On a Lock of Milton's Hair", Congress approves 1st pensions for government service, 1st steam-vessel to sail Great Lakes launched, 49th parallel forms as border between US & Canada and Handel's Messiah has its US premieres in Boston.

Illinois Statehood

1819

The people can't pay because the economy isn't doing well and as a result of the actions of the second Bank of the United States' policies money was hard to come by making it even more difficult for people to pay their debts. GDP is still shrinking and deflation is well under way, so the **people start losing their land, homes and business**.

96 miles of the **Erie Canal**, from Utica to Rome becomes navigable.

Savannah, the first oceangoing steamship, the sets sail to Europe. Seems when it was sighted off Ireland the locals thought it was afire and sent help.

> 1st successful agricultural journal "American Farmer" begins publication, 1st bicycles (swift walkers) in U.S. introduced in New York City, 1st savings bank in U.S. (Bank of Savings in New York City) opens its doors, 1st parachute jump in U.S, Manchester Massacre: English police charge unemployed, Thomas Blanchard patents lathe and 1st whaling ship arrives in Hawaii.

Dartmouth College v. Woodward the Supreme Court ruled that a state can't alter a contract despite its age and New Hampshire had to keep its' greedy little paws off Dartmouth College, a private enterprise.

> It should be noted that I grew up country and worked on farms as a kid, was a member of the Future Farmers of America and believe dirty hands are peaceable hands. This explains what some may consider a pre-occupation with agriculture in this narrative. Possibly so: but agriculture has played and still does play an important role in national and world economics and eating is a popular and preferred pastime.

The Panic of 1819 is widely considered the first truly 'American' generated Depression. As European agriculture recovered from the Napoleonic Wars, prices fell and demand for export was reduced; deep unemployment, foreclosures, many bank failures and major slowing in agriculture and manufacturing and a severe slide in real estate prices make this much like 1929 and 2007! GDP falls for the next few years.

Cotton prices had risen to around 33 cents a pound causing massive expansion in the cotton growing areas of the south and highly leveraged land buying in the hope of selling at this very high price. In 1819 cotton prices plummeted and the speculators and many established cotton growers in the south were ruined.

The regulatory actions by the second Bank of the United States, they called in loans and reduced the money supply, contributed to the panic and depression laying the foundation for Jacksonian-Democrats to stop national banking in 1836.

Politically this Panic and Depression widened the schism between the north and south. Largely because they had very different economies their interest seemed to oppose each other when it came to national economic policy.

Here come the judge, here come the judge. *I miss that guy.*

'The power to tax is the power to destroy.. .'

McCulloch v. Maryland came before the Supreme Court in 1819. Maryland imposed a tax on all 'notes', paper money, not issued by banks chartered in Maryland. As the Bank of the United States was the only bank operating in Maryland not chartered by that state the Supreme Court reasoned the law targeted the Bank of the United States. The case established two fundamental principles;

congress had implied powers for implementing express powers of the Constitution and states may not 'impede' proper and valid exercise of federal powers. Chief Justice John Marshall, the Federalist guy, wrote the opinion. '..the power to tax is the power to destroy..' **We will see this again!**

From the opinion written by Chief Justice Marshall … "After the most deliberate consideration, it is the unanimous and decided opinion of this court that the act to incorporate the Bank of the United States is a law made in pursuance of the Constitution, and is part of the supreme law of the land"

See Sections 8 & 10 of the Constitution.

England goes on the gold standard

Alison (England) says of the currency contraction brought on by the British gold resumption Policy: There can be no doubt that the reduction of interest has injured the holders of the available capital of the country nearly as much, in many cases, as the producing classes have been injured by the fall in the money-prices of their commodities. Probably it has reduced the incomes of creditors forty per cent. And so, on the other hand, what they might lose as creditors though an abundance of money and a general rise of prices would be more or less compensated by the buoyancy and activity of business, and by the enlarged revenues from real estate and taxed capital, which follow an increase in the volume of money. **From the Silver Commission of 1876**

This sounds a little bit like the rich people do not want to hustle to keep their money. *Just a passing thought.*

Alabama Statehood

1820

US government stops work on the National Road. *There seems to be a lack of funds or determination. Maybe it just didn't have enough political support because times were a changing.*

James Monroe is re-elected without opposition. That is correct. There was no major opposing candidate.

Land Act of 1820 reduced the price per acre to $1.25 per acre, the tract size to 80 acres and ***eliminated the credit program*** because too many folks had bellied up from the Panic of 1819. This had the effect of increasing the influence of 'western' lands as they became states and further isolated the south and somewhat less the northeast. Another result of this and other relief efforts was that the people in debt and those who had lost their lands and businesses, especially in the west began to understand they were a political might and passed state level debt relief laws, mostly in the south and west. Here comes Andrew Jackson! About now the Electoral College should start coming to mind, new states with smaller populations in the west and south. With the depression this can't have made the folks happy that bought land at the higher rate before this Act.

The Missouri Compromise kept the balance of free and slave states, as Missouri and Maine enter the union, and established 36°30' the northern boundary for slave states. *It just put the issue off.*

> The first 86 African American immigrants sponsored by the American Colonization Society started a settlement in present-day Liberia, Missouri Compromise passes, allowing slavery in Missouri, Venus de Milo is discovered on the Aegean island of Melos, Tomato is proven non-poisonous (*thank god*), Spain sells part of Florida to US for $5 million (*let those dumb Yankees deal with those crazy Seminoles*), Missouri imposes a $1 bachelor tax on unmarried men between 21 & 50 and Russian and British expeditions discover the Antarctic continent (separately).

William H. Crawford, Secretary of the Treasury, in a report to **Congress.**

> All intelligent writers on currency agree that when it is decreasing in amount, **poverty and misery must prevail.**

Cato Street Conspiracy Revolution and treason were in the air as some folks decided it would be a fine idea to kill off the British cabinet and take over the government. The British government found out about it and a few of the conspirators were hung and then decapitated with their heads placed upon spikes. *Ain't civilization great?*

Maine Statehood

1821

Relief Act of 1821 Effects of the depression caused by the Panic in 1819 left large segments of the nation crippled. People who'd bought land with the government credit plan, at higher prices before the 1820 Land Act, were unable to make their payments and many lost their land. The situation was so bad and wide spread the government made the following accommodations.

> Extended payment schedules.

> Let the people return the part of the land that would have been paid in full with the payments they'd already made and keep the part that could be considered paid for.

> They also got a large cut in price of around 37 percent if they paid off their original balance in full.

> There is a difference of opinion in the literature whether this worked well or not. At least the effort was made. In point of fact there had been several legislative efforts prior to this to help settlers retain their land.

> Mexico permits Moses Austin & 300 US families to settle in Texas (*are they ever gonna regret that*), Battle of Carabobo; Bolívar defeats royalists outside of Caracas, 1st edition of Saturday Evening Post, Failed liberal coup against French King Louis XVIII, 1st colonies along Santa Fe Trail, Costa Rica, El Salvador, Guatemala, Honduras & Nicaragua gain independence and Kentucky abolishes debtors prisons.

Speculation There were still investors buying large amounts of land with speculation in mind, *just a reminder.*

George Warde Norman serves as governor of the Bank of England from **1821-1872.**

England is now on the gold standard. [Notwithstanding the legal relation of value between the two precious metals established in 1792 in this country did not coincide exactly with the market relation, yet they circulated concurrently, with perhaps a preponderance of silver in the circulation until 1821, when the resumption of specie payments in gold by the Bank of England caused an advance in the value of gold and a consequent widening of the relation of value between the two metals.] In 1821, when the Bank of England resumed specie payments in gold, a change occurred in the relative value of the metals in the London market. Silver fell relatively to gold, but there was at that time no decrease in the demand in the world for silver, which was still accepted as money everywhere except in England. No change had then recently taken place in the relative production of the metals, nor had England any silver with which to frighten or affect the market.

The supply of and the demand for silver was unchanged at that period. It is clear, therefore, that in that instance the change in the relative value of the metals in the London market was not due to a fall in silver, but arose wholly from the new demand for gold and from a rise in its value. **Silver Commission of 1876**

Missouri Statehood

1822

Politically things are starting to get complicated. The Federalists haven't put a candidate in to the Presidency in over twenty years, *just a note.*

> Greek War of Independence from Ottoman Empire, Haiti invades the newly founded Dominican Republic, Denmark Vessy leads slave rebellion in South Carolina, Brazil declares independence from Portugal (National Day), eruption of Galunggung (Java), - Mexico officially recognized as an independent nation by United States.

Here we go again.

Recession of 1822 1815 to 1822 seems a big muddled mess. After a mild recovery from the 1819 Panic commodity prices peak then in early 1822 prices fall. With businesses failing unemployment rises again and imports cause a trade imbalance. GDP falls in 1823 and 1824 then rises again.

1823

The Monroe Doctrine written by Secretary of State John Quincy Adams. The New World, the Americas, should be free from more European colonization and European interference in sovereign countries' business. Also the United States intended to be neutral in European wars and their colonies but any new colonies or any interference with countries in the Americas would be considered hostile acts against the United States.

R J Tyers patents roller skates, 1st steamboat to navigate the Mississippi River, a fire destroys the ancient Basilica of Saint Paul Outside the Walls in Rome and Moroni 1st appears to Joseph Smith, according to Smith.

Nicholas Biddle becomes president of the second **Bank of the United States** and starts to run the institution the way it was supposed to but the damage is already done.

1824

There were 4 candidates for the **Presidential** election, John Quincy Adams a Democratic-Republican (Secretary of State), Andrew Jackson maybe sort of a Democratic-Republican (US Senator), Henry Clay, soon to be a Whig (Speaker of the House) and William H. Crawford Democratic-Republican (Treasury Secretary). The election results held to regional popularity and no candidate received a majority of the Electoral College. The election went to the House of Representatives. Adams and Jackson won by far the most states. Henry Clays' influence in the House gave him the leverage to sway the vote to Adams and Clay became Secretary of State. Jacksons' people deemed this the **'Corrupt Deal'**. The Federalists were pretty much nonexistent and couldn't even field a candidate.

During Adams term new political parties developed. Adams' followers took the moniker **National Republicans** and Jacksons' following picked up with **Democratic**. At this time nobody, but nobody, wanted to be affiliated with the word **Federalists**.

> J W Goodrich introduces rubber galoshes to the public, First Burmese War: The British officially declare war on Burma, Washing machine patented by Noah Cushing of Quebec, **General Lafayette returns to US** (*this was a truly grand event and tens of thousands turned out to greet him*) and a storm causes St Petersburg flood, killing 10,000.

Chemical Bank of New York is formed from New York Chemical Manufacturing Company, 1823.

Then the Supreme Court gets into the fray again!

Osborn v Bank of the United States also has to do with a state taxing the Bank of the United States. Ohio imposed a tax on the Bank of the United States because the bank, as had many others, lent money to people to buy federal lands in amounts beyond what the banks' credit allowed. The Bank of the United States required payments be made in hard cash or federal notes, paper money, and that type of money was in very short supply. Ohio figured that taxing the Bank of the United States would bring in funds for loans so folks could make their payments. Well the Bank of the United States said no and Ohio went and took the money from the bank. The Supreme Court said give it back and Mr. Osborn, the Ohio Auditor, returned all but two thousand dollars which he had paid his agents with for getting the money. The Supreme Court said give back the two thousand dollars and Ohio did. *It would have been interesting if Ohio had told them to go suck eggs.* Additionally, in this case, the Justices asserted Federal authority over all cases concerning the National Bank of the United States.

1825

John Quincy Adams becomes President 1825 to 1829 Last Democratic-Republican to become President

"America, with the same voice which spoke herself into existence as a nation, proclaimed to mankind the inextinguishable rights of human nature, and the only lawful foundations of government." **John Quincy Adams**

> Ezra Daggett & nephew Thomas Kensett patent food storage in tin cans, Charles X becomes King of France, Dutch King Willem I throws foreign students out, Erie Canal opens linking Great Lakes & Atlantic Ocean and the 1st public railroad using steam locomotive completed in England.

The **Panic of 1825** was primarily a stock market crash following a **'bubble'** in Latin American investments. (*Everybody sing that old Don Ho favorite, Tiny…..in the …*) Business growth slowed but it was generally mild. Panic also occurred in England.

1826

The first railroad in the United States was chartered and like all or nearly all others was given the right of eminent domain in a limited capacity to buy what land was needed if the owner declined to sell.

Railroads would become privately owned essential transportation enterprises, many of whom had been government sponsored.

> American Temperance Society, forms in Boston (*these temperance folks are persistent*), 1st US Rail Road chartered, Granite Railway in Quincy, Mass, USS Vincennes leaves NY to become 1st warship to circumnavigate the globe, Benjamin W. Edwards rides into Mexican controlled Nacogdoches, Texas and declares himself ruler of the Republic of Fredonia. *Really!*

1826 found England forbidding America to trade with English colonies. *Maybe they didn't like the Monroe Doctrine or something.*

> England sought to undermine the United States into and during the Civil War. Guess they did not like an ex-colony out trading them. Well, they really didn't. As the British Empire shrank so did their sources of income shrink and the Empire eventually collapsed. The erosion of the 'Colonial Era' began with the American Revolution and ended in the 1960's.

1827

United States issues counter trade prohibitions against England. Well why not?

Dutch Trade Company NHM gets opium monopoly on Java, 20,000 attend Ludwig von Beethoven's' burial in Vienna and William Rowan Hamilton presents his Theory of Systems of Rays.

1828

"Always vote for principle, though you may vote alone, you may cherish the sweetest reflection that your vote is never lost." **John Quincy Adams**

Recession of 1828 Credit tightened for New England businesses and trade income fell as the aforementioned prohibitions, not listed or cited, worked really well. *Yeah team! Or not!*

> The Russian-Persian peace treaty is signed, Brazil and Denmark sign a treaty of Commerce and Navigation, construction of the B&O Railroad begins (*yeah, one down three to go*), earthquake hits Japan 30,000 dead, Uruguay gains independence and US passes Tariff of Abominations (*the abominable feel abominated upon, may haps not grammatically correct but pointy.*)

The **Tariff of Abominations a.k.a. Tariff of 1828** was meant to protect north eastern, New England, manufacturers from low priced goods being sold by England that undercut American production costs. The south gave the tariff the moniker 'Abominations' as it hurt England's ability to pay for the cotton imported from the United States. As the western United States favored the tariff also, the south was adversely affected and further isolated by the rest of the nation aggravating an already hot political climate.

> *The way this works is England receives payments, in gold and silver, on the products in exports to the United States, mostly purchased in the North, uses that gold and silver to pay for the cotton it imports from the Southern United States. If the sales up north go south, that is lessened; the south cannot sell as much cotton to England, their primary customer for cotton or the prices drop because demand is less. But it isn't like England didn't have tons of money coming from other sources.*

Andrew Jackson wins Presidential election by a landslide.

1829

Andrew Jackson becomes President 1829 to 1837 Democratic.

The **Democratic Party** supported, states-rights and small government, opposed the Bank of the United States and paper currency, figured tariffs taxed the poor and supported the rich and pushed for expansion to the west. The Democratic Party was supported by rural regions with farmers and frontiersmen and immigrants in urban areas.

The states-rights support was heavily influenced by the issue of slavery as many urban people feared the entrance of former slaves into the labor market and land owners feared excessive competition from same said former slaves. The banking support was influenced by the agrarian suffering from debt and having to pay higher prices for items because of the protective tariffs. The banking and tariff activities had the effect of centralizing wealth in the East among those who were widely considered elite.

Despite riffs within the party on other issues the party solidly supported the slavery issue and continued to be the dominate party for the next 30 years in their support of slavery, states-rights, a weak central government and being against central banking.

The **National Republican** Party basically rallied around opposing Andrew Jackson and the philosophies of the Democratic Party. The National Republicans were not able to gain sufficient support to claim the Presidency and gradually became absorbed by the Whig Party.

Unruly crowd mobs White House during President Jacksons' inaugural ball. (*I'd bet, if available, they'd of had long neck Buds, Jack shooters and Tammy singing. I would have.*)

> William Austin Burt patents "typographer" (typewriter), London's Metropolitan Police Force goes on duty (*Scotland Yard*), Britain abolished "suttee" in India (widow burning herself to death on her husband's funeral pyre).

For the next few years we have negative inflation and growth in the GDP.

1830

Indian Removal Act and the Trail of Tears in 1831- You will have to look this one up as I had to delete my comments because they were too long and editing yielded ninety-three percent expletive deleted comments remaining.

> Great fire in New Orleans, New York Stock Exchange slowest day ever (31 shares traded), 1st regular steam train passenger service starts, Edwin Budding of England signs an agreement for manufacture of his invention, lawn mower (*ok so what do I do with the goats*), Revolution in France replaces Charles X with Louis Philippe.

1831

"The bold effort the present bank had made to control the government, the distress it had wantonly produced...are but premonitions of the fate that awaits the American people should they be deluded into a perpetuation of this institution or the establishment of another like it." **Andrew Jackson**

United States Population is now 13,235,000

> 1st US building & loan association organized, Frankford, Penn, Jan van Speijk blows up his gunboat in Antwerp, killing about 30, Soldiers marching on a bridge in Manchester, England cause it to collapse, "America (My Country 'Tis of Thee)" is 1st sung in Boston, - London Bridge opens to traffic, Michael Faraday demonstrates 1st electric transformer, HMS Beagle/Charles Darwin departs England for South America and Nat Turner's Slave Rebellion.

1832

The **Tariff of 1832** was a slightly watered down version of the Tariff of 1828 and still managed to tick-off southern states.

Anti-Masonic Party, platform self -explanatory, ran William Wirt for president gaining around 8% of the national vote.

> US population is 13.6 million and rising. Trinidad insurrection by negroes, anti-slavery society starts in Boston, choleras appears in Scotland and London, Joseph Smith is beaten, tarred and feathered in Ohio, Greece becomes an independent republic, 3rd national black convention in Philadelphia, cholera kills about 6,000 in lower Canada, opium is exempted from federal tariff duty (OOPS, wait, what was that. Opium exempted from tariff?), John Calhoun Resigns over differences with Andrew Jackson and South Carolina passes Ordinance of Nullification.

The **Ordinance of Nullification** declared the tariffs of 1828 and 1832 null and void in the state of South Carolina. It was felt these tariffs favored the Northern interests while hurting the south. Andrew Jackson issued the **Nullification Proclamation** of 1832 and sent a naval force south and threatened to send ground troops to force the collection of the tariffs. South Carolina, facing this military force, capitulated. This situation further alienated the south.

Andrew Jacksons' response to a bill to renew the charter of the second Bank of the United States…

> *"A bank of the United States is in many respects convenient for the Government and for the people. Entertaining this opinion, and deeply impressed with the belief that some of the powers and privileges possessed by the existing bank are unauthorized by the Constitution, subversive of the rights of the States, and dangerous to the liberties of the people, I felt it my duty…to call to the attention of Congress to the practicability of organizing an institution combining its advantages and obviating these objections. I sincerely regret that in the act before me I can perceive none of those modifications of the bank charter which are necessary, in my opinion, to make it compatible with justice, with sound policy, or with the Constitution of our country."*

Jackson was of the belief that only gold and silver minted as coin of the country should be allowed. Part of the problem was that there just wasn't all that much gold and silver around at the time.

1833

Tariff of 1833 was a compromise tariff act, guided through the confirmation process by Henry Clay, setting a schedule reducing the prior tariffs over a period ending in 1842. *While South Carolina capitulated on the Ordinance of Nullification it looks like they got what they wanted anyway.*

Whig Party formed. National Republicans, Anti-Masons and other smaller factions got together and became the Whig Party to confront the Policies of Andrew Jackson and his Democratic Party. Noteworthy leaders are John Quincy Adams and Henry Clay both former Democratic-Republicans.

The Whigs saw Jacksons' popularity as like a monarchy and took the name Whigs after patriots of the revolution who fought against the English monarchy. The Whigs supported a strong congress (because Jackson was a very strong president), tariffs to support industry and a means to modernization via industry financed by Banks, education and moral reform (anti-slavery) and internal improvements like roads.

> British seize control of Falkland Islands (seems this issue has been rather long standing), US and Siam sign a commercial treaty, soda fountain patented, Tsar Nichols bans public selling of serfs, John Deere makes their plow, 4th national black convention, Chicago is founded, British ban slavery in the colonies (700,000 are freed) **and Charles Darwin keeps floating around.**

"A power has risen up in the government greater than the people themselves, consisting of many and various and powerful interests, combined into one mass, and held together by the cohesive power of the vast surplus in the banks." **John C. Calhoun**

Bank of England notes are made **'legal tender'** in the United Kingdom.

A mild recession appears to have happened in 1833 and 1834.

1834

Andrew Jackson uses US troops to suppress a labor dispute among the workers at the Chesapeake and Ohio Canal.

In **Philadelphia Whigs and Democrats** stage a gun, stone and brick battle for control of a Moyamensing Township election, resulting in one death, several injuries, and the burning down of a block of buildings. *Look this last one up. It's a riot…!*

> Mexico imprisons Stephen F. Austin in Mexico City (*I don't believe this would have improved his attitude about Mexico*), hardhat diving suit patented and the 1st black to receive a US patent is Henry Blair for a corn planter.

Coinage Act of 1834 was passed by the United States Congress on June 27, 1834. It raised the silver-to-gold weight ratio from its 1792 level of 15:1 to 16:1. Silver became significantly undervalued in relation to gold and became scarce because folks took it to Europe where they got better value for it. Again?!

> *Also, after the change made in 1834 in the legal relation of value between the two metals, they circulated concurrently until about 1850, although, on account of the undervaluation of silver by the law of 1834, there was a constant tendency to an exportation of silver in the settlement of foreign balances.*
>
> *The legal relation of gold to silver of 1 to 15, originally established in 1792, was an undervaluation of gold and an overvaluation of silver. The change made in 1834, establishing a relation of 1 to 16, was as great an error in the opposite direction, but was acceptable to Georgia and the Carolinas, then in the flush of great hopes from recently-discovered gold mines, and satisfactory to the whole country on the theory that bank-notes could be expelled more certainly and readily from the smaller channels of circulation by gold than by silver coin.* **Silver Commission of 1876**

Senate censures President Andrew Jackson for taking federal deposits from the Bank of the United States and putting them in state banks. *Seems Old Hickory really hated that bank, he felt the bank was making favorable loans to people of influence.*

Seriously, there was a general feeling that the National Bank was favoring Industry and trade over development of the interior. This was likely the cases as these were fairly dependable investments and all those guys knew each other anyway. *The claim by Jackson made below is as* **likely** *to be as accurate, maybe more so.*

Andrew Jackson on the second **Bank of the United States**

> *"Gentlemen, I have had men watching you for a long time and I am convinced that you have used the funds of the bank to speculate in the breadstuffs of the country. When you won, you divided the profits amongst you, and when you lost, you charged it to the bank. You tell me that if I take the deposits from the bank and annul its charter, I shall ruin ten thousand families. That may be true, gentlemen, but that is your sin! Should I let you go on, you will ruin fifty thousand families, and that would be my sin! You are a den of vipers and thieves."*

Jacksons' statement represents a longstanding issue in the United States, Then as now and the times between when the bankers are successful they divide the spoils among themselves but when things go bad we 'the people' the government has to come bail them out or take the loss due to their failures.

As the west was settled Jackson and those of like mind felt it vital that those settling the west have the opportunities provided by accessible capital and what they thought best for those people. Others were more concerned with development of industry and modernization of the country. Who was or is right? Maybe they both are but are unable to entertain and execute a coordinated effort.

1835

Discovery of gold at Dahlonega Georgia forces Indians out as whites rush in. *This gold strike gave the United States its' first major internal source of gold!*

> The Republic of Indian Stream affair, Richard Lawrence fails to kill President Andrew Jackson when gun misfires (*bet the Indians hired him*), 1st edition of New York Herald, P.T. Barnum gets going (*There's a sucker born every minute*), Brazil has a revolution, second Seminole War begins, Texas Rangers get started, Hans Christian Anderson publishes a book of fairy tales and huge fire in New York City.

1836

Second Bank of the United States charter expires at the efforts of Andrew Jackson. **The National DEBT is virtually 'ZERO'.** This is the last time the National DEBT will ever approach ZERO. Over one hundred seventy-five years the United States has been in DEBT. *I also can't imagine those foreigners that owned 20% of the bank was very happy with Andrew Jackson and his followers.*

Davy Crockett arrives in Texas (*guess what's coming ... Remember the ....*), anyway, Sam Colt gets a patent for his revolver, Texas abolishes slave trade, Quanah Parker's mother is captured by the Comanche, Charles Darwin is running around, Whig Party's national convention (Federalists are defunct), and Betsy Ross (the flag LADY) and James Madison die. Cotton prices have been climbing and the west is being settled or invaded if you like.

The **Specie Circular of 1836** states that western lands can now only be purchased with gold or silver coin. This makes it a little harder for folks to buy Federal land but it is still readily available to those with adequate funds for speculation and puts more gold and silver in the federal coffers which was probably the idea anyway.

Deposit Act of 1836 has to do with distributing a federal surplus. Apparently the National DEBT had reached zero at this point. You wouldn't think getting money back would be contentious but it was very much so.

Martin van Buren easily elected to the Presidency on the tide of Andrew Jacksons' popularity.

"**Banks properly established** and conducted are highly useful to the business of the country, and will doubtless continue to exist in the States so long as they conform to their laws and are found to be safe and beneficial." **Martin Van Buren**

"**The connection which formerly** existed between the Government and banks was in reality injurious to both, as well as to the general interests of the community at large." **Martin Van Buren**

Arkansas Statehood

Since 1791 the United States has had a couple of rebellions, a secession/treasonous attempt by parts of New England, a Vice President gets arrested for treason, that same Vice President kills the former Secretary of the Treasury in a duel, the United States has had eight depressions/recessions/financial crisis, a Senator is put up for impeachment, had another war with the British and they start to play nice for a while, the Marines fight on 'the shores of Tripoli' making a line for their Hymn, Europe has gutted itself with war and the Federalists political party disappears because it fails to represent the most citizens as Jacksonian-Democrats appeal to the common man. The Whig party fills the void left by the Federalists.

The Supreme Court has a couple of land mark decisions concerning federal supremacy in banking, setting the stage for future fun and games.

Andrew Jackson pushed through the Indian Removal Act of 1830 leading to the Trail of Tears. *Bad dog!*

Economically the United States has been a tidal wave of enormous proportions. Europe accommodated the early success of the United States by tearing itself up in war and ordering supplies from the young country. Furthermore Europeans invested heavily in the United States.

The western lands were settled like a plague of locusts. Nearly everything was wide open and peoples' freedom from the European systems was a euphoric fever infecting all who could see a horizon. It was truly the 'promised land'.

Land has been sold by the federal government, to rich and poor alike, on credit leading to many foreclosures and ruined lives including Robert Morris. The rightly or wrongly hated National Bank system is over until 1863 creating the 'Free Banking Era' where banks are state chartered only`. Regulations on banking vary dramatically making the whole system, along with the stock market, wide open…. Much seems almighty familiar to today. Truly! Much more to come!

The state banks did have regulations on them and many served their communities well. It seems New England fared better, during this and the next era, better than most. Perhaps it was because it was well established. I do not know.

From here to 1863 the Supreme Court is not involved in banking cases concerning the National or Central Bank because there is no National Bank, only State Banks.

1837 to 1862 Free Banking Era, Dividing a Country & Oregon Trail

Free because there were only state chartered banks during this period with no federal interference and was it ever a 'free' for all.

1837

Martin Van Buren becomes President 1837 to 1841 Democratic

"As to the Presidency, the two happiest days of my life were those of my entrance upon the office and my surrender of it." **Martin Van Buren.** *Be careful what you ask for, the Gods may grant it.*

There are 700 or so banks in the United States.

The Free Banking Era began when the second National Bank of the United States charter ended and was not renewed in 1836. This left the United States with only state chartered banks who issued their own paper money against reserves of gold and silver. Each state established its own guidelines concerning reserves of gold and silver against the paper money issued, interest rates for deposits and loans and other guidelines.

The second Bank of the United States is gone leaving lending to finance the country's growth to state and private banks or foreign investors. Some banks began accepting payments only in hard money, gold and silver coins, and bank notes were not accepted making paper money undesirable. This blew up and the country went into a recession that seems to have lasted until 1843 and around 350 banks failed.

Michigan, in 1837, made accommodations for the basically automatic chartering of banks. Meaning the approval of each bank by the legislature was no longer required. The Michigan Act also *lowered oversight and state supervision.* The result was what is referred to as Wildcat Banking. A situation where a person or persons would open a bank, print 'bank bills' (*paper money*), against the supposed reserves of gold and silver and then screw it all up by printing too many, usually or just running off with whatever they could lay their hands on.. This would devalue the paper money from that bank. The result was that probably half of the banks opened in the Free Banking Era closed and left lots of folks in a hard place having *paper with only one of two uses.*

It is also important to realize that the fluctuating prices of gold and silver contributed to the difficulties of some banks. Not all banking during this or any period was unstable or unscrupulous. Many played important parts in the development of the nation and supplied people with much needed financial support. There were some banks that acted as a central bank and/or a clearing house for the other banks notes in the area. This made for a stable economic situation because the face value of the bills was honored at full or nearly full value.

> Vice President is chosen by the Senate, riots in New York because of poverty and flour prices jumping, Martin Van Buren President, Supreme Court now 9 members (was seven), Canada gave blacks right to vote, unemployment reaches record levels, Broad Street Riots in Boston (ethnic), Goodyear gets rubber patent, Queen Victoria begins reign of 63 years,

Tiffany jewelry store gets going, abolitionist printer Elijah P. Lovejoy killed by pro-slavery mob and a steam threshing machine receives patent.

The Panic of 1837 was a ripe and royal international mess.

Things had been **BOOM**ing for the past few years. Cotton prices had risen sharply resulting in lots of folks figuring it would just keep on that way so they speculated in buying more land and using excessive amounts of credit. Western land expansion with these good times had more folks buying homestead type land on credit until the Specie Circular of 1836. Much of the money to finance the expansion and growth in United States' internal improvements, industrialization and western expansion had come from Great Britain via ***Baring Brothers*** (*didn't they buy part of the Bank of the United States*) and others.

When the Bank of England, in 1836, noted that their reserves of real money had declined they decided to raise their interest rates over a period of time to five percent from three percent. A significant reason they had depleted reserves was because the wheat harvests had been very poor and they (Great Britain) had had to pay for foreign wheat. (Country to country is in real money, gold and silver).

Another version says the Bank of England one day simply refused to honor the credit of the United States by denying the value of American stocks and notes. This would have sent those holding that 'paper' into frenzy as they had expected to borrow funds and were suddenly unable to do business because they had no money. In either case the Bank of England put the sticks to Americas' economy.

> *YES, England is still financing much of Americas' economy as many banks are funded via England. This puts America at the mercy of England, still!*

To make a very long story short the result was rapid movements of gold and silver to England to the point that New York Banks began to pay less than face value, in gold and silver, for their own notes (currency) and the **BUST** starts with people running to the banks to get as much real money as possible before it runs out.

The result was severe unemployment, widespread business failures and prices dropping. It is generally accepted that this depression lasted for the next sixish years.

Partially because the **Deposit and Distribution Act of 1836** had federal money deposited in state banks around the country, there was less money in the industrial areas of the east and those banks had less money for lending. Some people blamed this for the Depression.

Because the United States had no central bank there was no structured, *under law*, way to come to the aid of the banks being run on. This demonstrated to some folks one of the reasons for a national or central banking system: not to bailout misdeeds but to provide for some stability when forces of nature and the acts of man elsewhere in the world create turbulence in the economy.

Because of the terrible economic times some banks and States defaulted on the loans made from creditors in Great Britain. *This really ticked off the British. Not only do we run them out of the country and cut into their trade markets but we go and take their money. I'd be ticked off too. This is also a good example of how international banking can affect the United States economy. Most of the loans were eventually repaid and the British did continue to finance American growth.*

It seems August Belmont and his buddy Peabody made a killing buying up stocks at bargain prices during this mess.

This might be a good time to talk about 'bank runs'.

Let's say we all get together and deposit $100,000 in the Bank of Forever Hopeful. The bank promises to pay us 2% interest on our deposits. The bank decides that normal withdraws for 'us the depositors' for a given period is going to be $10,000. The bank then decides to loan out $80,000 at an interest rate of 5% and keep $10,000 extra on hand just in case. Makes sense so far, after all the bank looks to make $2,000 or so.

The bank loans $60,000 to XY Railroad Company to start laying tracks and takes shares in the company as collateral because Railroad Shares are really BOOMing. A flash flood comes along and not only wipes out the tracks that have been laid but destroys most of the tracking material being held in a warehouse and the warehouse to boot. The Warehouse was financed by XY Railroad's president's mother-in-law.

I have $15,000 in the bank and after figuring that XY Railroad Company will likely not be able to pay off their loan, because I was standing on a hill watching the whole thing, I decide I better go get my money out of Forever Hopeful before it disappears. On my way to the bank I run into 'my brother Bill' sitting in a tree, he says he flew up there, I tell him what is up with the bank. Bill jumps down to join me in my trip to the bank so he can get his $7,000 out before it too has a chance to disappear.

When 'my brother Bill' and I are at the bank the teller says we can't have all our money at once because the bank only keeps so much on hand and we will have to come back for the rest later. At this point Bill and I have only been able to get everything we had but that $10,000 they had laying around for 'just in case' because the teller knew the boss would be mad if he didn't keep some operating capital on hand.

Mrs. Little was in line behind us and when we weren't able to get out all our money she decides to pull out her $4,000. She gets her money from the teller because everybody and their brother knows Mrs. Little has a bad temper especially when she neglects temperance as she apparently had been that morning and will run around breaking furniture and horses until a crowd gathers and the situation will leak out before the teller has a chance to duck home sans rope around neck and the entire county is going to want their money like NOW.

Mr. Bank President hasn't yet learned about the destruction caused by the flash flood and rides over to the owner of XY Railroad Company to tell him he has to call the loan because he has to keep so much on hand at the bank and is running a bit low. Oops! Not only has the material been destroyed but they have only $5,000 left of which $3,000 has to be paid to the employees for the time they have already worked.

Fast math equals short tens of thousands of dollars should people start wanting all of their money like NOW!

Meanwhile back at the Little house Chicken the third son of the Little's, hears Mrs. Little talking with Mr. Little about the financial sky falling and he, Chicken, promptly fulfills his moral obligation and runs around the county screaming about the financial sky falling and everybody 'runs to the bank', to get their money, which is now closed because Mr. Bank President knows there are going be lots of angry people wanting money that no longer exists and he might find himself wearing aforesaid rope if he doesn't take what there is left and head for Bermuda. On the way out of town Mr. Bank President runs into Mr. President of XY Railroad who also happens to be heading for Bermuda because he has decided to take all $5,000 leaving the workers without pay and besides he needs as much distance as possible before his soon to be ex-mother-in-law finds out what happened.

The result is lots of people are broke, loans are called in from the other $20,000 that was loaned out to local farmers and merchants and when the people can't pay they lose their land, businesses and homes.

That is one way political parties are motivated to get started.

Briscoe v. Bank of Kentucky established that state-chartered banks, state-owned banks, and the banknotes they created were Constitutional. So now the court has determined that a Central Bank and state banking are Constitutional but also that the currency issued by both is also constitutional.

Michigan Statehood

1838

The Caroline Affair A bunch of discontented Canadians wanted a republic and the Canadian government was not pleased at the idea. The rebels ran away to one Navy Island on the Niagara River, Canadian side, and proclaimed a Republic of Canada. *This Republic thing might be contagious.*

The American folks saw the Canadian Rebels on the island and after discerning their intent figured it was a good idea and it might be great fun to help them out. The Americans had access to the SS Caroline which they used to supply the new Republic of Canada with food, money and guns.

A couple of Canadian officers and their men, taking offense with the Americans and their interfering ways, grabbed the SS Caroline in Canadian waters, took her out to the current, set the poor dear afire and everybody enjoyed the show as she careened over Niagara Falls all ablaze. *Maybe some enjoyed the scene more than others.*

To retaliate for the SS Caroline some of the boys take the Sir Robert Peel, a British ship, and burn her. Alas the Sir Robert Peel was in Canadian waters at the time the boys nabbed her. This was not such a good idea, but after all this was the land of the free, brave and rebellious and the boys felt obliged to get even for the SS Caroline. So the President tells the army to go up to the border and get things under control as they seem to be getting out of hand. Oh dear, the army is partially successful as there are a few more battles before the respective governments sit down and make nice and almost every little body has a happy face.

Morse code used in telegraph, rebellion in Canada, fire destroys about half of Charleston, Frederick Douglas escapes from slavery, Mormons ordered to leave Missouri or be exterminated, Mexico declares war on France and Boers beat Zulu Chieftain in South Africa.

Meanwhile the **Aroostook War** got going over the International boundary between Canada and Maine. There were some casualties from civilian action but the military forces maintained cooler heads. The dispute was settled diplomatically in 1839 and signed off in 1842. *Seems the loggers took exception and good aim when they saw Canadians snooping around.*

New York passes a Free Banking Act.

1839

The Anti-rent War begins with the armed uprising in upper New York against a lease hold of land tenure (ownership) law. The governor calls out the militia which seems to tick off the tenants more and violence spreads. Then another governor declares martial law. The violence abates and a new constitution for New York abolishes the system establishing a more equitable method to change ownership.

> Steam shovel patented, riots in England, an Opium War begins in China, British occupy Beirut, cyclone hits India destroying thousands of ships about 300,000 people die, 1st photo of the Moon (French photographer Louis Daguerre), Thomas Henderson measures 1st stellar parallax (Alpha Centauri), Congress prohibits dueling in District of Columbia, 1st recorded use of "OK" [oll korrect] (Boston's Morning Post), 1st U.S. anti-slavery party, Liberty Party, convenes in New York and we have the Anti-Rent War starting.

Uncertain financial conditions in England

Henry Clay declares in Senate "I had rather be right than president." *He never was president.*

1840

With over 700 banks each printing their own notes, really credit drafts, how could a person be sure a note from a bank in Rhode Island was any god to a person in say Georgia? What people did was discount the notes. That is instead of giving $100 worth of value the seller might give only $80 of value. You can see how this could cause a great deal of uncertainty normally let alone the possibility of counterfeiting. These have contributed to several western and period novels' plots.

> First bowling match in US, Baltimore College of Dental Surgery, 1st in U.S., incorporated, American Charles Wilkes discovers Shackleton Ice Shelf, Antarctica, tornado strikes Natchez Miss, kills 317, Samuel Morse patents his telegraph and William H. Harrison elected President.

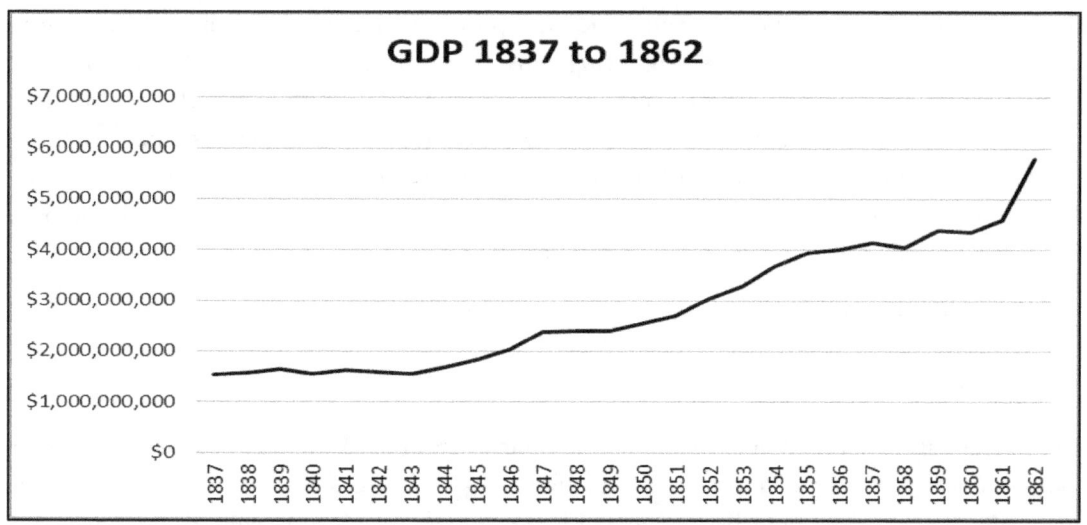

GDP 1837 to 1862

Nearly the entire mass of the metallic money of the continent of Europe consisted of silver, the gold standard being continued to Portugal and to the island of Great Britain. **From the Silver Commission of 1876**

1841

William Henry Harrison becomes President, lives one month Whig

"The prudent capitalist will never adventure his capital . . . if there exists a state of uncertainty as to whether the Government will repeal tomorrow what it has enacted today." **William Henry Harrison**

John Tyler becomes President to 1845 Whig, is drummed out of the party because he vetoed the re-establishing of a national bank, just like a good **Democrat** would have done.

"Wealth can only be accumulated by the earnings of industry and the savings of frugality." **John Tyler**

> China cedes Hong Kong to British, continuous filibuster in US Senate begins Feb. 28 and ends March 11(*this means that folks stood on the floor of the Senate and talked without giving the floor to any speaker in opposition – Look up Everett Dirksen, a man unfamiliar with the word brevity*), we have another rebellion (ain't freedom fun).

Preemption Act of 1841 a.k.a. The Distributive Preemption Act (I like to think of this as *the Lets Make More Squatters and Overrun the Frontier Act because this will inspire more people to go out and take the Indian lands and get out of our hair for a bit Act*)

Basically the act gave pre-emptive rights of ownership to folks already living on Federal lands and was widely used until the Homestead Act of 1862. There were still claims but lots left. The Act was officially repealed in 1891.

Squatters who were living on Federal land could buy up to 160 acres at not less than $1.25 per acre as long as they were; head of household, a single man over 21 or a widow, were or intended to become a citizen and were a resident on that land for a minimum of fourteen months and they had to stay there. (*Not just grab the land and sell it and take off, speculate*) They also had to make improvements to the land. Additionally Illinois, Missouri, Mississippi, Ohio, Indiana, Louisiana, Arkansas, Alabama and Michigan, or any state afterward admitted to the Union, would be paid 10% of the proceeds from the sale of such public land.

We have a rebellion. Yippee.

The Door Rebellion

Seems Rhode Island was still organized under a **Charter from 1663** that granted voting rights to landowners only. At the time most males were farmers so this was a moot point. The industrial revolution had reached America by this time (1841) resulting in large segments of the population living in the cities and were not owners of land and represented a percentage of the male population far greater than half. Understandably this caused a majority of the male population feeling left out and being under the thumb of the land owners. This was supposed to be the land of the free and, by now most of the states no longer required property ownership as a condition for voting.

Thomas Dorr and some of the boys took exception to this situation arguing that the Guarantee Clause of the Constitution was being violated. (*"The United States shall guarantee to every State in this Union a Republican Form of Government..."*)

As efforts to change the male suffrage situation over the preceding years had failed Dorr and the boys decided to hold a 'People's Convention' and wrote a new constitution giving voting rights to white males with residence over a year. The General Assembly of the state wrote their own 'Freemen's Constitution that gave into some demands.

Later that year, 1841, the Freemen's Constitution was defeated in the legislature and the People's Constitution was soundly supported in a Referendum. Each group had elections of their own in 1842. (*Both felt justified, I guess*) Door and Sam King were elected Governor of the state by their respective groups. Sam King wouldn't relent and things get rather dicey. King asks for Federal troops to quell the uprising. President Tyler instead sends somebody to look things over. Tyler says not yet, because it looks like it might be calming down, but he will uphold the Constitutional Guarantee should it come to that.

There is marching around of armed forces. Dorr's efforts fail and a warrant is put out for his arrest and big reward on his head. Dorr flees and the remaining parties to the disagreement get together and make nice and make the suffrage changes later that year. Dorr returns and is promptly convicted and thrown in the slammer in solitary. His fate does get resolved but not as nicely as I'd have liked so see.

Point is this was another step in the growth of freedom under the Constitution and the protection of citizens.

1842

Tariff of 1842 reverses the effects of the tariff of 1833 that had scheduled reductions each year. The Whigs and industrial interests put a lot of pressure to increase tariffs as they feared low prices from abroad. It also greatly helps the economic recovery from the Panic of 1837.

> First known sewing machine patented in US, John Greenough, Wash DC, 1st US child labor law regulating working hours passed (Mass), Over 500 Mexican troops led by Rafael Vasquez invade Texas, briefly occupy San Antonio and then head back to the Rio Grande, Ether was used as an anesthetic for 1st time by Dr. Crawford Long (GA), Karl Marx becomes editor-in-chief of Rheinische Zeitung, **Mount St Helens in Washington, erupts** (*many things have happened before and will happened again*), The University of Notre Dame is founded and The New York Philharmonic has its' 1st concert.

1843

During this 'Free Banking Era' there was also some fraudulent activity by the banks that were being inspected and audited as they often misrepresented the amount of specie they had on hand further generating a lack of confidence in the publics' mind?

> US & British settlers in Oregon Country choose government committee, Congress appropriates $30,000 "to test the practicability of establishing a system of electro-magnetic telegraphs" by the US, 1st wagon train, 1000+ depart Independence Missouri for Oregon, Sojourner Truth leaves NY to begin her career as antislavery activist, 1st blacks participation in national political convention (Liberty Party), Mt Rainier in Washington State has eruptive activity, 1st chartered mutual life insurance company opens and Charles Dickens publishes "A Christmas Carol," in England.

Leon Faucbet Researches upon Gold and Silver

> *If all the nations of Europe adopted the system of Great Britain the price of gold would be raised beyond measure, and we should see produced in Europe a result lamentable enough.*

1844

Peel Banking Act of 1844 was a measure taken in Britain which required that every bit of currency in circulation be backed by gold and silver. The general opinion in England at the time was too much currency floating around had been the cause of the financial panics and periods of uncertainty over the last 33 years. By making all currency it was believed panics would be no more, It doesn't seemed to have worked all that well because they still had panics in 1847, 1857 and 1866 when the government allowed more notes to be put into circulation to avoid financial ruin.

This will become important in 1847 and incidentally kinda puts the screws to England.

> United States military is dealing with Mexico again, Texan envoys sign Treaty of Annexation with the United States, Whig convention nominates Henry Clay as presidential candidate, Fire destroys US mint at Charlotte, NC, Iron ore discovered in Minnesota's

Mesabi Mountains, James K. Polk elected 11th president of USA, 1st dental use of nitrous oxide, Hartford, Ct.

1845

James K. Polk becomes President 1845 to 1849 Democratic

"Public opinion: May it always perform one of its appropriate offices, by teaching the public functionaries of the State and of the Federal Government, that neither shall assume the exercise of powers entrusted by the Constitution to the other." **James K. Polk**

American or Know Nothing Party was anti-Catholicism and pro; temperance, republicanism and Protestantism. The party campaigned to curb immigration as its members feared the country was being taken over by Catholicism. While the party had little success it was none the less affiliated with Millard Fillmore and US Grant in the mid-1850s.

"A Conservative government is an organized hypocrisy." **Benjamin Disraeli.** *I wonder if this had anything to do with that Peel Banking Act of last year.*

> Edgar Allen Poe's "Raven" 1st published (*once upon a midnight dreary…*), President Tyler signs a resolution annexing the Republic of Texas *(I do not believe the Mexican government was pleased with this)*, Congress appropriates $30,000 to ship camels to western US *(this has been referred to in Western Novels)*, rubber band patented *(I've seen a rubber band, I've seen a hot dog stand, I've even seen a needle wink its' eye, but I've seen everything when I've seen an elephant fly – couldn't help myself)*, Mexico drops diplomatic relations with US, 1st black lawyer (Macon B Allen) admitted to bar (Mass), 1,000 buildings damaged by fire in Pittsburg, Scientific American magazine publishes its first issue, 1st baseball team, NY Knickerbockers organize, adopt rule code and a hunger strike in Hague.

A **mild recession** that could have been a real recession but the Mexican–American War started and orders for military supplies jumped.

Manifest Destiny United States President James K. Polk announces to Congress that the United States should aggressively expand into the West. *Kind of a 'sea to shining sea' thing.*

Florida and Texas enter the Union

1846

Mexican American War

> The United States House of Representatives votes to stop sharing the Oregon Territory with the United Kingdom, the Milwaukee Bridge War, Juneautown and Kilbourntown unified as the City of Milwaukee, Wisconsin. Beginning of Mormon march to western US, Polish revolutionaries march on Cracow, but are defeated, California declares independence from Mexico, Oregon Treaty signed, setting US-British boundary at 49°N, Elias Howe patents sewing machine, Elizabeth Barrett & Robert Browning exchange last

letters before eloping, Johann Gottfried Galle & Heinrich d'Arrest find Neptune, Donner Party becomes trapped in the Sierra Nevada and Iowa becomes 29th state.

Henry David Thoreau (Walden Pond) jailed for tax resistance (you might try reading Emerson too).

I found it interesting that the over use of the land was an issue even earlier than this in the United States. Something else I found years ago, in a translation of Herodotus, concerned how around Babylon they had diverted the river and started controlled irrigation. The interesting part was ancient writings describing how the land became covered with salts. I guess they needed those floods.

1847

The Panic of 1847 is associated with the end of the early railway BOOM. The Bank of England requested a suspension of the Peel Bank Charter Act of 1844 and began to print more money and this caused significant inflation. The credit expansion related to the railway BOOM was very high and thereby allowed the stellar rise of railway stocks. When the BOOM began to BUST people ran out of money, funny thing about that.

> Michigan is 1st state to abolish capital punishment, Samuel Colt sells his revolver pistol to the United States government, Conspiracy in New Mexico against US, Doughnut created, Brigham Young & his Mormon followers arrive at Salt Lake City, UT, Charlotte Bronte finishes manuscript of "Jane Eyre", US Marines under General Scott enter Mexico City (halls of Montezuma, Frederick Douglass publishes 1st issue of his newspaper "North Star" and Indians kill Washington state pioneers Marcus & Narcissa Whitman, and 12 others in Walla Walla Oregon.

In Holland silver was the sole standard until 1816. In that year the double standard was adopted with the legal relation between the metals of 15.873 to 1, which undervalued silver and practically banished it from the circulation. In 1847 silver was again adopted as the sole standard, not in consequence of the discovery of gold in California, but just before that event. The principal reason assigned by the statesmen of Holland for this change in 1847 was, that it had proved disastrous to the commercial and industrial interests of Holland to have a money system identical with that of England, whose financial revulsions, after its adoption of the gold standard, had been more frequent and more severe than in any other country, and whose injurious effects were felt in Holland scarcely less than in England. Injurious effects were felt in Holland scarcely less than in England. They maintained that the adoption of the silver standard would prevent England from disturbing the internal trade of Holland by draining off its money during such revulsions, and would secure immunity from evils which did not originate in and for which Holland was not responsible. **From the Silver Commission of 1876**

Hum, it happened again.

1848

The **Free Soil Party 1848–1854** then new Republican Party after 1854 campaigned for 'Homestead' distribution of Federal lands to settlers as independent free 'yoeman farmers' as opposed to the selling of Federal lands to speculators and wealthy planters who would use slave labor on the best land leaving free men to farmer lesser ground. Its members were anti-slavery members of the Democratic and Whig parties striving to prevent new states entering the Union as slave-states.

An interesting effect of the Free Soil party in this election was that it may have provided enough of a split in the Democratic Party at the time to have caused Taylor, a Whig, to take the election.

James Marshall **finds gold**, Sutter's Mill in Coloma, California.

> Mexican American War ends. First commercial bank in San Francisco established, People's uprising in Palermo Sicily., first ship load of Chinese arrive in San Francisco, Treaty of Guadalupe Hidalgo ends Mexican War; US acquires Texas California, New Mexico & Arizona for $15 million (*I believe this was quite a bit less than what was offered before hostilities*), 2nd French Republic forms, a revolution breaks out in Hungary, state of siege proclaimed in Amsterdam, Jews of Prussia granted equality, Elizabeth Stanton & Lucretia Mott open 1st women's rights convention, Irish Potato Famine: Tipperary Revolt, 1st US homeopathic medical college opens in Pennsylvania, 1st US woman's medical school opens (Boston) and gas lights 1st installed at White House.

Cholera epidemic hits the nation, 5000 die in New York City alone. This epidemic is often mentioned in western novels and the Oregon Trail computer game. It was devastating all across the nation as it spread west and south.

France has another revolution! *Go boys and girls! Well, maybe not so much.*

As gold in America and Australia then silver in America produce unheard of before vast amounts of both metals the following excerpt from the 1876 Silver commission adequately explains the concerns and conversations in Europe which are then brought to America.

> In all the European discussions, alter 1848 and prior to the Genua ii demonetization of silver and its consequences, the point made was not that either metal had depreciated relatively to the other, but that by reason of extraordinary supplies of gold from California and Australia, supplemented about 1865 by new supplies of silver from Nevada, both metals had depreciated relatively to labor and commodities, and that those having fixed incomes were being injured by a rise in prices. So long as the double standard existed, a new supply of either metal was only an addition to and only affected the value of the "fall in gold," which Chevalier lamented in 1857, was its fall in relation to property. He pointed out how the double standard had prevented any change from occurring in its relation to silver, and how it would continue to do so until the silver of double-standard countries was exhausted. In order, therefore, to protect the interests of the income classes, it was claimed to be necessary to demonetize one of the metals, and gold being the metal which then promised the most abundant yield was selected for the purpose.

The Independent Treasury Act of 1848 required all business being with the government was to be transacted with gold or silver coins.

"**Money plays** the largest part in determining the course of history." **Communist Manifesto by Karl Marx**

Wisconsin Statehood

1849

Zachary Taylor becomes President Dies in office Whig

"**For more than half a century,** during which kingdoms and empires have fallen, this Union has stood unshaken. The patriots who formed it have long since descended to the grave; yet still it remains, the proudest monument to their memory. . ." **Zachary Taylor**

California Gold Rush is on. Along with the Australian gold strike the worlds' supply of gold increases to the point some feel it is becoming devalued. *The idea of demonetizing one of the currency metals starts to rise.*

> United States military at Smyrna, Gold Coinage Act authorizes $20 Double Eagle gold coin, Gold Rush is on, Benjamin Chambers patents breech loading cannon, British seize Tigre Island in Gulf of Fonseca from Honduras and Harriet Tubman escapes from slavery in Maryland.

Coinage Act of 1849 Because of the California gold fields the act allowed for a $20 and a $1 gold coin to be minted and expanded the money supply.   This expanding the money supply was rather important as people can't buy food, clothing, feel good medicines from the back of a wagon or pay taxes unless there is enough money floating around. Just think back to Shay's Rebellion.

1850

Compromise of 1850 basically allowed California to enter the Union as a free state and just delayed the inevitable Civil War.

> California Exchange opens, Adding machine employing depressible keys patented, New Paltz, NY, Nathaniel Hawthorne's "Scarlet Letter" published, Henry Wells & William Fargo form American Express, Levi Strauss makes his 1st pair of blue jeans, Fire destroys part of SF, Millard Fillmore sworn-in as president of US (replacing Taylor), "Swedish Nightingale" Jenny Lind (*Jenny is referred to in many western novels and histories*) gives 1st US concert and Congress passes Fugitive Slave Law as part of Compromise of 1850.

Belgium goes to a silver standard.

California Statehood

1851

Chemical Bank of New York parts ways with **New York Chemical Manufacturing Company** becoming a stand-alone organization.

United States military at Ottoman Empire and Africa, Gail Borden announces invention of evaporated milk *(I'd bet she had contented cows)*, Black abolitionists invade Boston courtroom and rescue a fugitive slave, 1st US alcohol prohibition law enacted (Maine), Isaac Singer patents sewing machine, Kentucky marshals abduct abolitionist minister Calvin Fairbank from Jeffersonville, Indiana, and take him to Kentucky to stand trial for helping a slave escape, "Moby Dick," by Herman Melville published and fire devastates US Library of Congress in Washington, destroys 35,000 volumes *(now that is a darn pity)*.

1852

Millard Fillmore becomes President to 1853 Whig – drummed out of the party.

"It is not strange . . . to mistake change for progress." **Millard Fillmore**

United States military at Argentina, Studebaker Brothers wagon company, precursor of the automobile manufacturer is established *(Studebakers were pretty cool cars back in the day and this is decidedly a matter of opinion)*, Harriet Beecher Stowe's "Uncle Tom's Cabin" published, Ohio makes it illegal for children under 18 & women to work more than 10 hours a day, 1st edition of Peter Roget's Thesaurus published, Massachusetts rules all school-age children must attend school, Congress authorizes US's 2nd mint (San Francisco, California), Franklin Pierce elected as president of US and Emma Snodgrass arrested in Boston for wearing pants.

Mr. R. M. T. Hunter, in a report to the United States Senate

Of all the great effects produced upon human society by the discovery of America, there were probably none so marked as those brought about by the great influx of the precious metals from the New World to the Old. European industry had been declining under the decreasing stock of the precious metals, and an appreciating standard of values; human ingenuity grew dull under the paralyzing influences of declining profits, and capital absorbed nearly all that should have been divided between it and labor. But an increase in the precious metals, in such quantity as to check this tendency, operated as a new motive-power to the machinery of commerce. Production was stimulated by finding the advantages of a change in the standard on its side. Instead of being repressed by having to pay more than it had stipulated for the use of capital, it was stimulated by paying less. Capital, too, was benefited, for* new demands were created for it by the new uses which a general movement in industrial pursuits had developed; so that if it lost a little by a change in the standard. It gained much more in the greater demand for its use, which added to its capacity for reproduction, and to its real value.

The mischief would be great, indeed, if all the world were to adopt but one of the precious metals as the standard of value. To adopt gold alone would diminish the specie currency more than one-half; and the reduction the other way, should silver be taken as the only standard, would be large enough to prove highly disastrous to the human race.

1853

Franklin Pierce becomes President 1853 to 1857 Democratic

"The revenue of the country, levied almost insensibly to the taxpayer, goes on from year to year, increasing beyond either the interests or the prospective wants of the Government." **Franklin Pierce**

> Unites States military at Nicaragua, Transcontinental railroad survey is authorized by Congress, Harriet Tubman began her Underground Railroad, helping slaves escape, Gadsden Purchase 29,670-square-mile (76,800 square km) from Mexico (now southern Arizona and New Mexico) for $10 million signed by President Franklin Pierce, 1st US World's fair opens (Crystal Palace NY), 1st round-the-world trip by yacht (Cornelius Vanderbilt), Austrian law forbids Jews from owning land.

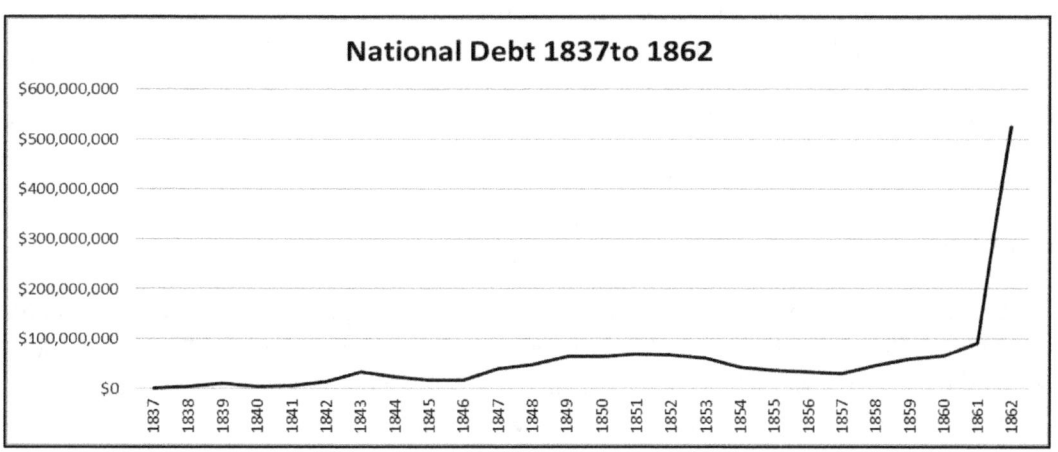

Commodore Matthew Perry and his expedition are running around Japan showing off US Naval ships and the troops trying to get Japan to open up for trade. Where there's a buck there's a will and a way.

The silver in coins was lowered so the coins would stay in circulation thus keeping the economy moving right along or so it was hoped. Remember when Jefferson had that little problem with US Silver coins leaving the country because the free market value of silver was higher in Europe.

A mild recession that looks a little like the dot.com bubble of 2001. Because interest rates rose and investment in railroad and other securities fell off. The result was a falling off of investment in businesses having little effect on the economy in general and the economy kept BOOMing.

And again

1854

The **Bloody Kansas Wars** begin as supporters of slavery and free-state ideals clash over Kansas' entry into the Union. The violence from this time extends through the Civil War and beyond as some of the most murderous activity against civilians in our history. Also out of this area and period came some of the worst outlaws and most famous lawmen of western American lore.

> The United States military operates in China and Nicaragua, Lincoln University, a black college, chartered (Oxford, Penn), Alvan Bovay proposes name "Republican Party," Ripon, Wisconsin, Franz Liszt's symphony "Orpheus," premieres, During the Crimean War, Britain & France declare war on Russia, Kansas-Nebraska Act repealed Missouri Compromise opens north slavery, Congress passes Confiscation Act, Smith & Wesson patents metal bullet cartridges, Henry David Thoreau publishes "Walden", John Fremont issues proclamation freeing slaves of Missouri rebels, Florence Nightingale and a staff of 38 nurses were sent to the Crimean War, Charge of Light Brigade (Battle of Balaklava, Crimean War), 409 die *(Into the valley of death rode the…an so on)*, Dutch army stops Chinese uprising in Borneo, Pope Pius IX proclaims Immaculate Conception, makes Mary, free of Original Sin and Pennsylvania Rock Oil Co, 1st in US, incorporated in NYC.

Still **BOOM**ing

1855

William Walker

Seems Mr. Walker was a fervent believer in the South and a proponent of slavery. To that end he ran around Baja, Sonora *(not so much)* and Nicaragua trying to establish colonies of which he would declare himself 'President' of each despite this being a clear violation of the Neutrality Act of 1794. The idea was to then have the colonies eventually join the United States as slave states thus maintaining the balance of slave and free-states. In this process he managed to enjoy the displeasure of, the United States via the Navy, Great Britton, **Cornelius Vanderbilt** and just about every South American country. In the end none of the schemes worked out well and the British Navy turned him over the Hondurans who promptly took him out and introduced him to the conveniences of a firing squad.

> United States Military operates at Uruguay and Fiji Islands, The bridge over the Mississippi River opens in what is now Minneapolis, Minnesota, Wisconsin Supreme Court declares US Fugitive Slave Law unconstitutional, US citizenship laws amended all children of US parents born abroad granted US citizenship, Louisiana establishes 1st health board to regulate quarantine, US adventurer William Walker conquers Nicaragua, reestablishes slavery, The Portland Rum Riot occurs in Portland, Maine, an edition of Walt Whitman's book of poems, titled Leaves of Grass, is published and 700 soldiers under American General William S. Harney avenge the Grattan Massacre by attacking a Sioux village, killing 100 men, women, and children.

1856

The **Republican** Party developed as the coalescence of the supports a strong central government, the National Bank, industry, modernization, and anti-slavery came together against the Jacksonian

Democratic notions.   **Know-Nothings, some Whigs, Barnburner Democrats and the Free-Soil folks** constituted the alliance to become the Republican Party.

United States military at Panama and China, John A Veatch discovers borax, Tuscan Springs, California(*twenty mule team and all that*), The American Party (*Know-Nothings*) convene in Philadelphia, Pennsylvania to nominate their Presidential candidate, former President Millard Fillmore, 1st national meeting of Republican Party (Pittsburgh), Gunpowder in church explodes killing 4,000 in Rhodes, Lawrence Kansas captured, sacked by pro-slavery forces, Violence in the Senate, South Carolina representative Brooks used a cane on Massachusetts Senator Sumner, Hurricane washes away 2-300 revelers at Last Island, Louisiana, The Second Opium War between several western powers and China begins with the Arrow Incident on the Pearl River and James Buchanan elected 15th US president.

1857

James Buchanan becomes President 1857 to 1861 Democratic

"There is nothing stable but Heaven and the Constitution." **James Buchanan**

7.9 earthquake shakes Fort Tejon Calif., National Association of Baseball Players founded, Congress outlaws foreign currency as legal tender in US, Dred Scott Decision: Supreme Court rules slaves cannot be citizens (*Balderdash*), Earthquake hits Tokyo; about 107,000 die, Elisha Otis' 1st elevator installed at 488 Broadway, NYC, - William Walker, conqueror of Nicaragua, surrenders to US Navy, Indian Mutiny begins with revolt of Sepoys of Meerut, Mountain Meadows Massacre, Mormons dressed as Indians murder 120 colonists in Utah and 1st production of Dion Boucicaults "Poor of NY".

The Tariff of 1857 There was a tax surplus and it seemed a good idea to take a load off the people by reducing tariffs; few objected and the south was elated. But when the Panic of 1857 came along the new Tariff was wrongly blamed and was removed a couple of years later. *What I cannot get my head around is how you can have a surplus when there is still a National Debt.*

Panic of 1857 a BUST! Touted as the first world-wide economic crisis!

Because the preceding years of prosperity had been so good many farmers, investors, bankers, merchants and industrialists over invested and borrowed to ride the **BOOM**. Since they were over invested and therefore cash poor when the **BUST** started they were hit rather quickly. It went rather like this.

March Dred Scott v Sandford_ The effect was, besides sticking it to Mr. Scott, that the Missouri compromise was unconstitutional. This meant that the western areas could become slave states. That political insecurity was enough to cause a bit a dip in railroad stocks. *This is the burp before the projectile vomiting.*

Meanwhile European demand for goods from Americas' western lands had eased off considerably because of their own economic slowdown. The obvious reduction in income for westerners caused bankers to become more cautious about lending and converting notes from western banks was halted by some eastern banks. Railroads had experienced a large expansion because of the tide of people moving to the west where opportunity abounded. Banks had extended large loans to the railroads to finance the expansion and the loans were as yet unpaid.

With the western economy slumping because of lower orders banks stopped lending and merchants and farmers slowed their orders from eastern industries sending the slowdown ripple to the east. Because the railroads depended on the western economy for shipping and passenger income they began to show lower income and profits threatening the viability of the loans they had taken from the banks.

Because demand for western goods was waning prices also fell. For example: grain had reached over $2.00 per bushel the year before. Before it was over the price had fallen by more than half. With farmers having loans on lands they had purchased for expansion they were unable to pay their loans and foreclosure was in the air.

Additionally American banks stopped paying in silver. *I imagine this caused some consternation in the international financial system.*

August brought the failure of the Ohio Life Insurance and Trust Company. The failure was largely due to fraudulent practices by management but none the less it failed. The failure caused a loss of confidence in banking and the result was runs on banks, lower industrial orders with the expected unemployment, foreclosures on western farm land and thousands of businesses closing.

Did this sound at all familiar? I mean really!

Although the economy showed significant stability by 1859 it was by no means strong and political hay was being made concerning banking in general and the role of the federal government in the economy. The south having weathered the panic better than most of the nation and encouraged by the Dred Scott decision began to push its position.

President Buchanan decided that the paper money was the cause of the panic and ceased the use of bank notes below twenty dollars hoping this would decrease the paper money supply and thereby decreasing inflation. *Hum, didn't we have a problem with too little money running around awhile back? I guess it depends on the point of view.*

Britain had suspended the 1844 rules and put more currency into circulation than was allowed. With this and failure of the American economy Britain joined the economic crisis.

The German States go to a silver standard. Under the appeals of Chevalier and others, several nations in Europe, notably Germany and Austria in 1857, demonetized gold. It is probable that the movement in that direction would have become universal in Europe but for the resistance of France.

Russia (silver standard) and the Argentine Federation suspend specie payments.

1858

William Wells Brown published 1st Black drama, "Leap to Freedom", John Brown holds antislavery convention, Great fire in London harbor, 1st use of fingerprints as a means of identification, Regular mail to Pacific coast begins, Britain's Queen Victoria telegraphs President James Buchanan, 1st Lincoln-Douglas debate (Illinois), 1st overland mail for California, In Paris, the Can-Can is 1st performed, Hamilton Smith patents rotary washing machine, Macy's Department store opens in NYC.

1859

Comstock silver lode discovered near Virginia City, Nevada.

Worlds' supply of silver rises dramatically, as other finds are made, and cause problems with bimetallism worldwide. The value of silver dropped as supply increased dramatically. This caused the value of silver coins to drop worldwide really messing up economies. It should be noted that the gold supply had increased significantly prior to this and in 1876 it was understood that the volume relationship of gold to silver was similar to levels.

Minnesota Statehood

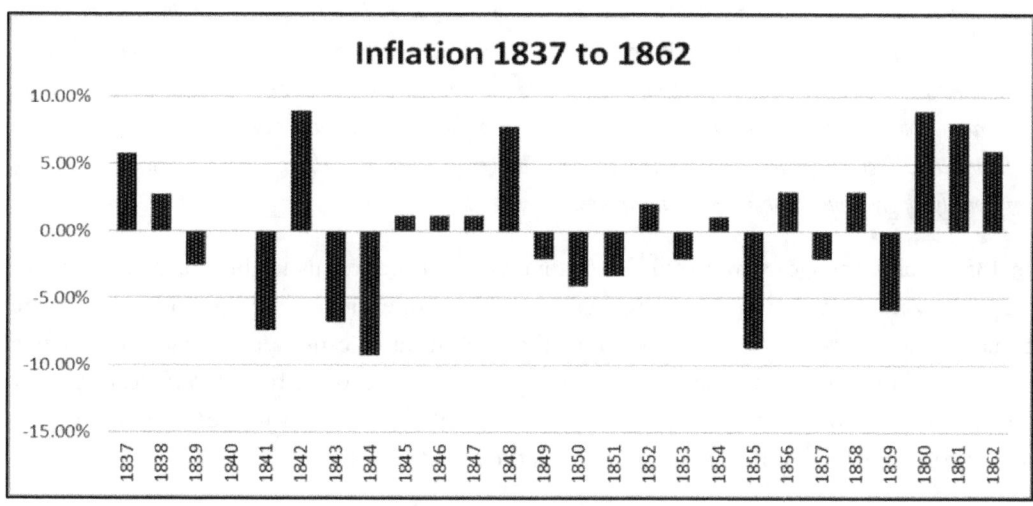

John Brown's raid at Harpers Ferry, The Codex Sinaiticus is discovered in Egypt, 1st use of "insanity plea" to prove innocence, Arkansas legislature requires free blacks to choose exile or slavery, Ground broken for Suez Canal, 1st successful oil well drilled, near Titusville, Penn by Edwin Drake, A geomagnetic storm causes the Aurora Borealis to shine so brightly that it is seen clearly over parts of USA, Europe, and even as far afield as

Japan, George Simpson patents electric range, Spain declares war on Morocco and South Carolina declared an "independent commonwealth".

The Pig War

When the Oregon Treaty of 1846 was signed the maps of the Strait of Juan de Fuca and the San Juan Islands were perhaps a little less than accurate and left some ambiguity concerning the international border in the region, specifically the San Juan Islands area.

Washington and London get some guys together to discuss the matter to see if they could come up with a resolution. This does not go so well and takes some time. While the boys are trying to figure it all out the Hudson Bay Company sets up a sheep farm on San Juan Island and a bunch of Americans move in figuring they had a right. Well one day an American shoots a pig, not an American pig, which is tearing up his garden. The pigs' owner gets upset and one thing leads to another and the locals call out the Military of each side. I mean ships, troops and cannon.

When London and Washington find out they wonder what the hell is in the water out there to get all this nasty about a darn pig and send word for everybody to just take a time out and get their heads out of their respect buts and get along until the dispute is settled diplomatically, which they do and everybody 'lives' happily ever after with the noted exception of said pig. It is unknown who eventually had the pig for dinner.

The Encyclopaedia Britannica, 1859 (article Precious Metals, by J. R. McCulloch)

A fall in the value of the precious metals, caused by the greater facility of their production, or by the discovery of new sources of supply, depends in no degree on the theories of philosophers, or the decision of statesmen or legislators, but is the result of circumstances beyond human control ; and although, like a fall of rain after a long course of dry weather, it may be prejudicial to certain classes, it is beneficial to an incomparably greater number, including all who are engaged in industrial pursuits, and is, speaking generally, of great public or national advantage.

When in 1859 such a change occurred in the relative value of the metals in the London market as to carry up the London quotation of standard silver to 62^^01.per ounce in gold, no recent change had then taken place in the relative production of the two metals to cause a change in their relative market value. Gold had been produced in unusual quantities since 1848, but the effect until 1859 had been merely to produce a gradual and not very great fall in the value of the two metals combined as compared with other things, but not in their relative value.

The demand for gold was as strong and steady as it had previously been. The commerce of gold-using countries was as active as ever, and the gold prices of commodities underwent no marked change during that year. But, on the other hand, there was an unprecedented demand for silver in England for export to Asia. In that single year the silver export from Great Britain to the East was £14,828,521, or over $70,000,000, which was double the amount of the then annual silver product of the entire world. The unprecedented price of silver in London in 1859 was therefore manifestly due to the extraordinary demand for it in that market, and not to a fall in the value of gold as compared with the value of all other things which it is the function of money to measure.

The sudden increase in demand for silver in England in 1859 is shown by the fact that British silver exports to the East rose from £4,753,933 in 1858 to more than three times that amount in 1859. **From the Silver Commission of 1876**

Oregon Statehood

1860

By now there are at least **9,000 or so differing bank notes** in circulation in the United States. Many of these notes were worthless because of widespread counterfeiting and many bank failures leaving the notes unredeemable. *These notes can also be considered toilet paper.*

> The United States military was operating at Portuguese West Africa and Columbia, 1st rabbi to open House of Representatives, Morris Raphall of NYC, Pre-emption Bill, 1st Pony Express reaches Sacramento Calif., Republican Party nominates Abraham Lincoln for president, 1st US "dime novel" published: "Malaseka, The Indian Wife of the White Hunter," by Mrs. Ann Stevens, the State Bank of the Russian Empire is established, 1st pro golf tournament held in Scotland, Abraham Lincoln (Rep-R-Ill) elected 16th American President, South Carolina votes 169-0 for Ordinance of Secession, 1st state to secede and Joseph Jefferson's "Rip Van Winkle," premieres in NYC.

A mild recession occurred this year and was kept mild as banks were supported by clearing houses. That is they understood the need to keep public confidence up to avoid a panic and the inevitable runs that would follow.

Abraham Lincoln wins the four way presidential race with 40% of the popular vote having had sufficient electoral votes. The Democratic Party was divided and thus gave the election to Lincoln. The Republicans dominated national politics for decades after this.

1861

Abraham Lincoln becomes President 1861 to 1865 killed April 15th shortly after starting second term as President Republican

"No man is good enough to govern another man without that other's consent." **Abraham Lincoln**

April 12 the Civil War officially starts

Victories by the South shake the North and bond sales slump as fear of even greater expenses related to a long duration of the war create fear of the government going off the gold standard. Subsequently depositor runs on banks begin.

December New York banks stop paying in gold.

> National Debt climbs. Pres. Lincoln declares slavery in Confederate states unlawful, Warsaw Massacre: Russians fire on crowd demonstrating against Russia, Edward Clark became Governor of Texas, replacing Sam Houston, who was evicted from the office for

refusing to take an oath of loyalty to the Confederacy, Baltimore riots-4 soldiers, 9 civilians killed, President Abe Lincoln suspends writ of habeas corpus, West Virginia secedes from Virginia after Virginia secedes from the Union, US, Congress authorizes paper money(*and did they print lots of it*), Brazil recognizes Confederacy, US levies its 1st Income Tax (3% of incomes over $800), 1st transcontinental telegram sent ending Pony Express and US banks stop payments in gold.

Revenue Act of 1861 act levied the first income tax and carried a 3% tax on all individuals whose annual incomes were above $800 per year. It also allowed for the issue of War Bonds that totaled over $3 billion by the wars end.

December Secretary of the Treasury asks Congress to establish national banks backed with government bonds instead of gold. Congress says no.

Kansas Statehood

1862

January Bank runs continue and banks throughout the country also stop paying depositors in gold.

February Congress passes Legal Tender Act causing the printing of $150 million of non-gold backed currency to be called 'Greenbacks'.

The Treasury of the United States stops paying in gold. Gold standard is kaput.

May Homestead Act of 1862 Made land available to; anyone who had never taken up arms against the United States government (including freed slaves and women); was 21 or older, or the head of a family; could file an application to claim a federal land grant. The grant process required a three step procedure: file an application, improve the land, and file for deed of title. The applicant was required reside on the land for five years, and 'show evidence' of having made improvements. This 'show evidence' clause would later be the stuff of many **western novels depicting** large cattle ranches sending the hands to make claims and then making false statement of 'showing evidence' of residence and improvements to officials. The large rancher would pay the cattle hand a nominal or even no fee for the land after title was issued

June Congress calls for another $150 million in Greenbacks.

Land Act of 1862 a.k.a. Morrill Land Grant Act sets up the land grant system from which many colleges of today started.

Internal Revenue Act of 1862 established the office of the Commissioner of Internal Revenue to collect all taxes and sell war bonds. It further established progressive income tax on individuals as follows; incomes were less than $600 were not taxed, greater than $600 and less than $10,000 paid 3% and were greater than $10,000 paid 5%. This was on individuals and was collected at the source of the income.

Julia Howe publishes "Battle Hymn of Republic, 1st US income tax (3% of incomes greater than $600, 5% of incomes greater $10,000), Agoston Haraszthy, 1st vintner in Sonoma Valley (*mighty glad that got started, good stuff that*), Slavery abolished in all US possessions (*hurray!*), Homestead Act becomes law: provides cheap land for settlement of West, Congress outlaws polygamy, Lewis Carroll creates Alice in Wonderland for Alice P Liddell, Land Grant Act endows state colleges with federal land, - Odore R. Timby patents revolving gun turret, Lincoln receives group of blacks to confer with US president, Sioux Indians begin uprising in Minnesota, Otto von Bismarck becomes German republic chancellor.

The South receives significant financing via the Erlangers.

1863 to 1900 Civil War Ends, National Returns, Cowboys & Indians and the Long Depression

January Congress calls for another $150 million in Greenbacks bring the total Greenbacks in circulation to $450 million. *I see inflation. Oh happy indebted people.*

At this point there are **Greenbacks (fiat money),** gold-backed currency (not that you can get any gold for it), gold coins and those state bank issued notes in circulation all together.

New York Draft Riots *Some folks just didn't think it was their responsibility to fight in Mister Lincolns' War.*

> Emancipation Proclamation (*ending* slavery) issued by Lincoln, Thomas Crapper pioneers one-piece pedestal flushing toilet thus was a new word introduced to American English (*liking this even better*), Army Medal of Honor awarded, Bread revolt in Richmond Virginia, Mexican forces attacked the French Foreign Legion in Hacienda Camarón, Mexico, black regiment (54 Mass) leaves Boston to fight in Civil War, Travelers Insurance Co of Hartford chartered (accident insurer), Very 1st National Bank opens in Davenport, Iowa, Battle of Gettysburg, 1st military draft by US (exemptions cost $100 and New York Draft Riots), orders barring Jews from serving under US Grant are revoked, Japanese battle cruiser shoots at Dutch warship Medusa, kills 4, Anti-draft mobs lynch blacks in NYC, Bread revolt in Mobile Alabama, Lincoln designates last Thursday in November as Thanksgiving Day, Lincoln delivers his address in Gettysburg; "4 score & 7 years ago…,etc.

The North receives significant financing via August Belmont. *Weren't Belmont and Peabody making big bucks off the 1837 Panic?*

It's back!

"The few who understand the system, will either be so interested from its profits or so dependent on its favors, that there will be no opposition from that class." **A. Rothschild**

This time instead of having a single location as the National Bank of the United States there are several National Banks. The National Banking system returns for good. Over the next few decades the Supreme Court is heavily involved with defining the place, role and functions of the National Banks as they compete with the State, members of the Republic, chartered banks and others.

National Bank Act of 1863 Congress offered charters to any bank that could provide sufficient capital and agreed to abide by strict regulations. Notes issued by these banks had to be of uniform design and also backed by the bank holding reserves of Federal Bonds. These banks could not offer branch offices in states other than the state they were chartered in and only if that state allowed branch offices. This created a fourth currency, Unites States Notes and expanded an already greatly expanded money supply even more laying the foundation for huge inflation.

West Virginia Statehood as it separates from Virginia.

1864

Gold dollar is equal to over $1.80 in the fiat greenback currency.

> 2nd German-Danish war begins, Rebecca Lee (US) becomes first black woman to receive a medical degree, Austrian Archduke Maximilian becomes emperor of Mexico, Geneva Convention signed by 12 nations.

The Coinage Act of 1864 altered the composition of the Cent and ordered the minting of a two cent coin.

National Bank Act of 1864 along with the 1863 National Bank Act established a uniform currency for the United States and an agency **The Office of the Comptroller of the Currency** to structure, supervise and audit the banks under the national banking system.

The banks bought securities from the federal government who held them for the inevitable rainy day and then received currency to distribute as a course of their business. While the system was sound enough when a national bank failed the securities were sold by the federal government and the note holders.

The currency at this time was beautiful. The engraving was of high caliber and depicted history of the United States. I have personally seen some and they really are a delight. The intricacy was also intended to stop counterfeiting.

Lincoln quoted from a letter

"We may congratulate ourselves that this cruel war is nearing its end. It has cost a vast amount of treasure and blood. . . . It has indeed been a trying hour for the Republic; but I see in the near future a crisis approaching that unnerves me and causes me to tremble for the safety of my country. As a result of the war, corporations have been enthroned and an era of corruption in high places will follow, and the money power of the country will endeavor to prolong its reign by working upon the prejudices of the people until all wealth is aggregated in a few hands and the Republic is destroyed. I feel at this moment more anxiety for the safety of my country than ever before, even in the midst of war. God grant that my suspicions may prove groundless."

"These capitalists generally act harmoniously and in concert to fleece the people, and now that they have got into a quarrel with themselves, we are called upon to appropriate the people's money to settle the quarrel."

November 29th Sand Creek Massacre

United States military volunteer forces numbering 700 attack an encampment of friendly **Cheyenne and Arapaho** killing and mutilating women and children. Of the massacre **Kit Carson** is quoted of saying….

Jis to think of that dog Chivington and his dirty hounds, up thar at Sand Creek. His men shot down squaws, and blew the brains out of little innocent children. You call sich soldiers Christians, do ye? And Indians savages? What der yer 'spose our Heavenly Father, who made both them and us, thinks of these things? I tell you what; I don't like a hostile red skin any more than you do. And when they are hostile, I've fought 'em, hard as any man. But I never yet drew a bead on a squaw or papoose, and I despise the man who would.

Nevada Statehood

1865

Andrew Johnson becomes President 1865 to 1869 Republican

"If the rabble were lopped off at one end and the aristocrat at the other, all would be well with the country." **President Andrew Johnson**

"The death of Lincoln was a disaster for Christendom. There was no man in the United States great enough to wear his boots and the bankers went anew to grab the riches. I fear that foreign bankers with their craftiness and tortuous tricks will entirely control the exuberant riches of America and use it to systematically corrupt civilization." **Otto von Bismark, German Chancellor**

By now the cost of living has gone up nearly double since the start of the war. Since the financial institutions are receiving payments on loans created during the inflationary period of the war and many of those loans placed early in the war they are getting less value in the payments they receive now and are becoming insistent of a change in monetary policy that is deflationary.

The **New York Stock Exchange** opens its first permanent headquarters at 10-12 Broad near Wall Street in New York City.

> JS Rock, 1st black lawyer to practice in Supreme Ct, admitted to bar, Columbia South Carolina burns down, Jefferson Davis signs bill authorizing use of slaves as soldiers, the Confederate Congress calls on black slaves for field service, General Robert E Lee and 26,765 troops, surrender at Appomattox Court House in Virginia to US Lieutenant General Ulysses S. Grant, US Secret Service created to fight counterfeiting, 1st edition of "Alice in Wonderland" is published and Horace Greeley advises his readers to "Go west young man".

March Hugh McCulloch becomes Secretary of the Treasury and declares his intent to bring back the gold standard.

December McCulloch heads over to Congress asking them to allow him to buy g back those nasty old Greenbacks.

Congress says OK and passes the Constriction/Redemption Act calling for $10 million in the next six months and $4 million a month after that to be pulled from circulation.

Meanwhile the country is in a postwar Recession of 1865 lasting about 2 years. The American Civil War ended in April 1865 which caused a 'post war' recession. This was also the start of a long period of deflation that apparently lasted until around 1896. Additionally the entire world was having some tough financial times.

1866

Reconstruction era turns out to be a nasty bit of business what with those carpet-baggers and all.

The **Southern Homestead Act of 1866** had little success in helping the tenant farmers and sharecroppers to become land owners as even the low expenses associate with the process proved unattainable for most.

> **Jesse James** holds up his 1st bank, Liberty, Missouri, New York Legislature forms NYC Metropolitan Board of Health, President Johnson vetoes civil rights bill; it later becomes 14th amendment, American Society for Prevention of Cruelty to Animals (ASPCA) forms, Congress authorizes nickel 5 cent piece (replaces silver half-dime), Italy declares war on Austria, fire destroys half of Portland Maine, Cholera epidemic kills hundreds in London, New Orleans's Democratic government orders police to raid an integrated Republican Party meeting, killing 40 people and injuring 150, Great fire in Quebec destroys 2,500 houses and national convention of Grand Army of Republic (veterans' organization).

The Fenian raids were a series of raids by Irish folks living in the United States against targets in Canada because they were ticked about the Irish Question in England. *There might have been a little indirect payback for England helping the south in the recent civil war too.*

The failure of **OVEREND & GURNEY** was the catalyst for a major change in how central banks manage financial crises.

Overend and Gurney was a bank that provided for banks in London. (London at the time was the worlds' financial center) When it went under in May lots of other smaller banks went under right along with it because they no longer had access to the funds they needed for operations. Basically it is referred to as a systemic collapse.

So the good old Bank of England gets together with a bunch of financial giants and they create a rescue fund and the Bank of England becomes the 'lender of last resort'. The idea is to help out banks that are having problems so the crisis does not spread to other banks and mess up the whole works.

National Labor Union is organized.

Excerpt from David Hume's Essay on Money:

> *It is certain that since the discovery of the mines in America industry has increased in all the nations of Europe. * * We find that in every kingdom into which money begins to flow in greater abundance than formerly, everything takes a new face ; labor and industry gain life ; the merchant becomes more enterprising, the manufacturer more diligent and skillful, and even the farmer follows his plow with greater*

*alacrity and attention. * * * It is of no manner of consequence with regard to the domestic happiness of a state whether money be in a greater or less quantity. The good policy of the magistrate consists only in keeping it, if possible, still increasing ; because by that means he keeps alive a spirit of industry in the nation and increases the stock of labor, in which consists all real power and riches. A nation whose money decreases is actually at that time weaker and more miserable than another nation which possesses no more money, but is on the increasing hand.*

Italy (double standard a.k.a. bimetallic) suspends specie payments.

1867

Patrons of Husbandry a.k.a. The Grange is established. Primarily concerned with Railroad reform, because of the pricing practices of the railroads, and also currency reform in looking to have more fiat (non-gold backed) currency in circulation. This is opposition to the Republican based banking/Industrial affiliation and support.

Seward's Folly United States buys Alaska from Russia for $7,200,000, two cents an acre.

> African American men granted the right to vote in Washington, D.C, Bricklayers start working 8-hour days, Johann Strauss' "Blue Danube" waltz premieres in Vienna, 1st ship passes through Suez Canal, 1st barbed wire patented by Lucien B Smith of Ohio (later to be cause of many conflicts in the west), Bank of California opens doors, Karl Marx' "Das Kapital," published, Garibaldi marches on Rome, US Congress commission looks into "impeachment" of President Andrew Johnson.

The 1865-1867 Recession is making a mess of things what with the post-war the thing and deflation screwing everybody up and congress hearing about it loud and strong so they, Congress, starts contemplating what to do and ends up with…

Kuhn, Loeb & Co. was as an investment bank founded by Abraham Kuhn and Solomon Loeb. The bank would grow via financing railways and companies such as Western Union, to rival JP Morgan.

Nebraska Statehood

1868

…**terminating the Constriction/Redemption Act** Over $40 million dollars had been taken out of circulation by this point.

Currency policy becomes and remains a major political issue on the national level for decades. Seems it wasn't much of an issue nationally when there was no National Bank System to issue fiat/paper money although currency from State-Chartered Banks had caused many problems. During the Free Banking Era the Federal Government only minted 'specie', gold, silver and copper coins as money of and for the use of the Federal Government. By use I mean in paying its bills.

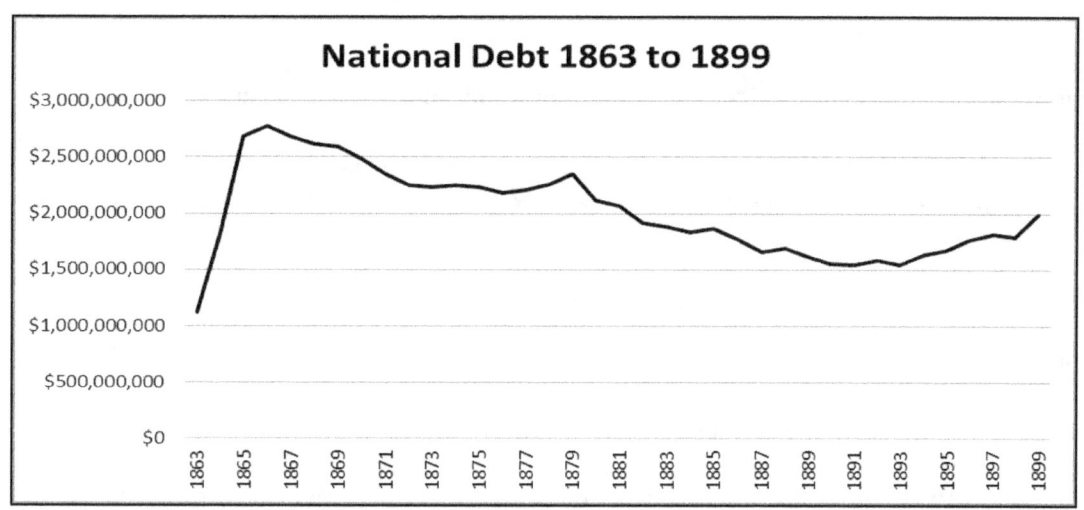

Now there is specie, Gold-certificates, Greenbacks and Federal Notes as well as the warrants and notes issued by state-chartered banks. The whole currency situation is a mess, especially as many of those state notes are worthless.

The same issue then as now is the effects of credit on the populace in a BOOM/BUST economy. If there is inflation then there is a BOOM conversely if there is deflation there is a BUST. By removing 'currency from circulation and creating deflation the government made it harder for folks to pay back their loans and made it better for the banks as the money they received in payments had greater value.

> Oscar J. Dunn, former slave, installed as Lt. Governor of Louisiana, 1st black cabinet member in South Carolina (Francis L Cardozo-Secretary of State), 1st use of tax stamps on cigarettes, Great Train Robbery-7 men (Reno Brothers) make off with $98,000 in cash, bonds and gold. Lots of southern states having conventions to organize for re-entering the Union, Cuba revolts against Spain, earthquakes cause severe damage in Peru, Chile and Ecuador, Edison patents electric vote recorder (*if he only knew about chads*), Battle at Washita River, Oklahoma, General Custer attacks a group of Native American Indians and Despite bitter opposition and President Johnson grants unconditional pardon to all persons involved in Southern rebellion (Civil War).

Ernest Seyd, 1868 (Bullion, page 613)

> *Upon this one point all authorities on the subject are agreed, to wit, that the huge increase in the supply of gold has given a universal impetus to trade, commerce, and industry, and to general social development and progress.*

United States Senate, June 9, 1868, Mr. Sherman, Chairman of the Committee on Finance:

The depreciation of the burden of debt is a loss to a class generally benefited by the increased values of fixed property, and better able to bear the diminution of their capital; but an increase of the burden of the debt to the debtor class often produces absolute ruin.

Peru and Austria (silver standard) suspend specie payments

1869

Ulysses S. Grant becomes President 1869 to 1877 Republican

"The Southern rebellion was largely the outgrowth of the Mexican war. Nations, like individuals, are punished for their transgressions. We got our punishment in the most sanguinary and expensive war of modern times." **Ulysses S. Grant**

American Museum of Natural History founded, Transcontinental Railroad completed at Promontory Utah with the driving of the 'golden spike' and the Wyoming Territorial legislature gives women the right to vote.

A little something about railroads would be good here specifically the Central Pacific. The 'Big Four', Central Pacific owners, are a perfect example of the effects of unregulated financial power and how it can affect the economy and individuals lives. After the nation was connected by the Transcontinental Railroad Union Pacific determined rates by forcing customers to open their books to them so the railroad could determine what rates to charge. The rate was determined by figuring out what the company could afford to pay and still remain in business. As the railroad had a monopoly their customers had to pay the rate or go out of business. It was so bad that some folks shipped goods over the ocean to England and then back to America so they could realize more than a subsistence profit. The general economic impact was devastating to locals as they were unable to realize and reinvest profits locally.

Black Friday of 1869, September 24

You may have heard of Jay Gould and Jim Fisk, or not. They were a couple of wily and experienced rascals who put together a scheme to corner the gold market.

President Grant was buying up greenbacks with gold backed currency. Gould and Fisk figured that if they could buy up lots of gold and get Grant to lay off his plans to keeping buying up the devalued Greenbacks they'd be able to make out in the gold market.

Being experienced rascals and rapscallions they knew they needed somebody to get them inside and a heads up guy if things started going south should Grant decided to sell more gold. So who do they get but Grants' brother-in-law as the insider who invites them to parties when Grant will be there. They go to the parties and with the brother-in-laws aide began talking up the idea of the government holding on to its' gold. The tipster was the guy who had the contract to sell the governments gold. If the sell order came he was to let Gould and Fisk know and they could dump their gold ahead of everybody else.

Things go along nicely for our rascals. They are buying lots of gold and the price is going up and up and up and Fisk and Gould are feeling pretty good. Then Grant decides to sell a bunch of government gold and the bottom drops out of the gold market.

Besides the whole scheme being a selfish and despicable thing to do to all those folks in the hinter lands, what with greenbacks not being worth so much, some speculators got ruined. Seems not a few investors borrowed money to buy the gold and when the prices dropped so did their pants, as it were.

Epilogue

Gould made out ok by selling early, the brother-in-law lost his pants, the tipster lost his position and Fisk got himself shot dead over a showgirl.

As promised here it comes.

The power to tax is the power to destroy

Veavie Banks v. Fenno Is a major states rights decision concerning the issuing of paper money. Historically both the state chartered banks and the federal government issued paper money against reserves of gold and silver. While there had been many instances of both issues of paper money becoming virtually worthless due to either lack of supporting reserves due to over issuing. Congress passed legislation to tax all non-federal notes (paper money). Veavie bank paid the tax but under protest and took the matter to court on the grounds that; a. That it was a direct tax and had not been apportioned according to population and b. That the act imposing the tax impairs a franchise granted by the State, and that Congress has no power to pass any law with that intent or effect.

In In a 5-2 opinion, Chief Justice Chase held that this use of Congress's taxing power was authorized.

Opinion of the Court

"It cannot be doubted that under the Constitution the power to provide a circulation of coin is given to Congress. And it is settled by the uniform practice of the government and by repeated decisions, that Congress may constitutionally authorize the emission of bills of credit. ... Having thus, in the exercise of undisputed constitutional powers, undertaken to provide a currency for the whole country, it cannot be questioned that Congress may, constitutionally, secure the benefit of it to the people by appropriate legislation. To this end, Congress has denied the quality of legal tender to foreign coins, and has provided by law against the imposition of counterfeit and base coin on the community. To the same end, Congress may restrain, by suitable enactments, the circulation as money of any notes not issued under its own authority. Without this power, indeed, its attempts to secure a sound and uniform currency for the country must be futile."

A uniform federal currency for the United States is now established without competition.

Earlier we saw the United States Supreme Court rule that a state may not tax a national bank.

National Bank v. Commonwealth establishes that a state may tax the shares of that bank held by, individuals or organizations, as the shares are not capital held by the bank for purposes of doing its business. The suit was brought by Commonwealth of Kentucky.

Before a French monetary convention in 1869 testimony of the late **M. Wolowski**, was given by **Baron Rothschild**, and by **M, Rouland**, governor of the Bank of France.

M. Wolowski said:

The sum total of the precious metals is reckoned at fifty milliards, one-half gold and one-half silver. If, by a stroke of the pen, they suppress one of these metals in the monetary service, they double the demand for the other metal, to the ruin of all debtors.

M. Rouland, governor of the Bank of France, said:

We have not to do with ideal theories. The two moneys have actually co-existed since the origin of human society. They co-exist because the two together are necessary, by their quantity, to meet the needs of circulation. This necessity of the two metals,' has it ceased to exist? Is it established that the quantity of actual and prospective gold is such that we can now renounce the use of silver without disaster?

Baron Rothschild said:

The simultaneous employment of the two precious metals is satisfactory and gives rise to no complaint. Whether gold or silver dominates for the time being, it is always true that the two metals concur together in forming the monetary circulation of the world, and it is the general mass of the two metals combined which serves as the measure of the value of things. The suppression of silver would amount to a veritable destruction of values without any compensation.

In the official resume of the doings of the French monetary commission of 1869, the arguments upon both sides were summed up.

In behalf of the gold standard it was said

The rise in price which has taken place within twenty years in a great number of articles of merchandise is evidently due to many causes, such as war, bad harvests, and increase of consumption; but it is very probable that the depreciation of the precious metals has contributed to' it, since there has been a striking coincidence between the rise of prices and the production of the new mines of gold and silver. The annual production of the two metals, which was only $80,000,000 in 1847, exceeds now $200,000,000. It has nearly tripled, and it is easy to see that the real value of the metals has diminished. It is difficult to estimate exactly what the diminution is; but, whatever it may be, it demands the attention of governments, because it affects unfavorably all that portion of the population whose income, remaining nominally the same, undergoes a yearly diminution of purchasing-power. As governments control the weight and standard of money, they ought, so far as possible, to assure its value. And as it is admitted that the tendency of the metals is to depreciate, this tendency should be arrested by demonetizing one of them.

In behalf of the double standard it was replied as follows

Many economists argue that the precious metals, having become very abundant, have lost 10 or 15 per cent, of their value, and that the situation must be redressed by making money scarcer by demonetizing silver. To this it may be answered that the great discoveries of gold of the last twenty years have injured nobody. The new mass of gold, spreading over the whole world, has found employment in stimulating all forms of business, and, as a consequence, the value of gold has fallen very little. According to Mr. Newmarch, the mass of gold and silver has augmented 3 per cent, per annum, while the mass of exchanges has augmented more than 3 per cent, per annum, so that the equilibrium has been maintained. And the present is an especially inopportune time to demonetize silver, because the annual production of gold has been falling off for several years. It was $200,000,000 in 1853, and it is now not more than $140,000,000. What will happen to the civilized world if silver is demonetized and if gold shall then fail? **From the Silver Commission of 1876**

Marcus Goldman gets into the Banking business.

1870

Owner Operated Agriculture and Labor begin national efforts to have a lose Green-Back type currency policy established to easy what they perceive as a heavy handed stranglehold of industrialists and banks. A convention calls for people to organize and support **the National Labor Reform Party**.

> Construction begins on Brooklyn Bridge, US mint at Carson City, Nevada begins issuing coins, John D Rockefeller incorporates Standard Oil, 173 Blackfoot (140 women & children) killed in Montana by US Army, Metropolitan Museum of Art forms in NYC, James W Smith of South Carolina is 1st black to enter West Point, 1st trans-US rail service begins, 3rd French republic proclaimed as they overthrow their king, Mayor William Tweed, of Tammany Hall, accused of robbing New York City treasury and Foot and Mouth Disease first reported in the United States.

Europe enters a major period of depression that last throughout the decade. This financial condition reduces foreign investment in the United States.

Kirk-Holden War Governor Holden of North Carolina declares Casswell County in a state of insurrection. Apparently Kirk who Holden put in charge of settling things down got a bit carried away. *OK, maybe more than a bit carried away.*

There are now over 1600 National Banks and a little over 300 state banks operating in the country.

The desire to a) create a national system of banking, b) create a common and uniform currency for the country, the currency was not discounted from national bank to national bank and c) create an secondary market for treasury bonds had been achieved. There were however some features of the system that had negative consequences attached.

One being the amount of currency a **National Banks** could have circulating at any one time was related to the **'market value'** of the Treasury securities it had on deposit with the **Office of the Comptroller of the Currency**. If the **'market value'** of those securities was up then the bank could place more currency into circulation, typically via loans. But when the **'market value'** of those securities decline then the amount of currency that bank had in circulation had to be reduced either by not making any loans and thereby slowly reducing the currency in circulation or if things were going south fast they would call-in outstanding loans. Imagine thinking you could walk down to the bank and get a loan to buy a couple pieces of farm equipment and they said no because the securities market was a little soft or thinking you had a couple of years to pay off the loan on aforementioned farm equipment and Mr. Banker man shows up and says **"I got to have the money right this moment"**. In either case you ain't gonna be happy and might be wondering why you should be doing business with the National Bank. The national banks had other restrictions too like no real estate loans and not more than 10% of on hand capital to any one person. This makes sense to me as it reduces risk of misadventure either by insider loans and not having too many eggs in a single basket.

Another issue was with the nature of agriculture. Farmers borrow money in the spring for planting and deposit money in the fall after harvest. This is a reasonable process until you consider that most rural banks were serving rather small specialized communities. So in spring when demand for currency was high the small banks had to go to the big banks to get the extra funds and in the fall they'd send currency back to the big banks. The big banks and everybody's uncle twice removed knew this and made accommodations for this cyclic occurrence. The big banks could borrow from a clearing-house (if they were a member of a clearing-house network), call in some loans or sell some bonds, securities, or some stock. All is well because everybody and their cousin twice removed know this is a normal occurrence and is no big deal.

The problem comes in when there are a lot of banks trying to sell securities or stock and driving the prices down. As the 'market value' of the securities on deposit with the Office of the Comptroller of the Currency drops the legal requirements for the Nation Banks is to further reduce currency in circulation typically resulting in 'loans being called-in'. When this happens the 'bank run story' kicks in and things turn to squatting residue. Who is left to pick up the pieces? The State Banks, not being 'hindered' by such regulations nor being subject to the whims of a security market, are able to pick up the pieces and get rich off the resulting financial crisis. We will see this again and again in the future.

Over the next four decades the National Bank system weakens and state banks expand precisely because of this situation.

To this point European trade with China was a deficit draining silver from Europe and additionally the ongoing wars in Europe had nearly emptied the coffers of silver coin.

France suspends specie payments.

1871

National Bank v. Lanier found that, as federal law forbade banks from owning their own shares, they were also prohibited from loaning money on those shares.

> Oleomargarine patented, 2nd German Empire proclaimed by Kaiser Wilhelm I & Bismarck, 1st Negro lodge of US Masons approved, New Jersey, US income tax repealed, Paris surrenders to Prussians, German Empire ends all anti-Jewish civil restrictions, Segregated street cars integrated in Louisville, Ky. , Ku Klux Klan trials began in federal court in Oxford Miss, Guatemala revolts for agrarian reforms, Great Chicago Fire (no cow involved, really), President Grant suspends writ of habeas corpus, Mob in LA hangs 18 Chinese, Susan B Anthony arrested after voting, National Rifle Association organized, Ku Klux Klan trials began in Federal District Court and Gilbert and Sullivan collaborate for the first time.

Merchants' Bank v. State Bank establishes the power of a national bank to certify checks.

Germany goes to the gold standard.

In respect to the disturbance in the relative market value of the metals which followed the German demonetization of silver, it could be shown from a comparison of prices in silver in 1873 and 1877 that that metal has more than maintained its purchasing power over everything except gold. **From the Silver Commission of 1876**

1872

Congress begins investigating The Crédit Mobilier Scandal. This involves the construction of the Union Pacific Railroad; the players being Union Pacific owners, Crédit Mobilier, lots of congressmen and lots of money being skimmed. **I mean big money as one of the 'Big Four' who owned the Union Pacific bragged about being able to buy any vote he wanted.** *Maybe this sounds familiar too!*

> 1st national convention of Prohibition Party, Yellowstone becomes world's 1st national park, Illinois becomes 1st state to require sexual equality in employment, 7.8 earthquake shakes Owens Valley, California, George B Brayton patents gasoline powered engine, Vesuvius erupts, Karl Marx speaks in Amsterdam, Montgomery starts his mail-order business, Bloomingdale's department store in NY opens, The Great Boston Fire of 1872, close to 1,000 buildings destroyed and HMS Challenger sets sail on 3½ year world oceanographic cruise.

Oulton v. German Savings and Loan Society establishes that national banks were not only depositories for savers but also loaned money and minted currency.

A note concerning Rome As Rome began to come undone they reduced the amount of gold in their coinage while expecting it to retain the same buying power, which kept the same name or token value, at least three times. This reduction in actual gold in Roman coins did nothing but ruin the reputation and international value of Roman coins.

1873

Timber Culture Act allowed up to 160 acres of land to a homesteader if he/she planted at least 40 acres of trees over a period of years. It could be added to an existing homestead claim.

> United States military goes to Columbia. Coinage Act of 1873, Congress abolishes bimetallism & authorizes $1 & $3 gold coins, The U.S. Congress enacts the Comstock Law, making it illegal to send any "obscene, lewd, or lascivious" books through the mail, Colfax Massacre in Grant Parish Louisiana, "Field & Stream" begins publishing, Colgate Company began selling dental cream and the Winchester '73 comes out.

Coinage Act of 1873 The United States went off a bimetal standard to use gold only. This really hurt the western silver industry. They got back in the game in 1878. Seems too much sliver is a bad thing because the value declines in relation to gold or some would have had the world believe at the time. The act also reduced the money supply in a growing economy bringing the better times to bad times. *That last part was a hint.*

Panic of 1873 The United States as well as parts of Europe had been expanding economically since the end of the Civil War particularly in railroads and the supporting industries. Much of the expansion was heavily finance through speculation in rising stock prices of the railroads. This part seems to be debated here and there. Anyway the bubble bursts! Banks start trying to raise money and reduce currency because of the National Bank requirements discussed earlier, people start running to the banks and the whole thing turns into a lousy mess.

When Germany went to an exclusively gold standard and dropped silver, in 1871, the demand for silver slid. The worlds silver supply had jumped over the last few years as there were many discoveries such as the Comstock Lode. This seemingly made silver less valuable in relation to gold making gold the preferred monetary standard for Bankers (creditors) and industrialists and demand for silver for currency fell off gradually worldwide as other European governments went off bimetal standards.

The coinage Act of 1873 took the United States off the silver standard as well and tightened the money supply making it harder for folks to pay their loans and in some cases get any money at all. Less money means higher interest rates, the old supply and demand thing. This situation existed not only in the United States but in much Europe as well.

The Silver Commission of 1876 found the facts concerning the relative volume of silver versus gold to such as to make the arguments presented since the Germans went to an exclusively gold standard in 1871 without merit. There were even hints that the Bank of England had precipitated the move to gold by refusing silver.

The event that contributed to the crash of the World Economy for 20 years!

Jay Cooke & Company ran into a shredder when they tried to raise money for railroad construction and a rumor went around that their credit was lousy. Bingo! Jay goes belly up, bank runs start, banks and businesses fail, unemployment rises, because money is tight or too expensive and it all goes down the tubes with the **New York Stock Exchange closing for like ten days**. We have a depression that lasts until about 1896 or so. This depression included Europe, Latin America and the Ottoman Empire. At the time this was called the **Great Depression**. Now it is mostly referred to as the **Long Depression**.

At the session (October 30, 1873) of the Belgian Monetary Commission, Professor Laveleye

> Debtors, and among them the state, have the right to pay in gold or silver, and this right cannot be taken away without disturbing the relation of debtors and creditors, to the prejudice of debtors', to the extent of perhaps one-half, certainly of one third. To increase all debts at a blow (brusquement) is a measure so violent, so revolutionary, that I cannot.......

"We sometime didn't get enough to buy oats for our horses. Most banks had very little money in them." **Frank James**

1874

Greenback Party is just beginning to get started.

April President Grant vetoes a bill that would have placed over $40 million in un-backed currency in to circulation.

> New York City annexes the Bronx, Battle between jobless & police in NYC, 100s injured, Gen J van Swieten conquerors Kraton Atjeh after 1000's die, NY legislature passes compulsory education law, Dutch 2nd Chamber passes child labor law, 1st recorded dam disaster in US at Williamsburg Mass, Freedmen's Bank closes, Social Democratic Workmen's Party of North America formed, Start of Sherlock Holmes Adventure, "Gloria Scott, Joseph F Glidden patents more barbed wire, The United States Greenback Party is established as a political party consisting primarily of farmers affected by the Panic of 1873

Tiffany v. National Bank of Missouri Established that federally chartered banks are allowed to charge the highest loan rates permitted under state law, even if state banks are restricted to lower rates. Also that federal law overrides state law when it comes to national banks. *This may eventually have something to do with credit cards.*

Mennonite Russians immigrated to Kansas with seeds for **"Turkey Red"** wheat, a drought-resistant strain that made the 'Great American Desert' the "Breadbasket of the World."

1875

Greenback Party is started. Their name refers to the Greenback currency issued during the Civil War which was 'not' backed by gold. Greenbacks are felt to be inflationary thereby causing bankers to be paid back with currency that has less buying power that the value of the initial loan.

This was favored by farmers and workers because they would be better able to pay back their loans. The Coinage Act of 1873 may have contributed to the Panic and ensuing Depression with the mutually related deflation the farmers were receiving less for their crops and had to pay higher prices for shipping too.

The party felt that the Greenback policy would better foster middle and small businesses and help break the iron fist of Eastern businesses and banks. As the Republican Party was in control of the government and favored business interests in the East the Greenback party found it was fighting an uphill battle.

The Railroad industry's policy of selling blocks of the land received from Congress as part of the Railway act contributed to the problem because the land was hardly able to be made profitable if at all so further alienating folks. Many Western novels refer to this situation.

> President Grant sends federal troops to Vicksburg, Miss, Electric dental drill is patented, Congress passes Civil Rights Act; invalidated by Supreme Ct, 1883, 238 members of "Whiskey Ring" accused of anti-US activities, Quake in Venezuela & Colombia kills 16,000, Alexander Graham Bell makes 1st voice transmission, The Herzegovinian rebellion against the Ottoman Empire begins and Violent bread riots in Montreal.

National Bank v. National Exchange Bank establishes that the bank can acquire stock. *This acquiring stock thing will pop up again and again.*

Farmers' and Mechanics' National Bank v. Dearing The Court decided that a state law forfeiting a bank debt in which excessive (usurious) interest had been charged was preempted by federal laws that allowed the bank in error to forfeit only the interest due and not the entire loan.

Specie Payment Resumption Act 1875 constricted the money supply in the United States and may have contributed to the 'Long Depression' as it returned the nation to the gold standard. This was largely in relation to European countries switching to a gold standard, making silver unacceptable for paying debts. Constricting the money supply for a growing nation would have the effect of slowing things down and taking money out of the hands of the populace making it harder for the common person to make ends meet.

Jacob Schiff, Solomon Loeb's son-in-law, joins the firm and under his leadership became a prestigious investment bank second only to J. Pierpont Morgan's, J.P. Morgan & Co.

More Europeans emigrate to Buenos Aries than to New York.

The Journal of the London Statistical Society (March, 1875) says:

Such is the development of credit in this country, that it has been roughly calculated that 97 per cent, of payments are ordinarily affected by checks, bills, and other expedients of credit; about 2 per cent, by bank-notes; and about 1 per cent, by coin.

In this country the proportion of money used in settling balances, recognizing both bank-notes and coin as money, is somewhat larger than in England, but is still small.

Both from the Silver Commission of 1876

1876

Indiana The Greenback Party has a platform of repeal of the Specie Resumption Act of 1875 and return to non-gold back currency so as to return the people to prosperity. Their candidate Peter Cooper gets up at the convention with this message, paraphrased.

"The paper currency, commonly called 'legal tenders' or 'greenbacks,' was actually paid out for value received as so much gold, when gold could not be obtained.....the commercial and industrial prosperity of a country do not depend upon the amount of gold and silver there is in circulation. **Our prosperity must continually depend upon the industry, the enterprise, and the busy internal trade and a true independence of foreign nations, which a paper circulation, well based on credit, has always been found to promote.**"

The Greenback Party, having support almost exclusively from farmers, did not fare well during this election

> The United States orders all Native Americans to move into reservations, Albert Spalding with $800 starts sporting goods company, A G Bell & Elisha Gray apply separately for telephone patents Supreme Court eventually rules Bell rightful inventor, US Congress decides to impeach Minister of War Belknap, Tchaikovsky completes his "Swan Lake" ballet, The April Uprising breaks out in Bulgaria, 1st player to hit for cycle (George Hall, Philadelphia Athletics), Tsunami's after earthquake floods NE coast of Japan, kills 28,000, Custer & 7th Cavalry wiped out by Sioux & Cheyenne at Little Big Horn, US law removes Indians from Black Hills after gold find, 1st carpet sweeper patented and Fire at Brooklyn Theater kills 295, trampled or burned to death.

"My failures have been errors of judgment, not of intent." **Ulysses S. Grant** *Thanks 'U'!*

General prosperity and a general fall in prices never did and never can co-exist. **From the Silver Commission of 1876**

The American Review (1876)

> Diminishing money and falling prices are not only oppressive upon debtors, of whom, in modern times, states are the greatest, but they cause stagnation in business, reduced production, and enforced idleness. Falling markets annihilate profits, and as it is only the expectation of gain which stipulates the investment of capital in operations, inadequate employment is found for labor, and those who are employed can only be so upon the condition of diminished wages. An increasing amount of money, and consequently augmenting prices, are attended by results precisely the contrary. Production is stimulated by the profits resulting from advancing prices; labor is consequently in demand and better

paid, and the general activity and buoyancy insure to capital a wider demand and higher remuneration.

The Silver commission of 1876 is formed as described below.

> **Resolved by the Senate and House of Representatives,** That a commission is hereby authorized and constituted, to consist of three Senators, to be appointed by the Senate; three members of the House of Representatives, to be appointed by the Speaker; and, not exceeding three in number, to be selected by and associated with them: with authority to determine the time and place of meeting, and to take evidence, and whose duty it shall be to inquire -

> **First** Into the change which has taken place in the relative value of gold and silver; the causes thereof, whether permanent or otherwise ; the effects thereof upon trade, commerce, finance, and the productive interests of the country, and upon the standard (of) value in this and foreign countries;

> **Second** Into the policy of the restoration of the double standard in this country; and, if restored, what the legal relation between the two coins, silver and gold, should it be;

> **Third** Into the policy of continuing legal-tender notes concurrently with the metallic standards, and the effects thereof upon the labor, industries, and wealth of the country; and

> **Fourth Into** the best means for providing for facilitating the resumption of specie payments.

Colorado Statehood

1877

Rutherford B. Hayes becomes President 1877 to 1881 Republican

"It is now true that this is God's Country, if equal rights—a fair start and an equal chance in the race of life are everywhere secured to all." **Rutherford B. Hayes**

> Reconstruction Era ends, President Hayes appoints Frederick Douglass marshal of Wash DC, electoral college vs. popular vote, Russia declares war on Turkey through Romania, Chase National Bank opens in NYC (later merges into Chase Manhattan) and Johnannes Brahms' 2nd Symphony in D, premieres in Vienna.

The **Molly Maguire's**, ten Irish immigrants, are hanged at the Schuylkill County and Carbon County, Pennsylvania prisons.

Great Railroad Strike of 1877 The economy was down the tubes so the railroads cut wages. The employees took remarkable exception to the cut in wages and proceeded to have demonstrations, marches and stayed from work. The railroad was running little if at all. Military shoots on striking railroad workers in Baltimore, killing 9. This was a very large strike and nearly crippled business as goods could not move.

Kuhn, Loeb raised funds for the Chicago and North Western Railroad

Excerpts from the 1876 Silver Commission report to Congress made in 1877

In respect to the disturbance in the relative market value of the metals which followed the German demonetization of silver, it could be shown from a comparison of prices in silver in 1873 and 1877 that that metal has more than maintained its purchasing power over everything except gold. In 1873, 6O d. in gold would purchase an ounce of standard silver in Loudon. In 1877 it only requires 54 d. to buy the same amount. It is within the knowledge of all that 54 d. will now buy, in England, or in any other country, more real estate, more labor, and more of the general commodities which the world deals in, except silver, than 60 d. would in 1873. The exchangeable value of an ounce of standard silver is therefore greater than it was four years ago. While the general purchasing power of silver has thus been maintained, it would be an inexcusable blunder to deprive it of its debt-paying power, and of its power, as money, to check the fall in prices which is now striking as with palsy the limbs of commerce and industry.

It is the single-standard countries which suffer the evils of falling prices caused by an enhanced value of their money, while it is the double-standard countries which enjoy the benefits of the use of a money which is the better because the steadier in value. It is the single-standard countries whose money metal is temporarily the dearer which pay these premiums, and it is the double standard countries which receive them. Thus, after 1821 this country sold gold to England at a premium of from 5 to 8 per cent. In more recent times France sold silver to India at a large profit, and at the present time the Germans are paying a heavy premium on gold, which is inaccurately described as the sale of silver at a discount. This premium on gold is for them a loss without any compensation, and so far as they have proceeded in the policy of establishing a gold standard, it has proved an unmitigated injury to the commercial and industrial interests of the world and especially of Germany.

Under the double standard the debtor may, at his option, avail himself of money coined out of either metal in the payment of his obligations. This option is of no practical importance, except when a variance between the legal and market relations of the metals becomes sensible. Neither does it work any injustice, nor is it, in fact, confined to one side of any transaction. The creditor is swift to avail himself of it when he lends money, and he never lends in the metal which for the time being happens to be the dearer one. He cannot claim, therefore, that it is his equity to be paid in the dearer metal, and he never is so paid unless, between the dates of lending and of being paid, the double standard is abrogated, so that he is enabled to exact what he did not lend. The debtor may justly complain if he is forced to pay in the dearer metal or money, which he never receives when he borrows. The enormous aggregate of debts in this country', public and private, were contracted by borrowing national paper currency or in the purchase of property at paper-currency prices.

It is urged that the debtors ought not to complain if they are forced to pay these debts in specie, and that they ought to have foreseen that the resumption of specie payments in the near future was probable, and that the right of paying in paper currency might be taken away from them. But it cannot be said that they ought also to have foreseen that the option of paying in silver, which had always been theirs, would be taken away, and that they would be condemned to pay in gold alone, and not only that, but in gold enormously appreciated in value, if other important double standard countries should follow our example and make it their sole standard of values.

The statement sometimes made that the two metals never in fact circulate indifferently and concurrently is not true. Notwithstanding the legal relation of value between the two precious metals established in 1792 in this country did not coincide exactly with the market relation, yet they circulated concurrently, with perhaps a preponderance of silver in the circulation until 1821, when the resumption of specie payments in gold by the Bank of England caused an advance in the value of gold and a consequent widening of the relation of value between the two metals. (See papers on the currency appended to the report made in 1830 by Mr. Ingham, Secretary of the Treasury.) Also, after the change made in 1834 in the legal relation of value between the two metals, they circulated concurrently until about 1850, although, on account of the undervaluation of silver by the law of 1834, there was a constant tendency to an exportation of silver in the settlement of foreign balances. The draining of a country of its silver coins is necessarily slow, as they are less in value than gold coins, and are consequently diffused among a vastly greater number of holders. It is for this reason that silver has less fluidity of circulation than gold, and presents greater obstacles to its concentration in large masses. The dangers of a financial panic occasioned by sudden and violent outflows of the money of a country are therefore less where the circulation is largely of silver than where it consists wholly or principally of gold.

The philosophy of the double standard is that a rise in the value of money and a fall in general prices are the greatest evils which can befall the world, and its object is to prevent, as far as possible, the occurrence of these evils. It takes no precautions against a fall in the value of money, because in the whole history of the human race not a single instance can be pointed out of a fall in the value of either or of both the metals which has not proved a benefaction to mankind; while, on the other hand, during every period and whenever a rise in the value of metallic money has occurred it has been attended by financial, industrial, political, and social disaster. An increasing value of money and falling prices have been and are more fruitful of human misery than war, pestilence, or famine. They have wrought more injustice than all the bad laws which were ever enacted. Under the double standard these evils could never occur, except by a rise in the value of both metals, while under the single standard they might be caused by a rise in the value of one of them.

1878

Bland–Allison Act of 1878 Congress required the Treasury to buy a large quantity of silver, at way above market value, and put it into circulation as silver dollars even though President had vetoed the bill. This was a return to bimetallism, gold and silver as the monetary standard. Unfortunately this caused problems because of silver being discovered all over the place it was 'perceived' as less rare and therefore less valuable even though the Silver Commission of 1876 had found the relative volume relationship nearly the same as 1848, before the California and Australian gold rushes and the Nevada silver Comstock Lode.

The Bland Allison Act was the first big success of the **'Free Silver'** movement to put more silver into circulation to relieve the effects of the depression that started in 1873. Things did get better and reduced the political pressure to maintain the bi-metallic monetary standard. However when things got a little worse again in 1884 and 1887 the pressure was on again.

> US Senate proposes female suffrage, US Supreme court rules race separation on trains unconstitutional, Greece declares war on Turkey, Thayer patents catcher's mask, John Tunstall is murdered by outlaw Jessie Evans, sparking the Lincoln County War in Lincoln County, New Mexico, Thomas Alva Edison patents gramophone (phonograph), Greenback Labor Party forms, US congress authorizes large-size silver certificate, Jack Johnson is 1st black to hold a heavyweight boxing title, Harley Procter introduces Ivory Soap, 1st unassisted triple play in organized baseball, by Paul Hines, Treaty of Berlin divide Africa up for colonization, - German anti-Semitism begins during the Reichstag election, 1st White House telephone installed, Joseph Pulitzer begins publishing "St Louis Dispatch".

1879

Around midyear the United States government **starts redeeming greenbacks with gold**, accepts greenbacks as payments for customs duties and is paying its debts in gold. Greenbacks now seem to have value! This may have dampened some of the hard feelings about currency while 'not so much so' with others.

> Cheyenne prisoners led by Dull Knife revolt at Ft Robinson, Zulu war against British colonial rule in South Africa begins, James Shields (D) elected US senator from Missouri after previously serving as US senator from Illinois & Minnesota, Joseph Swan demonstrates light bulb using carbon glow, Congress authorizes women lawyers to practice before Supreme Court, Fahlberg discovers saccharin, Trial of Standing Bear-Crook on Indians citizen rights begins, An F4 tornado strikes Irving, Kansas, Gilbert & Sullivan's "HMS Pinafore" debuts, Doc Holliday kills for the first time after a man shoots up his New Mexico saloon, NL owners meeting in Buffalo adopt reserve clause, giving each team exclusive rights to their players, In a 6-day footrace a Mr. Weston loses to a horse, 900 to 885 km, Elkins patents refrigerating apparatus.

1880

The **Greenback Party** is now the **Greenback Labor Party**. With the addition of labor the party now also supports an 8 hour work day, graduated income tax, women's suffrage and land should be given to settlers and not sold to speculators.

The Greenback Party in any form begins to fall apart in 1882. While the party elected several United States Congressmen its organizational abilities were not up to the task.

> Building of Panama Canal begins by French I think, 1st US sewage disposal system separate from storm drains, 1st town completely illuminated by electric lighting (Wabash, IN), 1st pay telephone installed, France annexes Otaheite (Tahiti), 1st commercial hydroelectric power planet begins, Grand Rapids, Michigan, John Philip Sousa becomes new director of US Marine Corps Band (*I love those marches*), Mexican soldiers kill Victorio, one of the greatest Apache military strategists.

1881

James A Garfield 1881 to 1881 killed in office Republican

"Whoever controls the volume of money in any country is absolute master of all industry and commerce." **James A Garfield**

Chester A Arthur 1881 to 1885 Republican

"If it were not for the reporters, I would tell you the truth." **Chester A. Arthur**

> Dr. John H Watson is introduced to Sherlock Holmes (A Study in Scarlet), Kansas becomes 1st state to prohibit all alcoholic beverages, China and Russia sign the Sino-Russian Ili Treaty, California becomes 1st state to pass plant quarantine legislation, Barnum & Bailey's Greatest Show on Earth opens (Madison Square Garden), Rioting takes place in Basingstoke in protest against the daily vociferous promotion of rigid Temperance by the Salvation Army, Anti-Jewish riots in Jerusalem, Bat Masterson fights his last gun battle, Anit-Jewish rioting in Kiev Ukraine, Frederick Douglass appointed recorder of deeds for Wash DC, 1st international telephone conversation, American Red Cross founded by Clara Barton, President Garfield shot by Charles J Guiteau, Booker T Washington establishes Tuskegee Institute, Sitting Bull surrenders to federal troops, Hurricane hits Florida & Carolinas; about 700 die, David Houston patents roll film for cameras, Shootout at OK Corral, American Federation of Labor (AFL) founded.

Kuhn, Loeb, & Co. does the financing for the Pennsylvania Railroad and the Chicago, Milwaukee & St. Paul Railroad

1882

Recession of 1882 to 1885 Primarily prices fell during this period because of the declined in railroad construction which also affected related industries.

Because of anti-monopoly laws, Standard Oil is organized as a trust, Richard Wagner completes his opera "Parsifal", Edmunds Act adopted by US to suppress polygamy in the territories, Chinese Exclusion Act: US Congress ceases Chinese immigration, Cyclone in Arabian Sea (Bombay India) drowns 100,000, Anti-colonization mass society of Alexandria Egypt kills 50 Europeans, Tchaikovsky's "1812 Overture" opens in Moscow, 10,000 workers march in 1st Labor Day parade in NYC and 1st World Series game, Cincinnati (AA) beats Chicago (NL) 4-0.

Parris Bourse Crash This is here as an example of what was happening on the international scene during this period so you know all this financial mess isn't just in the United States. The crash was generated by the collapse of a bank resulting in low capital for stock market traders causing the market to crash and a recession ensued. *Just think about that 'low capital for stock market traders' thing for a few decades herein.*

Marcus Goldman's son-in-law joins the firm.

1883

"The danger is not that a particular class is unfit to govern. Every class is unfit to govern."
Lord Acton

"Ladies Home Journal" begins publishing, Alabama becomes 1st US state to enact an antitrust law, Congress authorizes the 1st steel vessels in US navy, "Buffalo Bill"

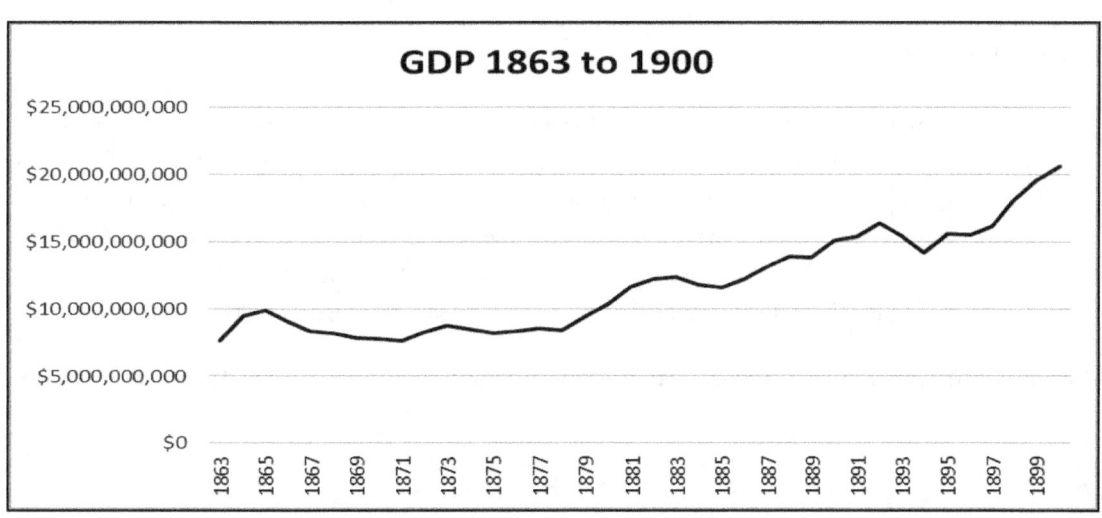

Cody put on his 1st Wild West Show, Italy signs military treaty with Austria-Hungary & Germany, 1st commercial electric railway line begins operation (Chicago El), Arabi Pasha declares a holy war in Egypt, Krakatoa, west of Java, explodes with a force of 1,300

megatons and kills approximately 40,000 people, Orient Express' 1st run, linking Turkey to Europe by rail and Supreme Court declares Civil Rights Act of 1875 unconstitutional (*WTFO*).

1884

Panic of 1884 was a panic during the Recession of 1882-85. National Banks stopped investment funds and called in loans. Europe was short of gold further reducing investments. Basically a cash shortage stopped funds from being invested and a panic ensued. The panic stopped when the clearing houses propped up some banks in danger of failing due to 'bank runs'. Even then thousands of smaller firms went under exacerbating the recession. The rules for national banks of reducing currency based on the value of the securities they had on deposit with the Comptroller of the Currency was still in effect.

> Police seize all copies of Tolstoy's "What I Believe In", Tornadoes in Miss, Alabama, NC, SC, Tenn., KY & In kill 800, Siege of Khartoum Sudan begins, London prison for debtors closed, Anti-Monopoly party forms in US, Anti-Monopoly party & Greenback Party forms People's Party in US, Dr. John Harvey Kellogg patents "flaked cereal", John Lynch (R-MS) chosen 1st black major-party national convention chair, Dow Jones published its' 1st stock average, Statue of Liberty presented to US in Paris, George Eastman patents paper-strip photographic film, Aluminum capstone set atop Washington Monument. *(at the time aluminum was more valuable than gold)*

1885

Grover Cleveland becomes President 1885 to 1889 Democratic

"A man is known by the company he keeps, and also by the company from which he is kept out." **Grover Cleveland**

> United States military is operating at Panama, Mark Twain's "Adventures of Huckleberry Finn," published, American Telephone & Telegraph (AT&T) incorporates, Congress passes Indian Appropriations Act (Indians wards of federal government), 2nd French government of Ferry resigns, "Good Housekeeping" magazine is 1st published, Battle of Batoche, French Canadians rebel against Canada, 1st gasoline pump is delivered to a gasoline dealer (Ft Wayne, Indiana) and France declares Madagascar a protectorate.

Marcus Goldman adds his son and another son-in-law and they become Goldman Sachs & Company

1886

Between now and 1929 over **130 bills** are introduced in Congress requesting a **'Deposit Insurance'**.

> 1st Tournament of Roses, Karl Benz patents 1st auto with burning motor, Pres. Cleveland declares a state of emergency in Seattle because of anti-Chinese violence, 1st US

alternating current power plant starts, Chemist John Pemberton begins to advertise for Coca-Coke, Sigmund Freud opens practice, 24 Christians burn to death in Namgongo Uganda, fire destroys nearly 1,000 buildings in Vancouver, BC, Apache Chief Geronimo surrenders, Spain abolishes slavery in Cuba and **The Folies Bergère** stages its revue..

1887

Interstate Commerce Act authorizes federal regulation of railroads.

"The worst thing in this world, next to anarchy, is government." **Henry Ward Beecher**

State banks are springing up everywhere!

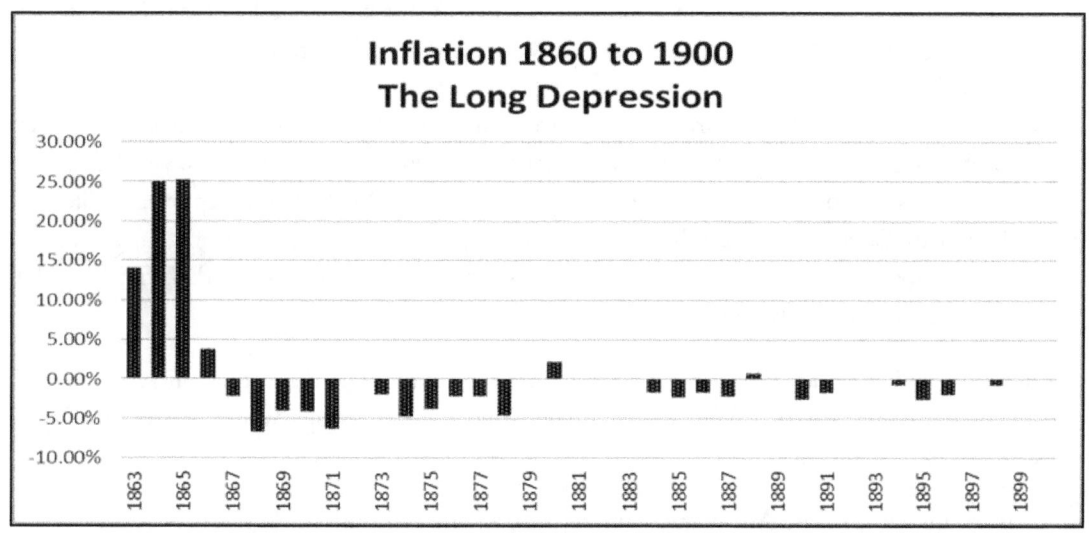

US Senate approves naval base lease of Pearl Harbor, to avoid disputed national elections, Congress creates Electoral Count Act, Union Labor Party organized in Cincinnati, Anne Sullivan begins teaching 6 year old blind-deaf Helen Keller, French/Italian Riviera struck by Earthquake; 2,000 die, Anarchist Haymarket Martyrs August Spies Albert Parsons, Adolph Fischer and George Engel are executed and Bloody Sunday clashes in central London.

The **Socialist Labor Party** stumped for a **graduated income tax**.

Recession of 1887 was a very slight recession as investments fell off.

Lord Collet serves as Governor of the Bank of England 1887 to 1889. He is also a partner of Brown Shipley Company of London for over twenty years.

1888

United States military operating at Korea, Haiti and Samoa, National Geographic Society founded (Washington, DC), The Convention of Constantinople is signed, guaranteeing free maritime passage through the Suez Canal during war and peace, Great blizzard of '88 strikes NE US, Congress creates Department of Labor, Philip Pratt unveils 1st electric automobile, "Jack the Ripper" butchers 2 more women.

1889

Benjamin Harrison becomes President 1889 to 1893 Republican

"The disfranchisement of a single legal elector by fraud or intimidation is a crime too grave to be regarded lightly." **Benjamin Harrison**

The United States Department of Agriculture (USDA) is established as a Cabinet-level agency, 1st train load of fruit (oranges) leaves LA for the east, Dakotas, Montana & Washington admitted to union, John T Reid opens 1st US golf course, Eiffel Tower officially opens, Oklahoma land rush officially started; some were "sooner", Johnstown Flood; 2,209 die in Penn, Great Fire in Seattle destroys 25 downtown blocks, Wall Street Journal begins publishing, in Colorado, Nicholas Creede strikes it rich in silver during the last great silver boom of the American Old West, New York World reporter Nellie Bly (Elizabeth Cochrane) began her attempt to surpass fictitious journey of Jules Verne's Phileas Fogg by traveling around world in less than 80 days She succeeded, finishing the trip in January in 72 days and 6 hours.

Jaybird-Woodpecker War was one of the post-reconstruction disputes concerning local government and representation. The Texas Rangers and military troops were needed to bring a semblance of peace to the area.

Paul M. Warburg joins Samuel Montague & Company, a bank in London.

France goes into a recession.

North Dakota, South Dakota, Montana and Washington Statehood

1890

Sherman Silver Purchase Act forced the US Government to buy double the amount of silver it had previously and drove up the price much to the delight of silver miners. The result was an increase of the money supply, causing inflation and an over valuation of silver as compared to gold. As people redeemed silver notes for gold the mandatory reserve limit was reached and gold redemption was halted.

United States military is operating at Argentina and Wounded Knee, Ellis Island designated as an immigration station, Congress passes Sherman Antitrust Act, Cy Young pitches & wins 1st game, Pres. of Mormon Church in Salt Lake City issues a manifesto advising members that teaching & practice of polygamy should be abandoned, Congress establishes Yosemite National Park, Daughters of American Revolution founded and US 7th Cavalry massacre 200+ captive Sioux at Wounded Knee, SD.

Panic of 1890 in England Remember Barings the bank that bought a bunch of shares of the first Bank of the United States and financed the Louisiana Purchase thereby financing an enemy of their country. Well they got all upside down with speculative loans in Argentina that went south and they needed a 'lender of last resort' to get bailed out so the Overend & Gurney thing from 1866 kicked in and averted a possible major financial crisis in England.

Germany experiences an economic downturn.

The Recession of 1890 in the United States is fairly brief and mild and things get BOOMing again.

Paul M. Warburg now is with the Banque Russe pour le Commerce Etranger in Paris.

Sherman Antitrust Act signed.

Idaho and Wyoming Statehood

1891

The **Populist Party a.k.a. the Peoples Party** was born from the plight of poor small farmers in parts of the Southern and Plains states due to low agricultural prices, middlemen cutting into profits, high railroad shipping costs and high interest rates and because they believed the Republican and Democratic parties were in bed with elitists, bankers and the landowners who had no caring for the needs of the small farmers. They readily included women in party affairs. Its greatest impact was in the elections of 1892 and 1896.

> United States military operating at Haiti, Bering Strait and Chile, French troops occupy Nioro, West-Sudan, 3000 killed, Mine explosion kills 109 at Mount Pleasant Pennsylvania, The attempt of a Portuguese republican revolution breaks out, Congress creates US Courts of Appeal, A Hatfield marries a McCoy, ends long feud in West Virginia it started with an accusation of pig-stealing & lasted 20 years, Painter Gauguin leaves Marseille for Tahiti, The Wrigley Company is founded in Chicago, Illinois, Jews are expelled from Moscow Russia, National Forest Service organized, 61°F, highest temp for July 1891, in Baltimore & Philadelphia, Electric self-starter for automobile patented, The gasoline-powered car debuts and Edison patents "transmission of signals electrically" (radio).

Briggs v. Spaulding *over turned 1997, establishes that officers of a bank may be sued for damages they cause through failure to act diligently in the performance of their duties.

From the decision…

> It was said at the bar that if such a rule be rigidly applied, a gentleman of property and means would hesitate long before accepting the position of director in a banking

95

association. This could not be the result if gentlemen of that class, becoming directors of such institutions, would exercise anything like the care and supervision they or any other prudent, discreet persons give to the management of their own business. They ought not, by accepting and holding the position of directors, give assurance to stockholders and depositors, whose interests have been committed to their control, that the bank is being safely and honestly managed, without doing what prudent men of business recognize as essential to make such an assurance of value. A banking corporation, publicly avowing that its business was to be wholly administered by executive officers, and that the directors would have nothing in fact to do with its management, would not long retain the confidence of stockholders and depositors; a fact which, of tse lf, shows that the abdication by directors of their duties and functions not only tends to defeat the object for the creation of such an institution, but puts in peril the interests of stockholders and depositors.

People being accountable for their actions, what a concept

American Express creates Travelers Checks

Paul M. Warburg goes to M.M. Warburg and Company in Hamburg, his family's bank founded in 1798.

1892

The **Populist Party's** platform for the national election included a graduated income tax and government control of telephones, telegraphs and railroads (*after all hadn't the government and therefore the people basically subsidized the Rail Roads in the first place*), direct election of Senators, an 8 hour work day and getting rid of the national banks.

The **Populist** candidates did rather well wining Nevada, Idaho, Colorado and Kansas as the Presidential Candidate garnered over a million votes nationwide.

> Britain & the US sign treaty on seal hunting in the Bering Sea, black longshoremen strike for higher wages in St Louis MO, George Sampson patents clothes dryer, Sierra Club forms, Dalton Gang ends in shoot-out in Coffeeville, "Nutcracker Suite," Peter Ilyich Tchaikovsky's ballet, premieres.

The Homestead Strike was a strike that culminated in a battle between strikers and private security agents. The battle was the second largest and one of the most serious disputes in U.S. labor history second only to the Battle of Blair Mountain. The strikers lost and labor was seriously set back.

Wyoming TA Ranch A battle of the Johnson County War. Cattle barons decided to eliminate their smaller neighbors buy hunting them down. Well, their neighbors got wind of the notion and nailed down the barons at the TA ranch and that put an end to that little escapade.

JP Morgan starts financing the New York, New Haven and Hartford Railroad.

Grover Cleveland becomes President again 1893 to 1897 Democratic

"It is the responsibility of the citizens to support their government. It is not the responsibility of the government to support its citizens," Grover Cleveland. This attitude may have been why he wanted off a dual/bi-metallic standard.

> Kingdom of Hawaii overthrown, Jaap Eden skates world record 1500m (2:35), Verdi's opera "Falstaff" premieres in Milan, 1st federal railroad legislation passed; required safety features, Congo cannibals killed 1000s of Arabs, Ivory Coast becomes a French colony, New Mexico State University cancels it's 1st graduation ceremony, its only graduate Sam Steele was robbed & killed the night before, The Critic reports that ice cream soda is our national drink, Whitcomb Judson, Chicago, patents a hook less fastener (zipper), Lizzie Borden acquitted in murder of parents in New Bedford Mass *(forty whacks and all that…)*, A revolution led by the liberal general and politician, José Santos Zelaya, takes over state power in Nicaragua, France issues 1st driving licenses, included required test, Chinese deported from San Francisco under Exclusion Act, tornado destroys coast of Savannah & Charleston, English author Beatrix Potter 1st tells the story of Peter Rabbit, Cherokee Strip, Oklahoma opens to white settlement for homesteaders, New Zealand is 1st country to grant all its women the right to vote, 1st auto built in US (by Duryea brothers), 3rd worst hurricane in US history kills 1,800 (Mississippi), , Anton Dvorak's "New World Symphony" premieres and Henry Ford completes his 1st useful gas motor.

Senate approves repealing **Sherman Silver Purchase Act of 1890**.

Things are about to get really nasty for a couple of decades.

Panic of 1893 is widely considered the worst economic depression in the country yet. The 1880s saw great expansion in the railroads creating a 'bubble', 'BOOM'. As 'bubbles' are often to do there was a 'BUST'. Affected was the investment in railroads and supporting industries for railroad construction. When railroad construction virtually stopped the 'Reading Railroad' was caught, as others were, with bond debt, with high interest rates attached and could not keep up payments on the bonds. Besides the Reading Railroad, made famous via the Monopoly game, the Union Pacific, Northern Pacific and the Atchison Topeka and Santa Fe Railroads failed.

The Free Silver Movement had forced the Silver Purchase Act of 1890 that drove up the price of silver. With the rise in inflation agriculture was happy because they could pay off their debts with inflated money. Additionally there was a run on gold as people ran to banks to redeem silver dollars for gold. This caused the Treasury to reach its' statutory threshold' of gold and stopped the issue of gold for silver. As things took a turn for the worse European investments withdrew and worsened the already fragile balance.

Many bank failures followed as they were run on and unemployment became high, around 18%. Because the growing middle class was hit hard by the unemployment and the loss of savings in failed banks, somewhere around 500, people simply walked away from their homes as they could no longer make the payments.

From the 'Panic Circular of 1893' "You will at once retire one third of your circulation and call-in one half of your loans etc……" Just think about this for a bit.

During this President Grover Cleveland suspended the Sherman Silver Purchase act as he felt was largely responsible for the panic and the depression that followed. The United States is back on the gold standard. This action did not stop the debate over whether gold or silver or both should be the national monetary standard. The issue of what the monetary standard should be continues to this day. At least in a few circles it does.

A low gold reserve at this time may have been a significant contributing factor.

Events in graph: Panic of 1873, Recession of 1882, Panic of 1884, English Panic of 1890, Panic of 1893, Panic of 1896 and 1899-1900 very mild Recession.

1894

North Carolina may have been the greatest success for the **Populist Party** as they, in coalition with Republicans, overran the states elections winning nearly all of the state and local seats.

United States military is operating at Brazil, Nicaragua, China and Korea, Columbus World's fair in Chicago destroyed by fire, Revolution in Sicily crushed by government troops, US flag fired on in Rio; prompt satisfaction exacted by Admiral Benham, female suffrage organization in Amsterdam forms, The Cripple Creek miner's strike, led by the Western Federation of Miners, begins in Cripple Creek, Colorado, Enforcement Act repealed, making it easier to disenfranchise blacks, anarchist Émile Henry hurls a bomb into Paris's Cafe Terminus, killing one and wounding 20, US & China sign treaty preventing Chinese laborers from entering US, 37 miners killed at Franklin, WA, Coxey's Army of the unemployed sets out from Massillon Oh for Wash, 11 strikers killed in riot at Connellsville, Penn, British & Belgian secret accord on dividing Central-Africa, 136,000 mine workers strike in Ohio for pay increase, 1st US poliomyelitis epidemic breaks out, Rutland, Vermont, Korea declares independence from China, asks for Japanese aid, Cleveland sends 2,000 troops to Chicago to suppress Pullman strike, In NYC, 12,000 tailors went on strike protesting sweat shops, vaccine for diphtheria announced by Dr. Roux of Paris and the Greenback (Independent) Party organizes in Indianapolis.

Democratic Party proposes income tax as the party absorbs Populist Party causes.

The Wilson–Gorman Tariff Act of 1894 generated a federal tax of 2% on incomes over $4,000. It was overturned by the Supreme Court in Pollock v. Farmers' Loan & Trust Co.

Coxey's Army 1 – Was a protest march on Washington DC protesting unemployment organized by Jacob Coxey in the second year of the worst depression to hit the US since the country began. The idea was to lobby the government to create jobs thru public works improvements, not unlike what FDR did in the 1930s and to have the labor paid for in paper currency. The paid in paper currency thing was part of the 'Populist philosophy running around at the time.

Coxey speaking in protest on the steps of the Capitol Building

> The Constitution of the United States guarantees to all citizens the right to peaceably assemble and petition for redress of grievances, and furthermore declares that the right of free speech shall not be abridged.

> We stand here to-day to test these guaranties of our Constitution. We choose this place of assemblage because it is the property of the people. . . . Here rather than at any other spot upon the continent it is fitting that we should come to mourn over our dead liberties and by our protest arouse the imperiled nation to such action as shall rescue the Constitution and resurrect our liberties.

> Upon these steps where we stand has been spread a carpet for the royal feet of a foreign princess, the cost of whose lavish entertainment was taken from the public Treasury without the consent or the approval of the people. Up these steps the lobbyists of trusts and corporations have passed unchallenged on their way to committee rooms, access to which we, the representatives of the toiling wealth-producers, have been denied.

> We stand here to-day in behalf of millions of toilers whose petitions have been buried in committee rooms, whose prayers have been un-responded to, and whose opportunities for honest, remunerative, productive labor have been taken from them by unjust legislation,

which protects idlers, speculators, and gamblers: we come to remind the Congress here assembled of the declaration of a United States Senator, "that for a quarter of a century the rich have been growing richer, the poor poorer and that by the close of the present century the middle class will have disappeared as the struggle for existence becomes fierce and relentless."

Montague Collet Norman goes to New York to work in the offices of Brown Brothers and becomes friends with W. A. Delano.

1895

Perhaps the Populists Party's successes in 1892 and 1894 were their undoing because the Democrats took up many of their causes for the Democratic Platform in the next years' election. After this the Populists slowing faded away. The 'Populists' brought national attention and support to their causes when the Democrats figured out they could enlarge their voter bases. The party faded into oblivion officially disbanding in 1908

> United States military operating at Columbia, Tchaikovsky's ballet "Swan Lake" premieres, St Petersburg, Oscar Wilde's "Importance of Being Earnest," opens in London, Cuban war for independence begins, Italian troops invade Abyssinia (Ethiopia), Russian scientist Alexander Stepanovich Popov demonstrates to the Russian Physical and Chemical Society his invention - the world's radio receiver, American frontier murderer and outlaw, John Wesley Hardin, is killed by an off-duty policeman in a saloon in El Paso, Texas, Belgium begins compulsory Roman Catholic education, Wilhelm Roentgen (Germany) discovers X-rays, Alfred Nobel establishes Nobel Prize and America's 1st auto race starts; 6 cars, 55 miles, the winner averaged 7 MPH.

Paul M. Warburg marries Nina Loeb, daughter of head of Kuhn, Loeb and Company.

Drexel, Morgan & Co. is renamed J.P. Morgan & Co. and supply the United States government $62 million in gold so they can do a bond issue and put the treasury to a surplus of $100 million.

1896

Davis v. Elmira Savings reaffirms that federal law overrode state law in the case of national banks when state law clashes with federal law. This does not mean state laws no longer have to be abided by.

> Fanny Farmer publishes her 1st cookbook, Emile Grubbe is 1st Dr. to use radiation treatment for breast cancer, Tootsie Roll introduced by Leo Hirshfield, Battle of Adua: 80,000 Ethiopians destroy 20,000 Italians, announcement of gold in Yukon, US Supreme court affirms race separation (Plessy v Ferguson), Dow Jones begins an index of 12 industrial stocks (closing is 40.94), Tsunami strikes Shinto festival on beach at Sanriku Japan 27,000 are killed, 9,000 injured, with 13,000 houses destroyed and Yosemite becomes a National Park.

Panic of 1896 Commodity prices fell sharply, the stock market dropped and silver reserves dropped. The result was further devastation in an already severely depressed nation. Additionally, there seems to have been some rather nasty shenanigans going on in the Chicago banking community.

Goldman Sachs & Company invited to join the New York Stock Exchange maybe because they had become so good at use 'Commercial Paper' for entrepreneurs looking to start a business.

Senator Henry M. Teller of Colorado and a mess of other western Republicans formed the **Silver Republican Party** to support silver and William Jennings Bryan

Utah Statehood

1897

William McKinley becomes President 1897 to 1901 Republican

"Unlike any other nation, here the people rule and their will is the supreme law. It is sometimes sneeringly said by those who do not like free government, that here we count heads. True, heads are counted, but brains also . . ." **William McKinley**

> The Greco-Turkish War, also called "Thirty Days' War", is declared between Greece and the Ottoman Empire, Dracula, a novel by Irish author Bram Stoker is published and later brings fame and fortune Bella Lugosi, The Boston subway opens, becoming the first underground rapid transit system in North America, Lattimer Massacre - a sheriff's posse kills twenty unarmed immigrant miners in Pennsylvania, 1st frontier days rodeo celebration (Cheyenne Wyoming), Peter Pan opens in NY at Empire Theater.

"It could probably be shown by facts and figures that there is no distinctly native American criminal class except Congress." Mark Twain

Kuhn, Loeb & Co. with Schiff at the helm engineered the reorganization of the Union Pacific Railroad.

1898

> Spanish American War (*remember the Maine, William Randolf Herst*) USS Maine sinks in Havana harbor, cause unknown-258 sailors die, US Military operates in China, Black postmaster lynched, his wife & 3 daughters shot in Lake City South Carolina, in France, Emile Zola is imprisoned for writing his "J'accuse" letter accusing government of anti-Semitism & wrongly jailing Alfred Dreyfus, Battle of Atbara River, Anglo-Egyptian forces crush 6,000 Sudanese, President McKinley asks for Spanish-American War declaration, Louisiana adopts new constitution with "grandfather clause" designed to eliminate black voters, Social Democracy of America party holds 1st national convention, China leases Hong Kong's new territories to Britain for 99 years, 1st amusement pier opens in Atlantic City, NJ, Teddy Roosevelt & his Rough Riders charge up San Juan Hill, The shooting death of crime boss Soapy Smith releases Skagway, Alaska from his iron grip, Will Kellogg

invents Corn Flakes, 20,000 Paris construction workers go on strike, Race riot in Wilmington NC and Scientists Pierre & Marie Curie discovers radium.

1899

Auten v. United States National Bank establishes that a bank may borrow money. *Get that! A bank may borrow money!*

> Philippine American War, lawn mower patented, Brazo River in Texas floods 12 miles wide causing $10 mil damage, National Brotherhood of Electrical Workers, forms, 8.3 earthquake shakes Yakutat Bay Alaska, 2nd quake in 7 days (8.6) hits Yakutat Bay Alaska, J S Thurman patents motor-driven vacuum cleaner, South Africa Boer Republic declares war on England.

Recession1899–1900 Very mild if at all

1900

US currency goes on gold standard, silver certificates, silver dollars and greenbacks could be redeemed for gold. This just might pull some of those out of circulation and some peasants might be too happy about that even though the paper money was backed by gold.

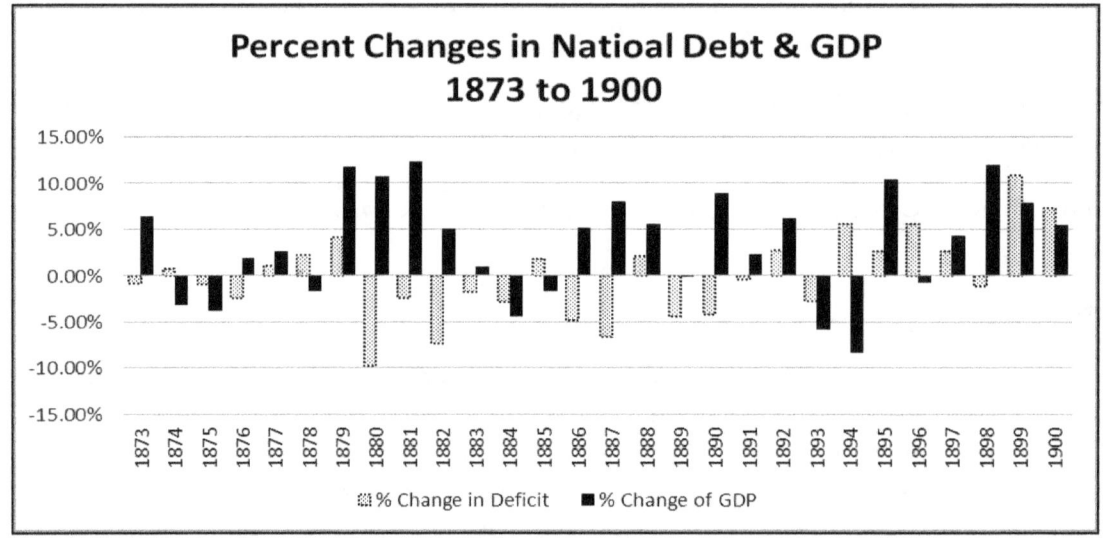

Events in graph: Panic of 1873, Recession of 1882, Panic of 1884, English Panic of 1890, Panic of 1893, Panic of 1896 and 1899-1900 very mild Recession.

> John Hay announces the Open Door Policy to promote trade with China. The United States Senate accepts the Anglo-German treaty of 1899 in which the United Kingdom renounces its claims to the Samoan islands., Social Democrat Party of America (Debs'

party) holds 1st convention, Labor Party forms in England, Russia responds to international pressure to free Finland by tightening imperial control over the country, US Steel Corporation organizes, In France the length of the workday for women and children is limited to 11 hours by law., US Navy's 1st submarine made its debut, US troops arrive in Beijing, help put down Boxer Rebellion, King Umberto I of Italy is assassinated by Italian-born anarchist Gaetano Bresci and 6,000 killed when a hurricane & tidal wave strikes Galveston, Texas.

JP Morgan and Company: At some point Morgan owns around 20% of the company's assets. The balance is owned by the Rothschild family.

1901 to 1940 Getting a Federal Reserve, WWI, Great Depression, Glass-Steagall & A Walk to War

Theodore Roosevelt becomes President 1901 to 1909 Republican

"To announce that there must be no criticism of the president, or that we are to stand by the president, right or wrong, is not only unpatriotic and servile, but is morally treasonable to the American public." **Theodore Roosevelt**

> Unites States military operating at China some more and Columbia into 1902, Australia declares independence from federation of UK colonies, Oil discovered in Texas, Congress creates National Bureau of Standards, in Dept. of Commerce, A showing of seventy-one Vincent van Gogh paintings in Paris, 11 years after his death, creates a sensation, 55 die as Rock Island train derailed near Marshalltown Iowa, Anti-Semitic riot in Budapest, Fire destroyed 1,700 buildings in Jacksonville, Florida, Gustave Whitehead and Marconi receives 1st transatlantic radio signal, England to US.

The Panic of 1901 was the result of Morgan, Hill, Harriman, Standard Oil Money and Schiff wrangling over control of the Northern Pacific Railway. The result was the ruin of lots and lots of smaller investors and the participants eventually got together and formed the Northern Securities Company. *Nobody got hung for this one either. Moral of the story: The big boys play rough!*

1902

"Issue of currency should be lodged with the government and be protected from domination by Wall Street. We are opposed to what provisions would place our currency and credit system in private hands." **Theodore Roosevelt**

> Philippine American War ends. Denmark sells Virgin Islands to USA, China's empress Tzu-hsi forbids binding woman's feet (about time too), The "Electric Theatre" a full-time movie theater in the United States, opens in Los Angeles, California, J C Penney opens his 1st store in Kemmerer, Wyoming (*I've been there*), Marie & Pierre Curie isolate the radioactive element radium chloride (they died as a result of their exposure to radiation in developing a scientific miracle that save millions from great suffering), Portugal bankrupt by revolt in Angola and Oliver Wendell Holmes Jr. became Associate Justice on Supreme Court.

Recession of 1902 to 1904 was mild but distinct and lasted 2 years.

1903

Colorado Governor James Peabody sends the state militia into the town of **Cripple Creek** to break up a miners' strike.

> United States military operating against Philippine Insurgents continue effort until 1913, President Theodore Roosevelt shuts down post office in Indianola Mississippi for refusing to accept its appointed postmistress because she was black, US Department of Commerce

& Labor forms, due to drought the US side of Niagara Falls runs short of water, Dr. Harry Plotz discovers vaccine against typhoid and an unsuccessful uprising of Macedonians against Turkey.

1904

Kinkaid Act which granted larger homesteads up to 640 acres, to homesteaders in western Nebraska.

Construction begins by the United States on the **Panama Canal**.

United States military operating at Morocco and Korea, Herero people of South West Africa, now Namibia, begin uprising, 179 die in coal mine explosion at Cheswick, Pennsylvania, Japan & Russia declares war after Japan's surprise attack on Russian fleet at Port Arthur disabled 7 Russian warships, Schron finds microbe that causes photosynthesis, Dutch troops occupies Kuto Reh, Sumatra, killing all inhabitants, train derails on bridge in Eden Colorado during a flash flood, kills 96.

Theodore Roosevelt confirms **Monroe-Doctrine** with **Roosevelt Corollary**.

1905

"Speak softly and carry a big stick." **Theodore Roosevelt**

Bloody Sunday in Russia, French government of Combes falls, Hungarian premier Tisza resigns, Earthquake in Kangra India, kills 20,000, US Supreme court judges maximum work day unconstitutional, Norway dissolves union with Sweden (in effect since 1814), Warsaw & Lodz revolt against Russian occupation, Electric tramline opens in Rotterdam, Swedish mine workers win 5 month strike for minimum wages and Arthur Griffith forms Sinn Fein in Dublin.

During this period Winslow Homer, Frederic Remington and Charles Russell were busy painting America in life and landscape. Frank Lloyd Wright was redefining American architecture, Art Nouveau declined and Arts and Crafts continued to be popular. In literature 'Oz' became, Zane Grey was active and the Virginian became, then and now, the singular best western novel.

Urbanization was a critical social issue and this is widely considered the first decade of consumerism and materialism. During this decade, Broadway musicals flourished. Irving Berlin and George M. Cohan opened on Broadway.

1906

Einstein introduces his **Theory of Relativity**

United States military operating at Cuba, Dutch law makes driver's license mandatory, WK Kellogg & Ch. Bolin found Battle Creek Toasted Corn Flake Co, Finnish Senate accepts universal suffrage, except for poor, Mount Vesuvius erupts and devastates Naples, Mutiny on Portuguese battleships Dom Carlos & Vasco da Gama, Pure Food & Drug Act & Meat

Inspection Act adopted and in the presence of the king and before a great crowd, Leonardo Torres Quevedo successfully demonstrates the invention of the Telekino in the port of Bilbao, guiding a boat from the shore, in what is considered the birth of the Remote Control.

San Francisco earthquake & fire kills nearly 4,000 & destroys 75% of city.

Wyman v. Wallace further establishes that a bank may borrow money to keep operating. In this matter a third out of state party was involved and they were allowed collection after the bank decided to close and liquidate its assets.

Goldman Sachs & Company handles the IPO for Sears, Roebuck and Company.

Something wicked this way comes!

The set-up!

April The San Francisco earthquake pulls funds from the capital centers to finance the rebuilding and pay insurance claims.

July The Hepburn Act goes into effect giving the Interstate Commerce Commission the power to set railroad rates. Interest in Rail Road stocks wanes and the stock prices go down.

Autumn – The annual harvest purchases cause a reduction of capital available in the market centers.

> **Bank of England raises interest rates to attract capital.** This means less money from England is injected into the American market to support the fall harvest purchases and general investment. *Seems like they have done this sort of thing before at inopportune times.*

September – Stocks start a long slide well into March 1907

The stock market is facing a reduction in available funds to operate on and a major segment of the market is suffering losses. The market is showing weakness and perhaps the beginnings of a loss of confidence with investors.

1907

United States Congress raised their salaries to $7500 a year.

> Unites States military participation in Cuba that continues until 1913, 1st federal corrupt election practices law passed, English suffragettes storm British Parliament & 60 women are arrested, , 1st involuntary sterilization law enacted, Indiana, Finland is 1st European country to give women the right to vote, Bubonic Plague breaks out in San Francisco, taxis 1st began running in NYC, Government of Transvaal sends home 50,000 Chinese day workers, 44 nations meet in 2nd Hague Peace Conference, Pope decree forbids

modernization of theology, world's 1st air force established (US Army), French troops occupy Casablanca (*best movie ever*), Bank of Italy opens 1st branch at 3433 Mission Street, San Francisco, Britain & Russia sign treaty with Afghanistan, Persia & Tibet and

Coal mine explosions in Monongah, West Virginia, kills 361 and 239 workers died in a coal mine explosion in Jacobs Creek, Pennsylvania, Explosion at Yolande Alabama, coal mine kills 91.

"The Money Trust caused the 1907 panic, and thereby forced Congress to create a National Monetary Commission." Congressman Charles Lindbergh, Sr.   The National Monetary Commission is headed up by Nelson Aldrich who just happens to be the father-in-law of one John D. Rockefeller, Jr.

Panic of 1907

Stop!   Enough is enough!

Some countries experience bank runs during the middle six months of the year.

June – New York City tries to sell bonds to keep afloat, the effort fails. The city is running out of money and everybody knows this.

August – Standard Oil gets hits with an antitrust fine of some $29 million. *More doubt is raised in another segment of the market as antitrust laws are enforced.*

By the end of August the stock market is down over 20%.

During this uncertainty the Heinze brothers, Otto and Augustus, and Charles Morse, get together and develop a scheme to corner the stocks on one United Copper. Otto figures, that since his family owns a 'majority' of the stock of United Copper and lots of the outstanding shares had been borrowed, to sell shorts against the stock they could buy the share price up. This way the guys borrowing shares to sell shorts would be against the wall and be looking for shares to cover their shorts.

The problem was the boys didn't have enough money for the scheme. So they went to see Charles T. Barney, president of the city's third-largest trust, the Knickerbocker Bank, figuring he'd help out because they'd done some scheme business with the man before. But alas Barney says, thanks anyway boys but I think I'll sit this one out. *Bummer for the boys.*

Otto says what the hell I'll do it anyway and proceeds and things are looking good. The price rises sharply as Otto buys the price up and he decides to call in the shorts figuring he had them over the barrel. NOT! The shorts cover and the price tanks. I mean really tanks! Otto is not only on his way to the poor house and his Brokerage goes belly up but brother Augustus is looking to skin him alive.

Why? Because when the stock price tanked Augustus' shares tanked too and he'd had them tied into a bank in Montana that is now insolvent because the price has dropped. It doesn't stop there. The Montana bank is tied to another bank that Augustus is the president of but the Board of the bank thinks Augustus was involved with his brother and kicks him out. Alas, the bank gets run on anyway. That might have been it but for folks getting all nervous and running to banks Augustus is involved with and Chuck Morse's banks get run on because everybody knows these two work together, lots of banks get run on.

Panic is in the air. *Blood is the water and the sharks are circling. Folks are going to be circling their wagons and burying their money in the back yard.*

J.P. Morgan gets ahead of the curve because he knows the bad boys have worked with Barney's Knickerbocker Trust Company of New York before, or maybe he just don't like Barney, and next thing you know the National Bank of Commerce, JP Morgan, says it would not be a clearing house for Knickerbocker anymore and throws The Trust Company of America under the bus to boot. It did not help any when New York's newly appointed Superintendent of Banks, Luther Mott, took a look at Knickerbockers books and quit his nice new job practically on the spot. Everybody sees this as meaning Knickerbocker and American are in big trouble and the **run** is on. Besides old JP didn't like Barney any way ……, the Trust Company of America had a run and soon a run took place at the Lincoln Trust Company

Panic ensues and people run-a-muck taking their money home to their mattresses leaving banks and trusts lying in the dust deader than ants after a 'Raid' attack. *I'll have to call the company and see if I can get free Raid for life.* The Banks et al, left standing are being tight, holding on to their cash and don't want to make any loans.

J.P. Morgan organizes other banks and the US Treasury to put cash into the several banks and trusts left standing to keep them solvent and thereby stop the run. The banks now having some cash decide it best to hold onto the cash just in case. Without the usual short-term loans the Wall Street traders needed the stock market began to crash.

Morgan gets together with a bunch of New York bankers, again, and arranges some $23 million to be made available to the brokers so the market can stay open. That deal works out ok for a day but the market starts to crash again the next day. Morgan gets the bankers to pledge more funds but it is less than half of the funds from the day before. So Morgan says no **margins sales** to be made with this money and it works out, sort of.

To make a longer story shorter Morgan and other bankers keep things going and in the process Morgan acquires Tennessee Coal, Iron and Railroad Company (TC&I) when the Brokerage house that owned it was about to go broke as it had pledged TC&I as collateral for the money it borrowed during the recent crisis. Additionally several rival banks have gone under and JP and his 'boys' pick up the mess for a song, or so, after JP and his two new favorites Henry P. Davison and Benjamin Strong Jr. had decided which banks would get help and which would not. The point was also well made that the good old United States of America needed a 'Central Banking System'. At least it sure seemed like that at the time.

Despite Morgan's efforts to avert a greater panic the economy went on to suffer for the next couple of years and Morgan was vilified for having picked up TC&I in the process of trying to save the day.

Moral of the story: An already jittery and perhaps over leveraged market was pushed over the edge by unscrupulous twits. *Unscrupulous twits also seem to be a recurring theme.*

The other Moral to the Story: Buy when things are falling apart.

The benefit of this mess was the creation of the **Federal Reserve**. An additional down side was the creation of the **Federal Reserve**. *We'll get to that diametric opposition later.*

Paul Warburg, a recent immigrant from Germany, begins six years of lecturing on the need for bank reform while on salary from Kuhn, Loeb & Company. *Hummmmmm?*

Montague Collet Norman elected to the court of the Bank of England.

Oklahoma Statehood

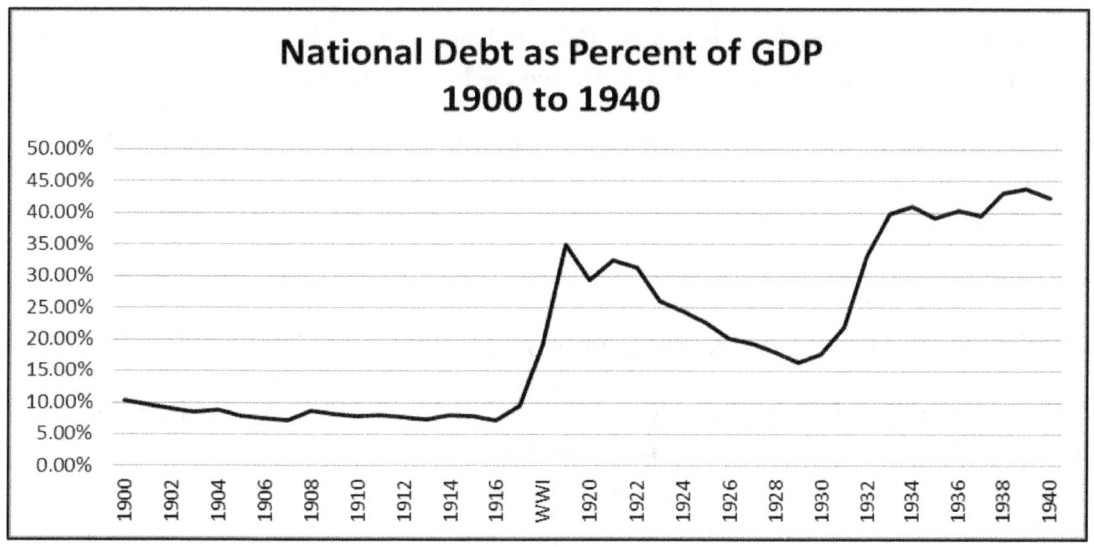

1908

Supreme Court rules a union boycott violates Sherman Antitrust Act

Rhoads Opera House fire in Boyertown, PA killing 171 people., US & Great-Britain demand end of abuses in Congo, fire makes 17,000 homeless in Chelsea Massachusetts, 1st federal workmen's compensation law approved, Fourth German Navy Bill is passed authorizing the financing the building of another four major warships., giant fireball most likely caused by the air burst of a large meteoroid or comet impacts in Siberia (Tunguska

Event), Bulgaria declares independence from Ottoman Empire (Turkey), Serbia & Montenegro sign anti-Austria-Hungarian pact, Dutch capture Venezuelan navy, Haiti's president-General Alexis Nord flees from military coup, child Emperor Pu Yi ascends the Chinese throne at the age of two and Earthquake strikes Messina, Italy (nearly 80,000 died).

Banks start using affiliates to invest in stock market. The camels' nose is firmly in the tent and fleas are running all about.

The Democratic Party has income tax in its platform.

At **Masjed Soleyman**, in southwest Persia, the first major commercial oil strike in the Middle East is made. The rights to the resource are quickly acquired by the United Kingdom.

The Aldrich–Vreeland Act came about because of the Panic of 1907. The Act created the National Monetary Commission to study the causes of the Panic of 1907 (which would recommend the Federal Reserve Act of 1913) The Act also allowed National Banks to form currency associations and be able to issue 'emergency currency" backed by bonds other than government bonds and that currency would be taxed (*that tax the currency thing has come up before*). Railroad bonds were initially proposed but resistance was too great because it was felt the associated increase in railroad bonds favored Eastern Banks, and that just wouldn't fly what with the outrage the public still felt against Wall Street and the Eastern Banks.

Harriman v. ICC In a split decision the ICC was denied the power to force answers from the railroad and banker guys, Kuhn, Loeb & Company concerning the Union Pacific and others about the purchase and transfer of stock.

1909

William Howard Taft becomes President 1909 to 1913 Republican

"Next to the right of liberty, the right of property is the most important individual right guaranteed by the Constitution." **William Howard Taft**

The **Enlarged Homestead Act** changed the 1862 Homestead Act to 320 acres. The idea was to enable dry land farming in less fertile and wet areas with the additional acreage it was felt the homesteaders would be better able to make a living. The net result was the **Dust Bowl** because it was not understood how to farm the land properly.

1st federal legislation prohibiting narcotics (opium), National Association for the Advancement of Colored People (NAACP) forms, Serbia mobilizes against Austria-Hungary, Amsterdam Social-Democratic Party (SDP) forms, North Pole reached by Americans Robert Peary & Matthew Henson, Sultan of Turkey Abdul Hamid II is overthrown, White firemen on Georgia RR strike to protest hiring blacks, Collier's magazine accuses U.S. Secretary of the Interior Richard Ballinger of questionable dealings in Alaskan coal fields, US invades Nicaragua.

1910

"The intoxication of power rapidly sobers off in the knowledge of its restrictions and under the prompt reminder of an ever-present and not always considerate press, as well as the kindly suggestions that not infrequently come from Congress." **William Howard Taft**

> British miners' strike for 8 hour working day, British-Russian military intervention in Persia, China ends slavery, US forbid immigration to criminals, anarchists, paupers & the sick, Belgian parliament rejects socialist motion for general voting rights, Passage of Earth through tail of Halley's Comet causes near-panic, Pygmies discovered in Dutch New Guinea, 50th British Golf Open: James Braid shoots a 299 at St Andrews Scot, Mann Act passed (no women across state lines for immoral purposes), Russia absorbs Finland, Portugal overthrows monarchy, proclaims republic.

The Panic of 1910-1911 was a slight economic depression that followed the enforcement of the Sherman Anti-Trust Act. It mostly affected the stock market and business traders who were smarting from the activities of trust busters, especially with the breakup of the Standard Oil Company. *Somewhat similar to the Dotcom bubble losses.*

The National Monetary Commission

In November a "duck hunt" on Jekyll Island proceeds with **Senator Nelson Aldrich**, his secretary **Arthur Shelton**, J.P. Morgan & Co. partner **Henry P. Davison, Charles D. Norton**, president of the Morgan-dominated First National Bank of New York, a former Harvard University professor of economics **Dr. A. Piatt Andrew**, Kuhn, Loeb, and Co. partner **Paul M. Warburg** and National City Bank president **Frank A. Vanderlip** spend a few days writing up what would essentially become the structure of the Federal Reserve System. Ostensibly this so called 'duck hunt' was done in secret because public sentiment was rather high against big bankers and both political parties were against the idea of a central bank that would put the issuance of the nations' money and credit in the hands of a privately controlled central bank.

Later **Bertie Charles Forbes**, founder of Forbes Magazine describing the meeting wrote.

"Picture a party of the nation's greatest bankers stealing out of New York on a private railroad car under cover of darkness, stealthily vying hundreds of miles South, embarking on a mysterious launch, sneaking onto an island deserted by all but a few servants, living there a full week under such rigid secrecy that the names of not one of them was once mentioned lest the servants learn the identity and disclose to the world this strangest, most secret expedition in the history of American finance.

I am not romancing; I am giving to the world, for the first time, the real story of how the famous Aldrich currency report, the foundation of our new currency system, was written . . . . The utmost secrecy was enjoined upon all. The public must not glean a hint of what was to be done. Senator

Aldrich notified each one to go quietly into a private car of which the railroad had received orders to draw up on an unfrequented platform.

Off the party set. New York's ubiquitous reporters had been foiled . . . Nelson (Aldrich) had confided to Henry, Frank, Paul and Piatt that he was to keep them locked up at Jekyll Island, out of the rest of the world, until they had evolved and compiled a scientific currency system for the United States, the real birth of the present Federal Reserve System, the plan done on Jekyll Island in the conference with Paul, Frank and Henry . . . . Warburg is the link that binds the Aldrich system and the present system together. He, Warburg, more than any one man has made the system possible as a working reality."

Salomon Brothers, a Wall Street investment bank, gets started by brothers Arthur, Herbert and Percy and Ben Levy.

1911

Supreme Court dissolves Standard Oil (Sherman Antitrust Act)

Belgian Mining law introduces 9½ hour work day, Portuguese expel Jesuits, failed assassination attempt on premier Briand in French Assembly, Great fire destroys downtown Constantinople/Istanbul Turkey, Victor Berger (Wisconsin) becomes 1st socialist congressman in US, US sent 20,000 troops to Mexican border, NY Giant Fred Merkle is 1st to get 6 RBIs in an inning, 1st Indianapolis 500 car race, Ray Harroun wins at 74.59 MPH (120 KPH), R.M.S. Titanic launched, Mona Lisa stolen from Louvre (*I guess they got it back*), ground breaking begins in Boston for Fenway Park, Italy declares war on Turkey, starting the Italo-Turkish War, Yanks steal 15 bases & get 13 walks, beating Browns 16-12; with a major-league record 6 stolen bases in 1 inning, Sun Yat-sen's revolutionaries overthrow Manchus (Taiwan National Day), Chevrolet officially enters the automobile market in competition with the Ford Model T and Marie Curie receives her 2nd Nobel Prize.

Kuhn Loeb & Company gets a partnership going with Rockefeller to get control of the Equitable Trust Company

1912

"Money is a new form of slavery, and distinguishable from the old simply by the fact that it is impersonal – that there is no human relation between master and slave." **Leo Tolstoy**

1st National Hockey Association game (Victoria), The International Opium Convention is signed at The Hague, Martial law declared in textile strike in Lawrence, MA, Coal miners' strike in England, Pitcher Cy Young retires from baseball with 511 wins, 1st Japanese cherry blossom trees planted in Wash DC, Titanic sinks at 2:27 AM off Newfoundland as the band plays on, Soviet Communist Party newspaper Pravda begins publishing, Massachusetts passes 1st US minimum wage law, The eruption of Novarupta in Alaska begins. It is the second largest volcanic eruption of the 20th century, Progressive (Bull Moose) Party nominates Theodore Roosevelt for pres., US passes Anti-gag law, federal employees right to petition government, Edgar Rice Burroughs' publishes "Tarzan of the Apes", War between Turkey & Montenegro breaks out in Albania, "Keystone Comedy" movie released, beginning of 1st Balkan War, Denmark, Norway & Sweden declare neutrality in Comende war.

Miller v King   Further establishes that National banks are subject to state laws in their operations as a bank.

Republican Party split into Progressives and Old Guard factions over Payne–Aldrich Tariff Act causes Woodrow Wilson to win the Presidential Election. *Big money backing all three might have had a lot to do with determining the outcome. Really big point here, big banks got what they wanted in the process.*

New Mexico and Arizona Statehood

1913

Woodrow Wilson becomes President 1913 to 1921 Democratic

"The government, which was designed for the people, has got into the hands of the bosses and their employers, the special interests. An invisible empire has been set up above the forms of democracy." **Woodrow Wilson**

There is a lot of literature concerning **Colonel Edward M. House**. Col. House was Wilson's advisor during his Presidency. Much of the talk is about a book entitled **"Philip Dru: Administrator."**

> Bread & Roses Strike begins, British House of Commons accepts Home-Rule for Ireland, Franz Kafka stops working on "Amerika"; it will never be finished, Jim Thorpe relinquishes his 1912 Olympic medals for being a pro, 1st prize inserted into a Cracker Jack box, 1st US law regulating the shooting of migratory birds passed, Flood in Ohio, kills 400, Coal mine explosion kills 263 at Dawson New Mexico, Henry Ford institutes moving assembly line, Mohandas K Gandhi arrested for leading Indian miners march in South Africa.

Recession of 1913–1914 was a general decline in income and production that lasted until demand rose with the start of World War I. During this recession the Federal Reserve System was made law as a response to the 1907 Panic.

Amendment 16 -The Congress shall have power to lay and collect taxes on incomes, from whatever source derived, without apportionment among the several States, and without regard to any census or enumeration. This Amendment was sponsored by Nelson Aldrich.

The marketing campaign for the 16th Amendment touted the income tax as on only one percent of income under $20,000, with an assurance that it would never increase. The largest payers of the income tax would be the wealthy. But alas, the wealthy had already started putting their riches into tax exempt Foundations.

"In questions of power then let no more be heard of confidence in man, but bind him down from mischief by the chains of the Constitution." **Thomas Jefferson**

17th amendment provides for election of senators by popular vote.

CLEMENT NATIONAL BANK v. STATE OF VERMONT

The state of Vermont had a taxation policy upon the deposits in state banks. The Vermont legislature expanded this tax to the deposits in National Banks operating within the state. Clement National Bank objected.

The Supreme Court essentially said the tax was ok because it was a tax on the individuals and not the bank and the tax was uniform throughout the states' financial industry thereby not singling out the National Bank.

"A great industrial nation is controlled by its system of credit. Our system of credit is concentrated in the hands of a few men. We have come to be one of the worst ruled, one of the most completely controlled and dominated governments in the world--no longer a government of free opinion, no longer a government by conviction and vote of the majority, but a government by the opinion and duress of small groups of dominant men." **Woodrow Wilson**

"Power tends to corrupt and absolute power corrupts absolutely." Lord Acton

Federal Reserve Act of 1913

There was great debate before, during and after the creation of the Federal Reserve System around whether it should be formed, its structure and purpose should it become a reality and who would run it and how.

After the financial debacle of 1907 many folks had come to believe that the injection of funds by bankers would never be sufficient to hold off bank runs and a central bank would be the only means of averting financial collapses in the future.

Others believed the 1907 Panic was the fault of those same bankers referred to as the 'money trust'.

A central banking system was established with 12 Federal Reserve Banks each with a geographic area to serve with the idea of stabilizing the economy and preventing further panics. These banks were to be a lender of last resort, make emergency short term loans, for member banks in their areas, print and issue money (Federal Reserve Notes) and act as the fiscal agent for the U.S. government. The 12 private banks could have branches. The system was headed by a Federal Reserve Board, later called the Board of Governors that had to be appointed by the president. Initially the Treasury Secretary and the Comptroller of the Currency sat on the Federal Reserve

Board as government representatives. They no longer are part of the Federal Reserve System. *I wonder what Alexander Hamilton would say about that?*

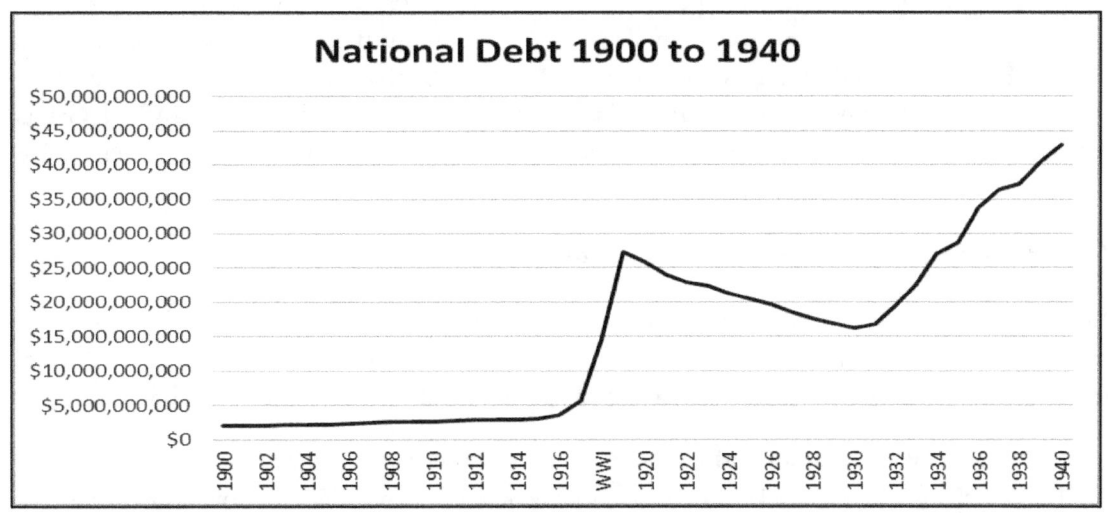

The Debt as Percent of GDP & this chart exhibit similar slopes.

Membership in the system was required of all nationally chartered banks and state chartered banks could join. Any member bank was required to have reserves at the Federal Reserve banks. Additionally they were required to be under supervision of the Federal Reserve System. By being members these banks were able to borrow funds from the Federal Reserve.

Sounds great except some banks and other financial organizations weren't interested in the being supervised part and stayed out of the system. Later some would remove themselves from the system or spin off enterprises as economic conditions changed.

> **"This Federal Reserve Act** establishes the most gigantic trust on earth. When the President Wilson signs this bill, the invisible government of the monetary power will be legalized....the worst legislative crime of the ages is perpetrated by this banking and currency bill." — **Congressman Charles A. Lindbergh**

Woodrow Wilson would later bemoan his signing of the Federal Reserve Act

> I wonder how this Federal Reserve thing was supposed to work on the National Debt.

1914

World War One, WWI, is raging in Europe. America is still embracing an isolationist attitude as popularized with the 'Monroe Doctrine' and the 'Roosevelt Corollary'. The feeling is the United States was founded, in part, so the people could be rid of the European systems and constant wars.

With the advent of WWI countries suspend the gold standard but not the United States.

Ford Motor Co wages jump from $2.40/9-hr day to $5.00/8-hr day, Stock brokerage firm of Merrill Lynch founded, US Congress approves Burnett-anti-immigration law, Charlie Chaplin debuts "The Tramp", first stone of the Lincoln Memorial is put into place, 1st successful blood transfusion (in Brussels), US signs treaty of commerce with Ethiopia, Franz Ferdinand, Archduke of Austria and his wife Sophie are assassinated in Sarajevo by young Serbian nationalist Gavrilo Princip at 10.45 , the' casus belli' of World War I, Giants outfielder Red Murray is knocked unconscious by lightning after catching a fly ball, ending 21 inning game, Giants win 3-1.

Coxey's Army 2 another march on Washington

Ludlow Massacre, Colorado Reports vary about the number of deaths, from 69 to 199 men, women and children. The deaths occurred over a period of several days and started when the tent town of the strikers was attached with various weapons including machine guns and burned.

Henry Davison, of **JP Morgan and Company** hits the mother lode. He goes to England and gets the **Bank of England** to have JP Morgan & Co. become the sole underwriter of **'War Bonds'** for England and France even gets thrown in. So JP Morgan is the 'fiscal agent' of the Bank of England and the Bank of England is the 'fiscal agent' of JP Morgan. Neat deal huh! Gets better, JP Morgan also starts investing in war supplies. They are making money all over the bloody place. *Yes that was a puny and pointed comment.*

1915

Albert Einstein publishes his **"General Theory of Relativity"**.

House of Representatives rejects proposal to give women right to vote (*you have to know what some of those guys ain't getting for a while*), Earthquake in Avezzano Italy kills 29,800, Neon Tube sign patented, Thomas Edison invents telescribe to record telephone conversations, U.S. Supreme Court hands down its decision in Guinn v. United States 238 US 347 1915, striking down an Oklahoma law denying the right to vote to some citizens, 10,000 blacks march on 5th Ave (NYC) protesting lynching's, John Gruelle patents his Raggedy Ann doll, 25,000 women march in NYC, demanding right to vote and Jack Johnson is 1st black world heavyweight boxing champion.

People who will not turn a shovel full of dirt on the project nor contribute a pound of material, will collect more money from the United States than will the People who supply all the material and do all the work. This is the terrible thing about interest ...But here is the point: If the Nation can issue a dollar bond it can issue a dollar bill. The element that makes the bond good makes the bill good also. The difference between the bond and the bill is that the bond lets the money broker collect twice the amount of the bond and an additional 20%, whereas the currency, the honest sort provided by the Constitution pays nobody but those who contribute in some useful way. It is absurd to say our Country can issue bonds and cannot issue currency. Both are promises to pay, but one fattens the usurer and the other helps the People. If the currency issued by the People were no good, then the bonds would be no good, either. It is a terrible situation when the Government, to insure the National Wealth, must go in debt and submit to ruinous interest charges at the hands of men who control the fictitious value of gold. Interest is the invention of Satan." **Thomas Edison concerning the Muscle Shoals Dam project**

1916

"Poncho" Villa invades United States. *Did he ever have some juevos!*

> 1st bombings of Paris by German Zeppelins, Emma Goldman arrested for lecturing on birth control, Great Arab Revolt begins, Mary Pickford becomes the first female film star to get a million dollar contract, 40,000 Amsterdam demonstrators demand general voting right, T E Lawrence (of Arabia) meets with Fasal Hoessein and The Everett Massacre takes place in Everett, Washington as political differences lead to a shoot-out between IWW organizers and local police.

The **Stock-Raising Homestead Act of 1916** Settlers could get up to 640 acres of public land for ranching.

Montague Collet Norman becomes deputy governor of the Bank of England

1917

Congress passes 1st **excess profits tax** on corporations.

> Congress overrides Wilson's veto, curtailing Asian immigration, February revolution begins in Russia, US Supreme Court upheld 8-hr work day for railroad employees, US passes Selective Service act, Gen Pershing & his HQ staff arrived in Paris, Supreme Court decision (Buchanan v Warley) strikes down Louisville KY ordinance requiring blacks & whites to live in separate areas and New York allows women to vote.

President Woodrow Wilson is re-elected on the slogan **"He Kept Us out of War".** Then what happens we jump right in and we get the **Dough-Boys** fighting in the trenches. Notable circumstances for the United States entering World War One; the Lusitania was sunk carrying 128 Americans and 'war supplies' in violation of 'neutrality'. The war was basically at a stalemate and the combatants were going broke at the time the United States entered the war, just saying.

Ernest Hemingway would later write some great novels about this war.

Green Corn Rebellion – Some folks in rural Oklahoma took exception to the draft for the war in Europe, WWI. Seems the Socialist Party and the Industrial Workers of the World organization, these two might be one and the same, got a bunch of the tenant farmers all riled up about being taken away from their already difficult existence to fight somebody else's war thereby putting their land and homes to further risk. As early as 1916 there had already been some violent hostilities in the area because of unfair interests being charged to the farmers. In August of 1917 there was some dry-gulching, raiding and burning of bridges and what-not.

These farmers consisted of whites and African Americans with some Native Americans thrown in for the rebellion and intended a march to Washington, along the way eating 'Green Corn'. The farmers got themselves organized and started their march but when they came upon armed resistance and shots were fired, killing three folks, it all fell apart and bunch of them and members of the Socialist Party got arrested, tried and sent to jail. *This Green Corn Rebellion seems to have similarities to Shay's Rebellion.*

1918

"Some people call me an idealist. Well, that is the way I know I am an American. America is the only idealistic nation in the world." **Woodrow Wilson**

Spanish Flu Pandemic occurred between 1918 and 1920. Hundreds of millions are infected and from 20 to 100 million die worldwide!

"Tarzan of the Apes," 1st Tarzan film, premieres at Broadway Theater (*saw a copy of this in a movie appreciation class*), Finnish Civil War: Rebels seized control of the capital, Helsinki, and members of the Senate of Finland go underground, last Carolina parakeet dies in captivity at the Cincinnati Zoo, Spanish flu occurs, the start of a devastating worldwide pandemic, Food riot in Amsterdam, The Sedition Act of 1918 is passed by the U.S. Congress, making criticism of the government an imprison able offense, House of Representatives passes amendment allowing women to vote, Lightning kills 504 sheep in Utah's Wasatch National Park, 6 US soldiers are surrounded by Germans in France, Alvin York is given command & shoots 20 Germans & captures 132 more, Poland proclaims independence from Russia after WW I.

The Armed Forces employed **2.9 million** people for WWI.

Post WWI Recession was caused by reduction in manufacturing orders and high unemployment because of the returning solders. It last several months then things got moving again.

1919

Prohibition ratified cutting government income from liquor taxes and creating more government expenditures to enforce it. *Told you those Temperance ladies were persistent.*

National Socialist Party (Nazi) forms as German Farmers Party, 2 million gallons of molasses flood Boston MA, drowning 21, Fascist Party forms in Italy by Benito Mussolini, British Parliament passes a 48-hour work week with minimum wages, Cincinnati Reds are 10½ games back in NL, & win World Series.

With the end of WWI many countries **return to the gold standard but** inflation with price levels having doubled in the United States and as much as quadrupled in places like Italy. Such conditions made it nearly impossible to return to the classic international gold standard eventually bringing the practice to a halt internationally. The United States, as a result of the war was now a creditor nation in a strong international monetary position.

Labor strikes in the iron/steel industry and later is the coal miners' strike.

"**The history of liberty** is the history of limitations of governmental power, not the increase of it."
Woodrow Wilson

1920

Here comes the "Roaring Twenties", a huge economic BOOM for most of the country and also seems to be a turning point in the industrial/agricultural nature of the country.

10,000 US union & socialist organizers arrested in the Palmer Raids.

> NY Yankees purchase Babe Ruth from Red Sox for $125,000, 1st Black baseball league, National Negro Baseball League, organizes, Amsterdam actors decide to strike for retirement benefits, League of Nations established, silver reaches record $1.37 an ounce, 14,000 Rotterdam/Amsterdam harbor workers strike, Palm Sunday tornado outbreak of 1920 affects the Great Lakes region and Deep South states, Duluth lynching's in Minnesota, Mussolini's squad begins terror, 11 die in Bologna Italy, 8.5 earthquake rocks the Gansu province in China, killing an estimated 200,000 and Yugoslav government bans communist party and in the US a railroad strike.

A bomb explodes in the **J.P. Morgan** bank building in New York City, killing 30 and injuring over 200. There was a warning note: "Remember we will not tolerate any longer. Free the political prisoners or it will be sure death for all of you. American Anarchists Fighters." The FBI eventually retired the case as they couldn't solve the matter.

Kuhn, Loeb & Company is run by Otto Kahn and Felix Warburg after Schiff's death.

The **Battle of Matewan** was a shootout in the town of Matewan, West Virginia in Mingo County between coal miners and the mine owners' heavies of the Baldwin-Felts Detective Agency.

The Depression of 1920/1921 lasted 18 months, might well be considered and extension of the post WWI recession. There was a brief surge in the economy several months after the end of the war. This surge was not sustained as the 'Boys' were discharged from the services and tried to enter the work force. This mass influx of workers was one the largest ever.

The period had _huge_ deflation, many unemployed and large defaults on credit extended for products that caused an increase in inventory for producers. The increase in work force and increase in inventory led producers to cut wages, work force and production.

The period saw business failures triple and profits decline well over 50%. The stock market fell drastically to nearly half its high before the recession began.

Although there was some calls for direct government intervention President Harding produced the Emergency Tariff of 1921, the Fordney McCumber Tariff, cut the federal budget drastically and cut tax rates.

This recovery seems to have gone as well or better than some of the federal intervention recoveries since, maybe even better. No new debt too!

119

"I am a most unhappy man. I have unwittingly ruined my country. A great industrial nation is controlled by its system of credit. Our system of credit is concentrated. The growth of the nation, therefore, and all our activities are in the hands of a few men. We have come to be one of the worst ruled, one of the most completely controlled and dominated Governments in the civilized world no longer a Government by free opinion, no longer a Government by conviction and the vote of the majority, but a Government by the opinion and duress of a small group of dominant men." **Woodrow Wilson**

1921

Warren G. Harding becomes President 1921 to 1923 dies in office

"My God, this is a hell of a job! I have no trouble with my enemies, but my darn friends, they're the ones that keep me walking the floor nights." **Warren G. Harding**

Consider that by 1920 there were more banks in the United States than the rest of the world combined. During the 'Roaring Twenties' about 500 of banks failed each year, mostly small rural banks. Maybe the 1920s roared in a different way for some folks not popularly celebrated.

Emergency Tariff of 1921 - An Act Imposing temporary duties upon certain agricultural products to meet present emergencies, and to provide revenue; to regulate commerce with foreign countries; to prevent dumping of foreign merchandise on the markets of the United States; to regulate the value of foreign money; and for other purposes. Things were bad in the economy and the American people were becoming very agitated, especially the agricultural areas, so the government set this up as a protection from lower cost imports.

The Battle of Blair Mountain was the single largest armed rebellion since the Civil War as West Virginia coal miners battled the coal company thugs for five days.

"Half a dozen men at the top of the big finance banks could upset the whole fabric of government finance by refraining from renewing Treasury Bills." **London Times September 26**

1922

The Fordney–McCumber Tariff of 1922 raised American tariffs to protect industry and agriculture. At the same time congress provided huge loans to Europe which was buying American products while reviving from WWI.

The **Teapot Dome Scandal** Secretary of the Interior Albert B. Fall was convicted of taking bribes for leases of Oil Fields reserved for the Navy. Fall was fined $100,000 and did a year in the big house. He also has the dubious honor of being the first Presidential cabinet member to go to prison for doing No-No's while serving in the Cabinet. The oil fields were returned to the Navy in 1927.

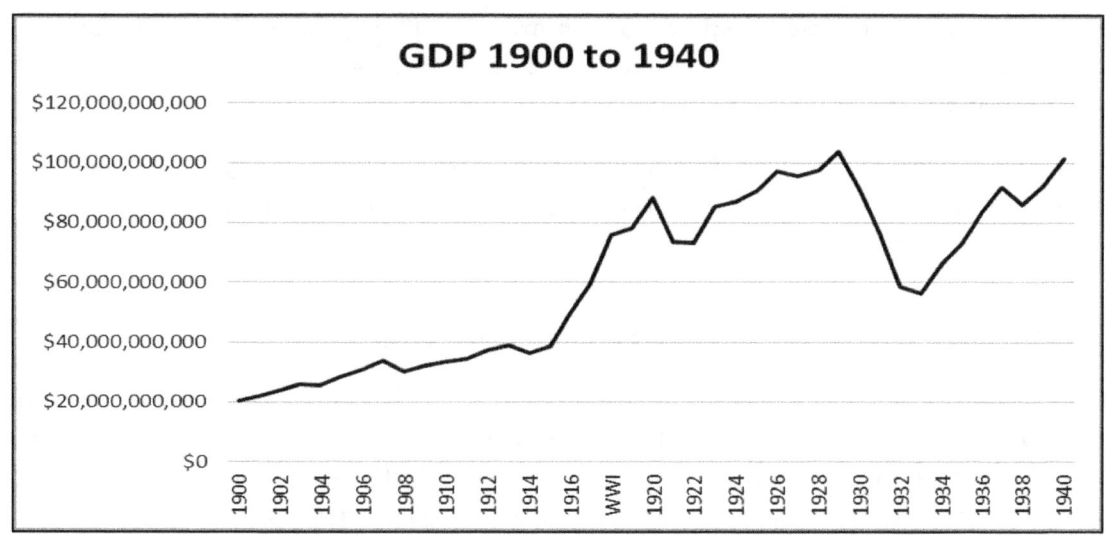

The Great Railroad Strike of 1922 was a nationwide strike by the railroad shop workers that began on July first.

The Railroad Labor Board decided hourly wages would be cut by seven cents on July first.   So the various shops decided to vote on a strike.   Strike, it is and come the first of July the entire railroad system comes to a halt.

Things get nasty as the Railroads call in strike breakers, the National Guard gets called in and a couple thousand US Marshalls to keep the trains running and disrupt pickets and union meetings.

Attorney General Harry M. Daugherty gets Federal Judge James H. Wilkerson to issue a wide ranging injunction against striking, assembling, picketing, and a bunch of other union type stuff. This gets the handle the **"Daugherty Injunction."**

This brings about more striking but fades away leaving a bitter memory for not just the railroad workers but much of the nation as people empathize with the Union workers.

1923

Calvin Coolidge becomes President as Harding dies in office 1923 to 1929 Republican

"The business of America is business." Calvin Coolidge

The Recession of 1923 was mild with but a tiny decrease in overall production.

> **Union of Socialist Soviet Republics established**, Ethyl gasoline 1st marketed, Dayton, Ohio, Coal mine explosion at Dawson, New Mexico kills 120, British Egyptologist Howard Carter finds sarcophagus of Tutankhamen, Jean Sibelius' 6th Symphony premieres, mass arrests in U.S. of mafia, Time magazine debuts, Frank Silver and Irving Conn release "Yes, We Have No Bananas", general harbor strike begins in New York City,

7.9 earthquake strikes Tokyo and Yokohama, kills 142,000, Garrett Morgan invents and patents traffic signal and Cecil B DeMille's 1st version of "Ten Commandments" premieres.

From now to **1929 the Federal Reserve** expands the money supply over 60%. To me this expansion is similar to the expansion of the housing market in the 1990s and beyond.

1924

NATIONAL BANK IN ST. LOUIS v. STATE OF MISSOURI

The state Of Missouri sought to prohibit the National Bank in Saint Louis from operating a branch bank according to the banking laws of the state of Missouri. The court held that the appropriate banking act of the United States clearly stated that National Banks were required to adhere to the state laws concerning this subject and the National Bank in Saint Louis was forbidden its second operating building.

A main point here is National Banks powers were limited to those stated in federal laws and because the Federal law made the National Banks subject to State law in this matter it was therefore Federal Law. *This was not a unanimous opinion.*

Opinion by Justice Sutherland

Clearly, the state statute, by prohibiting branches, does not frustrate the purpose for which the bank was created or interfere with the discharge of its duties to the government or impair its efficiency as a federal agency. *A line taken from the opinion that I believe states the decision succinctly.*

Dissenting opinion by Justice Vandevanter Basically says screw the law the Federal government is supreme and the state has no right to place any impediment in the way of the National Bank to do the business of the United States. *There's an attitude for you! Let's just toss the whole republic thing out the window. This also rings some bells.*

> 1st Winter Olympic games open in Chamonix, France, Russian city of St. Petersburg renamed Leningrad, George Gershwin's "Rhapsody In Blue" premieres at Carnegie Hall (New York City, IBM Corporation founded, trial against Hitler in Munich begins, coal mine explosion kills 171 at Castle Gate Utah, Hitler sentenced to 5 years labor, tubular steel golf club shafts approved for championship play, 119 die in Benwood West Virginia coal mine disaster, Pulitzer Prize awarded to Robert Frost, "Jelly-Roll Blues," is recorded by blues great, Jelly Roll Morton, Ziegfeld Follies opens on Broadway, military revolt in Sao Paulo Brazil, Comic strip "Little Orphan Annie," by Harold Gray, debuts, Jim Bottomley bats in 12 RBIs in 1 game, NHL franchise, Boston Bruins founded and Edwin Hubble announces existence of other galactic systems.

The **World War Adjusted Compensation Act or Bonus Act** was a federal law vetoed by President Coolidge on May 15 and overrode on May 19, 1924, becoming law. It gave a benefit to veterans of American military service in World War I and could be redeemed in 1945 or be used as collateral for loans as it was basically an insurance policy.

1925

"Banking was conceived in iniquity and was born in sin. The Bankers own the earth. Take it away from them, but leave them the power to create deposits, and with the flick of the pen they will create enough deposits to buy it back again. However, take it away from them, and all the great fortunes like mine will disappear and they ought to disappear, for this would be a happier and better world to live in. But, if you wish to remain the slaves of Bankers and pay the cost of your own slavery, let them continue to create deposits." — **SIR Josiah Stamp, who happen to be filthy rich and, President of the Bank of England in the 1920's.**

Nellie Taylor Ross became governor of Wyoming, 1st woman Governor in USA, 1st all-female U.S. state supreme court appointed, Texas, Miriam (Ma) Ferguson sworn in as Texas Gov., nation's 2nd woman governor, Moving picture of a solar eclipse taken from dirigible over Long, dogsleds reach Nome with emergency diphtheria serum after 1000-km, 1st issue of "New Yorker" magazine published, Tennessee makes it unlawful to teach evolution, John T. Scopes arrested for teaching evolution in Tennessee, Tigers' Ty Cobb is 1st to collect 1,000 extra-base hits (ends 1,139), Jury selection took place in John T Scopes evolution trial, Monkey Trial ends-John Scopes found guilty of teaching Darwinism, Italian army takes Somalia, water skis patented and Col William "Billy" Mitchell court-martial for insubordination.

The **Gold Standard Act** of Britain eliminated the return of gold coin to the realm. It did make gold bullion the redemption for gold.

1926

1926 Recession was an unusual and mild recession, thought to be caused largely because Henry Ford closed production in his factories for six months to switch from production of the Model T to the Model A. *That would make for a little bit of a burp.*

George Burns marries Gracie Allen, Ford Motors announces 8 hour day and $5 daily minimum wage, 1st public demonstration of television, John L Baird, London, Walt Disney Studios forms, **run on Belgian banks**, riots between Moslems and Hindus in Calcutta, At 41, Walter Johnson pitches his 7th opening day shutout, British coal-miners go on strike, British general strike-3 million workers support miners, "Five Foot Two, Eyes of Blue" by Gene Austin hits #1, France forms a bunch of different governments, Spain leaves League of Nation due to Germany joining, John C Garand patents semi-automatic rifle and Josephine Baker in Amsterdam.

"It is well that the people of the nation do not understand our banking and monetary system, for if they did, I believe there would be a revolution before tomorrow morning." **Henry Ford**

From the **League of Nations' World Economic Conference** 'the time has come to put an end to tariffs', and to move in the opposite direction.' Gold was the preferred method of payment at the time. Sounds like free trade.

> Communist uprising in West Java, Harlem Globetrotters play 1st game (Hinckley, Ill, U.S. and Mexico battle over oil interests, President Coolidge creates Federal Radio Commission (FCC), U.S. Marines land in China to protect American property, Pan American Airlines incorporates, U.S. government doesn't sign League of Nations disarmament treaty, Bavaria lifts ban on Hitler's speeches, Johnny Weissmuller set records in 100 and 200 m free style, "Black Friday" on Berlin Stock Exchange, Supreme Court ruled bootleggers must pay income tax, 8.3 earthquake strikes Nan-Shan China, 200,000 killed, Assay Office in Deadwood, South Dakota closes, Babe Ruth hits record setting 60th home run, off Tom Zachary, Duke Ellington opens at Cotton Club in Harlem and Grand Ole Opry makes its 1st radio broadcast, in Nashville, TN.

McFadden Act allowed National Banks to branch but only in accordance with state laws if a state allowed branching and prohibited interstate branching. *See also The Riegle-Neal Interstate Banking and Branching Efficiency Act of 1994.*

"**Mr. Montague Collet Norman**, the Governor of the Bank of England, is now head and shoulders above all other British bankers. No other British banker has ever been as independent and supreme in the world of British finance as Mr. Norman is today. He has just been elected Governor for the eighth year in succession. Before the war, no Governor was allowed to hold office for more than two years; but Mr. Norman has broken all precedents. He runs his Bank and his Treasury as well. He appears to have no associations except his employees. He gives no interviews. He leaves the British financial world wholly in the thick as to his plans and ideas." **Wall Street Journal**

1928

Tariff of 1928 was the highest set of tariffs and likely began a global slowdown in international commerce as retaliatory tariffs from trading partners were threatened. I have to wonder what officials were thinking about with this tariff. There had been an International conference calling for the end of tariffs and our trading partners were warning us this would bring retaliations. Really, without trade the growth economy slows and then busts.

> 1st U.S. air-conditioned office building opens, San Antonio, 450 die in St. Francisquito Valley Dam burst, Noel Coward's musical "This Year of Grace," premieres in London, Mae West's New York City debut in a daring new play "Diamond Lil", Buddy, a German Shepherd, becomes 1st guide dog for the blind, England lowers age of women voters from 30 to 21, Pulitzer prize awarded to Thornton Wilder for (Bridge of San Luis Rey), Mickey Mouse made his 1st appearance, Velveeta Cheese created by Kraft, Alfred Hitchcock's 1st film, "Case Of Jonathan Drew," is released, Baseball Hall of Famer Ty Cobb got his

4,191th and final career hit, Katharine Hepburn's New York stage debut in "Night Hostess", hurricane hits West Palm Beach-Lake Okeechobee Florida; 3,000 die, 1st recording session in Nashville (Warmacks' Gully Jumpers), 1st issue of Time magazine and George Gershwin's "An American In Paris" premieres (New York City).

Goldman Sachs & Company starts a closed end investment fund. Oops! See next year.

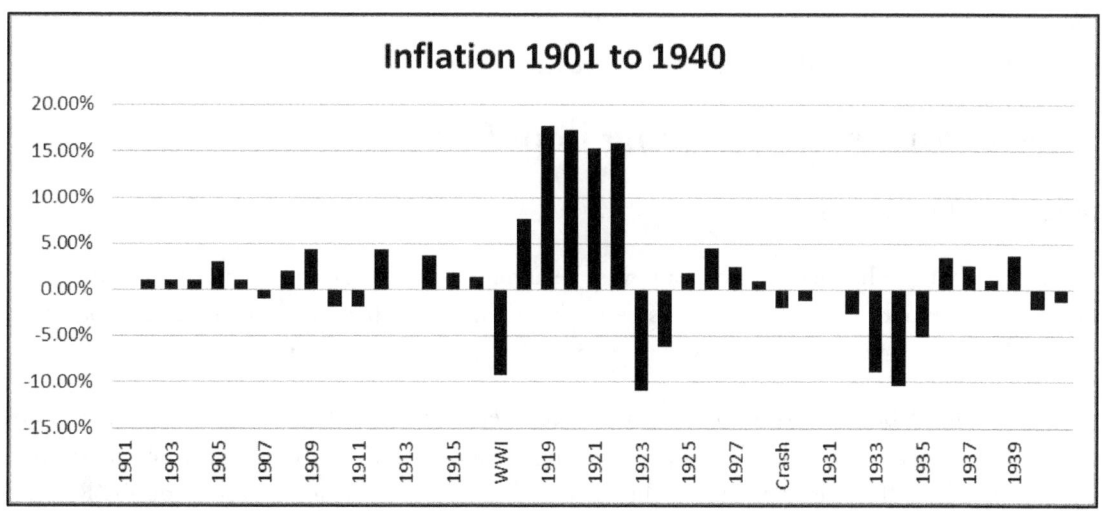

1929

Herbert Hoover becomes President 1929 to 1933 Republican

"Blessed are the young, for they shall inherit the national debt." **Herbert Hoover**

Income tax rates are currently around .0375 % at the lower end and 25% at the upper end. Remember this is the tax rate during 'good times'. Check out 1932 when everything is all hosed up.

Stock Market Crash

From 1923 to September 1929 the New York Stock Market had a steady rise, a result of an expanding economy. Employment was high and the world was basically at peace. Construction was strong, cars and refrigerators were selling, supporting industries like steel were doing great, home construction was booming and people were doing pretty well.

There are too many whys' for the crash and too many varying opinions for the reasons for the crash in the literature to go into that. Instead I will present the general conditions chronologically that are in the common body of knowledge.

> Between 1923 and 1929 the Federal Reserve expanded the money supply by over sixty percent. Today we see the Federal Reserve expanding the money supply drastically again, just saying.

Here we go folks, the times they are a changing.

A few pertinent factors going into 1929

Agriculture/Commodities

As seems want to happen Agriculture was beginning to have issues. Industrialization was producing machinery that was more cost effective than traditional labor intensive methods and increased yields. Another problem was the yields themselves, specifically the wheat crop.

Note grains have been a major commodity since, well since man began farming and gave up wandering. An excellent example is Egypt feeding Imperial Rome. Rome relied heavily on the grain surplus from the Nile to the point that it sometimes drained the gold reserves on the Roman Empire. When Egypt had smaller than expected harvests the world at that time shuddered. *This is one of those look it up things as the flow of gold impacts the financial security of a nation.*

The point is that grains are imported and exported widely and often impact the balance of payments between nations as well as the internal economy. When the harvest is larger than the demand then prices go down and the growers have less income. That reduction in income could simply mean a few less trinkets or maybe as severe to cause poverty and an inability make required payments and then loss of the land and income completely.

1929 brought a significant grain surplus and a winter wheat crop was in the ground. This surplus caused a severe drop in wheat prices that meant wheat farmers faced going belly up and finding something else to do. The problem with finding something else to do was it was improbable. When an agricultural area is in a local recession or depression there is no 'other' work available. Additionally mobility was not nearly has easy then as it is today. In the early part of 1929 the economy was still going gang busters and some jobs in manufacturing areas could be found, later not so much.

Anyway the wheat crop in 1929 turned out to be rather small and things started looking good because other regions of the world were facing difficult times for their wheat harvests and prices rose to the point it appeared most American farmers would be doing just fine. Then in August Europe announced great harvests and prices went down the tubes and the wheat areas were looking at an untenable financial situation.

Agricultural commodities are keenly important to the stock market for a few reasons. One is credit stability. When loans are being paid off and banks and other lending institutions are sound and cash flow is as projected then society and the market are secure and people don't run to the bank to pull their money out. When loans are not being paid then the bank has way less money than it needs to meets depositors and creditors demands and people run to the bank to get their money before the bank runs out.

Note that there were somewhere around 30,000 banks in the United States at the beginning of 1929. Many, I mean very many, of these were small local and regional banks whose success was tied to their respective economies. So if an agricultural area suddenly began to have money problems these banks would be in dire straits. During the 'Roaring Twenties' some 500 banks failed annually with most being small local rural banks often referred to as unit banks.

Another reason is demand for goods and services. When a fairly large segment of the population has less money they tend not to by a radio, that car they were thinking about, less new clothes and on and on. This means there 'will' be a reduction in demand for not only finished products but also the manufacturers of the parts and back all the way to the people who process the raw material.

1929, in the agricultural segment of the economy was a bit of yoyo, yoyos are uncertain things. *You would know this if you had ever broken Granny's favorite lamp in the living room, a place where you were never allowed anyway.*

August 1929 the agricultural segment is hit by price declines that threaten a reduction in demand. I do not know if that reduction in demand would have been enough to slow the growth of the economy by itself or even if it would have been enough to actually result in a decline or if those in the agricultural segment could have been successfully absorbed in other segments of the economy and neither did anybody then.

The point is a significant part of the economy was dangerously threatened and had been having troubles for several years. .

Money/Credit

Too Much Easy Money

From 1923 to 1929 the Federal Reserve had increased the money supply by over sixty percent. Interesting especially as the Federal Reserve was required to have gold reserves to cover 40% of the outstanding Federal Reserve Notes.

Large amounts of money were on loan at the time of the crash that was invested in the stock market or businesses both listed in the stock market and not listed.

Many people were invested in the market using margins. Buying stocks on Margin is where a stockbroker lends a percentage of the purchase price against the stock being bought. The percent loaned can be from 90%, not usually this high, to 50%. Say I want to buy stock in Edison of New York, which was doing very well and paying nice dividends, but I only have $400 which was about the price of one share. I go to the broker to make the purchase and he and I come to an agreement where he lends me another $1,200 so I can buy four shares. This works out great if the stock goes up fast enough to cover the interest on the loan and not so great if it falls. If the stock falls the broker has to get more money from me. If I do not have the money available the broker sells the stock and I still owe him some money to cover the loan against the purchase price. Apparently during the crash few brokers went under as they apparently kept sufficient reserves to cover losses. Meanwhile lots of folks who bought on margin had few reserves as many were working folks and usually had insufficient savings to cover their losses.

Manufacturing and Business

Manufacturing and business had been doing well during the 1920s realizing steady profits and growth throughout the period. Capital was readily available to finance expansion and improvements. Inventory was built up in reserve. Dividends were paid regularly and were of an attractive size making it tempting to invest in the stock market.

The business community during the late 1920s had borrowed money for improvements and expansion and why not. The economy was booming and people were buying their products. That borrowed money would haunt then.

Politics

The mood in the country was widely split about the boom in the stock market. Herbert Hoovers' incoming administration saw speculation as an evil and wanted to curtail the speculation and tighten the money supply, this of itself would have decidedly slowed things down. While business generally saw things as moving along rather nicely and found no significant reason for all the doom and gloom.

Sequence of events

February Federal Reserve bulletin states they would restrain the use of "credit facilities in aid of the growth of speculative credit." (*To slow down the use of credit in speculation*)

March The stock market drops but rises after bankers reassure the public that everything is fine. *Didn't that happen in 2007 and early 2008?*

> **Paul M. Warburg says he believes the wild speculation in the Market would lead to a crash.**
>
> Smoot-Hawley Tariff Act is introduced in the House of Representatives. This made more than a few people nervous and made more people nervous as the countries we imported from began talk of retaliation if it passed. Retaliation would reduce exports and result in a reduction of gold and silver coming into the United States as well as income for American

businesses. *Just might put the world in the toilet too if all the other countries are leveraged like the United States.*

May The winter wheat harvest looks great and wheat prices drop.

July Stock prices rise on profits and earnings. This seems familiar too.

August There is over $8 billion on loan.

Federal Reserve Bank of New York raises discount rate to 6%. They are trying to slow investment and speculation in the stock market.

September It is worth noting that there are differences in the literature concerning the general health of businesses at this time. As a guide the Price to Earnings Ratio estimates vary from 9:1 to 30:1 and higher. *30:1 is not a good position to be in when things toughen up as some of the Wall Street Bankers in 2008 found out. This is one of those why did they ever think it couldn't happen to them things.*

Dow Jones Industrial Average peaks at 381.17.

 Prices on the New York Stock Exchange fall.

The Bank of England raises its discount rate from 5.5 to 6.5. The English were also heavily investing in the New York market. This caused gold to leave England to the States. (*Country to country payments were still in real money, gold and silver*). The raising of the discount rate was considered an acceptable means of improving the reserve ratios because loans would slow down and payments/receipts would build. This action also meant there would be less money available to support that margin investing activity.

The Hatry Case panicked England's markets. Clarence Hatry's company fell apart when it was found he'd used faked collateral when buying United Steel (*Bad, Bad Dog*). Billions were lost by the investors and the underlying lack of confidence probably undermined confidence in the American stock market and American companies causing a reduction in financing for loans to stock brokers in America for the margin market.

October Likely in response to the Hatry Case Phillip Snowden, England's Chancellor of the Exchequer, described America's stock market as a "speculative orgy." *I can see where a comment like this from such a person in the world of finance might cause some to pause.*

The "speculative orgy" quote was widely printed as well as United States Secretary of the Treasury Mellon saying "people acted as if the prices of securities would infinitely advance." *This seems almighty familiar too!*

Investment trusts sold to investors increased 2.5 fold from 1928 through the first eight months of 1929. Additionally stocks were heavily used as leverage/collateral against loans.

> *Get that? Stocks are used as collateral against loans. So if the value of a stock drops the lender will demand that the borrower hand over some money to cover the change in risk the lender is facing because the value of the stock has dropped. Seems like this is similar to the 2008 financial situation were the MBSs*

(Mortgage Backed Securities) lost value and folks started demanding money to cover the risk causing the big five to basically go under or change their status and stick us with the bill under the too big to fail philosophy.

October 16 -- On Wednesday, October 16, stock prices again declined.

Even now business conditions seemed rather stable as retail trade was brisk with low interest rates and the investment trusts had large amounts of money for investment. The possible downside was influenced by lower agricultural prices, higher stock prices, new common stocks, an increase in loans by brokers and the general nervous conditions to this point and perhaps most important was the Public Utilities regulators.

October 17 Stock Market prices decline yet again and are reported as a crushing blow. Communication very rapid and news disseminated quickly.

The October 19, 1929 issue of the Commercial and Financial Chronicle identified the main depressing influences on the market to be the indications of a recession in steel and the refusal of the Massachusetts Department of Public Utilities to allow Edison Electric Illuminating Company of Boston to split its stock. The explanations offered by the Department — that the stock was not worth its price and the company's dividend would have to be reduced — made the situation worse.

 In the days leading up to the crash, the market was severely unstable. Periods of selling and high volumes of trading were interspersed with brief periods of rising prices and recovery. Economist and author Jude Wanniski later correlated these swings with the prospects for passage of the Smoot–Hawley Tariff Act, which was then being debated in Congress

October 21 Monday the market went down again and margin calls went up that night for the next day.

October 22 Tuesday Dutch and Germans sell calls awaited the Tuesday morning opening and out-of-town banks and corporations called in $150 million of call loans. Wall Street was a mess before the Stock Exchange even opened. As the market fell from the opening margin holders were forced to sell as foreign investors liquidated and short sellers forced the market lower exacerbating the situation for margin holders.

October 23 Wednesday the stock market falls sharply on a huge selling wave. Newspaper headlines tout the market as collapsing and in a panic setting the stage for the next day.

October 24 Black Thursday. The market lost eleven percent of its value at the opening as everybody and his brother, sister; aunt and uncle flooded the floor of the exchange with sell orders. Margins collapsed and the Panic was at full force as volume was nearly three times the average for the year to date. There was an effort to quell the tide by placing large purchase orders for blue chip stocks but it failed and the crash continued. Additionally some companies reported lower than expected earnings reinforcing the idea that the upward run was over.

Throughout the year lower car sales and housing construction along with lower steel orders were harbingers of a slowdown but people kept buying anyway.

October 25 Friday Stocks rise.

 October 26 Saturday Hoover remarks on the excellent state of the business climate but backhands the housing market slowdown as being caused by high interest rates caused by the 'orgy of speculation'.

October 27 Sunday newspapers indicated regulation of utilities to be less than friendly giving foundation to the notion that utility stock prices would fall.

October 28 Black Monday. Down 13% as more investors run for cover.

October 29 Black Tuesday. All of the gains in the stock market for the past year are gone and the market as the guide to the American economy and confidence goes right down the tubes. Another article on utilities comes out indicating an unfavorable climate about rates.

Share prices fell globally during this period.

October 31 The market continues to fall.

November 13 The stock market hits a bottom at 198.60.

November 14 A rally begins.

> U.S. and Canada agree to preserve Niagara Falls, "Buck Rogers," 1st sci-fi comic strip, premieres, Popeye makes 1st appearance, in comic strip "Thimble Theater", "NY Daily Mirror" columnist Walter Winchell debuts on radio, Rudy Vallee recorded "Deep Night", St. Valentine's Day Massacre in Chicago, 7 gangsters, 4 Charles Curtis (R-Kansas) becomes 1st native American Vice President, Louie Marx introduces Yo-Yo, Police kill 19 Mayday demonstrators in Berlin, Lou Gehrig hits 3 consecutive home runs, 1st regularly scheduled TV broadcasts (3 nights per week), George Eastman demonstrates 1st Technicolor movie, Russian-Chinese border fights, 1st U.S. roller coaster built, 1st manned rocket plane flight (by auto maker Fritz von Opel), former Interior Sec Albert Fall convicted of accepting $100,000 bribe, New York City Museum of Modern Art opens and Lieutenant Commander Richard E. Byrd sends "My calculations indicate that we have reached vicinity of South Pole".

A little venting seems in order.

This does not look to me like the Federal Reserve System did anything but drive the economy into the ground instead of keeping things on an even keel to avoid just this occurrence. Why, the hell, have a Federal Reserve System if it can't or won't function as it was touted? I mean REALLY! This is also the case concerning the 2008 BUST.

"**The Autumn of 1929 was**, perhaps, the first occasion when men succeeded on a large scale in swindling themselves." **John Kenneth Galbraith**

"A splendid storehouse of integrity and freedom has been bequeathed to us by our forefathers. In this day of confusion, of peril to liberty, our high duty is to see that this storehouse is not robbed of its contents." **Herbert Hoover**

April 17 Rally closing peak of 294.07

June the **Smoot–Hawley Tariff Act** was enacted and the Dow dropped again. This tariff was the second highest in US history with the idea of protecting American businesses and starting a recovery. It resulted in retaliatory tariffs by U.S. trading partners slowing world trade and driving economies around the world even lower. It is widely considered to be the event that starts the great depression as world trade tumbles.

> Note that during this time imports were around 5% of GDP, a rather small amount until you consider a possible domino effect of an already rocky situation. Additionally, should this 5% loss of exports represent a reduction in labor and reduction in profits of 5% or less, it would impact the economy. Should the economy be growing and unemployment be decreasing that labor force would be absorbed in the rest of the market. If unemployment is steady or rising the impact would affect a broader range of businesses with lower sales and on and on.

Unemployment was at 7.8% in 1930.

President Hoover was popularly blamed for the Depression thus the shanty towns that cropped up around the nation were referred to as **Hoovervilles**.

Dust Bowl starts as weather conditions across the 'great plains' and south start crippling the agricultural industry of the region. Wind storms brought walls of dust several hundred feet high across the central region. This is something that really should be looked up. Farming practices of the time in dust bowl areas evidently exacerbated the effects of the drought.

> Mao Tse-tung writes "A Single Spark Can Start a Prairie Fire", "Mickey Mouse" comic strip, 1st radio broadcast of "Lone Ranger" (WXYZ-Detroit), William Howard Taft, resigns as chief justice for health reasons, The Communist Party of Vietnam is established, French government of Tardieu, falls, 1st red & green traffic lights installed (Manhattan NYC), Coolidge Dam in Arizona dedicated, Mahatma Gandhi starts civil disobedience in India, Constantinople & Angora changes names to Istanbul & Ankara, Motion Pictures Production Code is instituted, imposing strict guidelines on the treatment of sex, crime, religion and violence in film for the next thirty eight years, Twinkies invented, White women win voting rights in South-Africa, Veterans Administration created, Construction begins on Boulder (Hoover) Dam, mob estimated at 2,000 lynch two young black men, Thomas Shipp and Abram Smith in Marion Indiana, disappearance of supreme court justice Joseph Crater, 1st appearance of comic strip "Blondie", Betty Boop debuts in Max Fleischer's animated cartoon Dizzy Dishes, Nazis gain 107 seats in German election,

bloodless coup d'état in Brazil, Vatican approves rhythm method for birth control and Bette Davis arrives in Hollywood under contract to Universal Studios (*gotta love those eyes*).

The stock market starts another long and steady slide down that ends in July 1932 at the lowest level of the century. This slide was over 40% of market value and 89% of market value from the 1929 high.

Unemployment was over 16%.

The **Creditanstalt** of Austria fails. This is often considered proof of the destructive power of the Smoot-Hawley Tariff.

Sidney Weinberg has control of **Goldman Sachs & Company** and moves the focus to investment banking instead of trading.

1931

England is forced off the gold standard, at this point a bullion standard, as speculators, feeling the country was unable to support the necessary convertibility to gold, charged upon the British Pound thereby forcing the United Kingdom to creating 'monetary policy' via interest rates.

> Identification of 'heavy water publicly' announced (*used in the making of atomic bombs*), Alka Seltzer goes on sale, Chinese People's Republic proclaimed by Mao Tse Tung, DuPont introduces synthetic rubber, Al Capone convicted of tax evasion, sentenced to 11 years, 1st infra-red photograph, Britain abandons gold standard/pound devalues 20%, Japanese troops conquer Mukden, South Manchuria, France & USSR sign neutrality/no attack treaty, Grasshoppers in Iowa, NB & SD destroyed thousands of acres of crops, Poland & USSR sign friendship & trade treaty, Austrian government of Ender falls, Norway occupies East-Greenland, Belgian government of Jaspar falls, Empire State Building opens, Egypt & Iraq sign peace treaty, Spain becomes republic with overthrow of King Alfonso XIII, "Star Spangled Banner" officially becomes US national anthem, 1st Dracula movie released, French government of Steeg falls, Hungary-Austria sign peace treaty.

The Federal Reserve has loaned over **$140 million in gold to foreign Central Banks**. *This looks like a move that will haunt the Fed because it reduces the amount of currency available to the United States, the 40% reserve formula.*

"By a continuous process of inflation, governments can confiscate, secretly and unobserved, an important part of the wealth of their citizens. By this method, they not only confiscate, but they confiscate arbitrarily; and while the process impoverishes many, it actually enriches some", **John Maynard Keynes** concerning inflation.

1932

U.S. imports from Europe decreased from 1929 highs by about 70% and U.S. exports to Europe decreased by nearly the same percentage. Over all, world trade decreased by some 66% between 1929 and 1934.

Crash of 1932 might be considered 'greater' than the one in 1929

Unemployment was at 24.9% or so in 1932

Income tax lower end rate is about 4% and the upper end is over 60%. *Lordy, that had to bite.*

Unemployed March on Washington in January.

"We have, in this country, one of the most corrupt institutions the world has ever known. I refer to the Federal Reserve Board. This evil institution has impoverished the people of the United States and has practically bankrupted our government. It has done this through the corrupt practices of the moneyed vultures who control it". — **Congressman Louis T. McFadden**

> France's Laval government falls, Eddie Arcaro won his 1st race, El Salvador army kills 4,000 protesting farmers, Japan occupies Shanghai, Japan occupies Harbin, China, George Burns & Gracie Allen debuted as regulars on "Guy Lombardo Show", Riots at Ford-factory Dearborn Michigan, German police raid Hitler's Nazi-headquarter, Jack Benny debuts on radio, Dominion of Newfoundland: 10,000 rioters seize the Colonial Building leading to the end of self-government, Emperor Haile Selassie of Ethiopia ends slavery, Yellow fever vaccine for humans announced, Pulitzer prize awarded to Pearl S Buck (Good Earth), "We Want Beer!" parade in NY, Carlos Davila coup against Pres. Juan Montero of Chile, Revenue Act of 1932 is enacted, creating the gas tax in the United States, at a rate of 1 cent per US gallon, French government of Herriot falls, Fred Astaire & Ginger Rogers, 1st joint movie (Flying Down to Rio).

June brings the **Bonus Army march on Washington**. The group wanted their WWI bonuses paid early because they were starving. President Hoover orders the Bonus Army removed from Washington, General Douglas McArthur, with Major Dwight David Eisenhower as a junior aide, and Major George S. Patton proceed to do so.

"Some people think the Federal Reserve Banks are the United States government's institutions. They are not government institutions. They are private credit monopolies which prey upon the people of the United States for the benefit of themselves and their foreign swindlers" **Louis T. McFadden, Chairman of the Committee on Banking and Currency**

Glass-Steagall Act of 1932 made the following pertinent provisions as the structure of emergency measures the Federal Reserve Board was supposed to use in extreme circumstances

It authorized Federal Reserve Banks to lend to five or more Federal Reserve System member banks on a group basis or to any individual member bank with capital stock of $5 million or less against any satisfactory collateral, not only "eligible paper," and issue Federal Reserve Bank backed by United States government securities when a shortage of "eligible paper" held by Federal Reserve banks would have required such currency to be backed by gold.

The Pecora Commission was established by the U.S. Senate to study the causes of the 1929 crash. Hearings started early in 1933. Many of their findings result in the structure of the banking acts over the next few years.

Over the next few years stock markets around the world started policies to stop trading when panic sell-offs started to avoid damage similar to historically similar events.

Paul M. Warburg dies while chairman of the Manhattan Company. He was also a director of the Farmers Loan and Trust Company of New York, Western Union Telegraph Company, First National Bank of Boston, Bank of Manhattan Trust Company, American I.G. Chemical Company, Union Pacific Railroad, Baltimore & Ohio Railroad, Los Angeles & Salt Lake Railroad and the Warburg and Company of Amsterdam.

1933

Franklin Delano Roosevelt becomes President 1933 to 1945 dies in office Democratic

"Better the occasional faults of a government that lives in a spirit of charity than the consistent omissions of a government frozen in the ice of its own indifference." **Franklin D. Roosevelt**

"Is there any reason why the American people should be taxed to guarantee the debts of banks, any more than they should be taxed to guarantee the debts of other institutions, including merchants, the industries, and the mills of the country?" **Carter Glass**

"in politics, nothing happens by accident. If it happens you can bet it was planned that way." **Franklin Delano Roosevelt**

"As soon as Mr. Roosevelt took office, the Federal Reserve began to buy government securities at the rate of ten million dollars a week for 10 weeks, and created one hundred million dollars in new currency, which alleviated the critical famine of money and credit, and the factories started hiring people again." — **Eustace Mullins.** *Sounds similar to the desires of the Populist Parties*

Unemployment was at 25.1%.

More than **10,000 of the nation's 26,000** American banks have closed over the past four years.

March Roosevelt signs executive order 6102 making it illegal for the possession of monetary gold by any individual, partnership, association or corporation.

March 5 – Roosevelt order for a **banking holiday** goes into effect thereby closing all banks. This avoided further runs on banks.

March 9 - The **Emergency Banking Relief Act** of 1933 is passed the evening of the day it was introduced to congress with a single copy to view with these provisions and others. *At least they had one copy to see before they voted on it instead of having to vote on it so they could read it.*

> ### Part 1
>
> > Section 1 Affirms any orders or regulations the President or Secretary of the Treasury had given since March 4, 1933.

<u>Section 2</u> Gives the President the ability to declare a national emergency and have absolute control over the national finances and foreign exchange of the United States in the event of said an emergency.

<u>Section 3</u> Authorizes the Secretary of the Treasury to order any individual or organization in the United States to deliver any gold that they possess or have custody of to the Treasury in return for "any other form of coin or currency coined or issued under the laws of the United States".

<u>Section 4</u> Makes it illegal for a bank to do business during a national emergency (per section 2) without the approval of the President.

Part II

Enables the Comptroller of the Currency to take complete control of and operate any bank in the United States or its territories and to establish the terms and conditions under which bank is administered.

Part III allows banks to not allow debt to extinguish the use of stock.

Part IV

<u>Section 1</u> Allows the Federal Reserve banks to convert any US debt obligation into cash at par value and any check, draft, banker acceptance, etc. into cash at 90% of its apparent value.

<u>Section 402</u> Allows the Federal Reserve banks to make unsecured loans to any member bank at an interest rate of 1% over the prevailing discount rate.

<u>Section 403</u> Allows Federal Reserve banks to make loans to anyone for up to 90 days if the loan is secured by a general obligation of the United States (such as a Treasury bond, for example).

Part V

<u>Section 501</u> Is an appropriation of $2,000,000 to the President for carrying out this legislation.

This pretty much ended the bank runs that had crippled the nation financially.

March 13 Banks reopen as people stood in line to redeposit their cash.

June Congress makes the ownership of monetary gold illegal supporting Roosevelt's executive order.

Made the FDIC a temporary government corporation and gave the FDIC authority to provide deposit insurance to banks and to regulate and supervise member banks and state chartered non-member banks. The FDIC is initially funded with around $290 million loan. It further stopped banks from paying interest on checking accounts. It also allowed national banks to branch in states that allowed branch banking.

Work on Golden Gate Bridge begins, French government of Paul Boncour falls, German government of Von Schleicher falls, German president von Hindenburg appoints Hitler chancellor, US Senate accept Blaine Act: ending prohibition, 1st genuine aircraft carrier christened, USS Ranger, "King Kong," premieres, Mount Rushmore dedicated, FDR proclaims 10-day bank holiday, Dachau, 1st concentration camp, completed, FDR announces US will leave gold standard, Spanish anarchists call for general strike, Federal Emergency Relief Administration & Agricultural Adjustment Administration form to help the needy & farmers, Tennessee Valley Act (TVA) Act signed by FDR, to build dams, 50,000 demonstrate in Antwerp against fascism, Congress passes 1st minimum wage law (33 cents per hour), Germany began mandatory sterilization of those with hereditary illness, Vatican state secretary Pacelli (Pius XII) signs accord with Hitler, Iraqi Government slaughters over 3,000 Assyrians, Coup on Cuban president De Cespedes by Fulgencio Batista, Black Blizzard snowstorm-dust storm rages from SD to Atlantic, Josephine Baker performs in Amsterdam and Fox signs Shirley Temple, age 5, to a studio contract.

International trade had fallen over 60 percent, economies were failing around the world and the people were in the streets either starving or protesting. The world was in turmoil. *Something governments tend to pay attention to or fear, depending on the way you look at it, is people in the streets.*

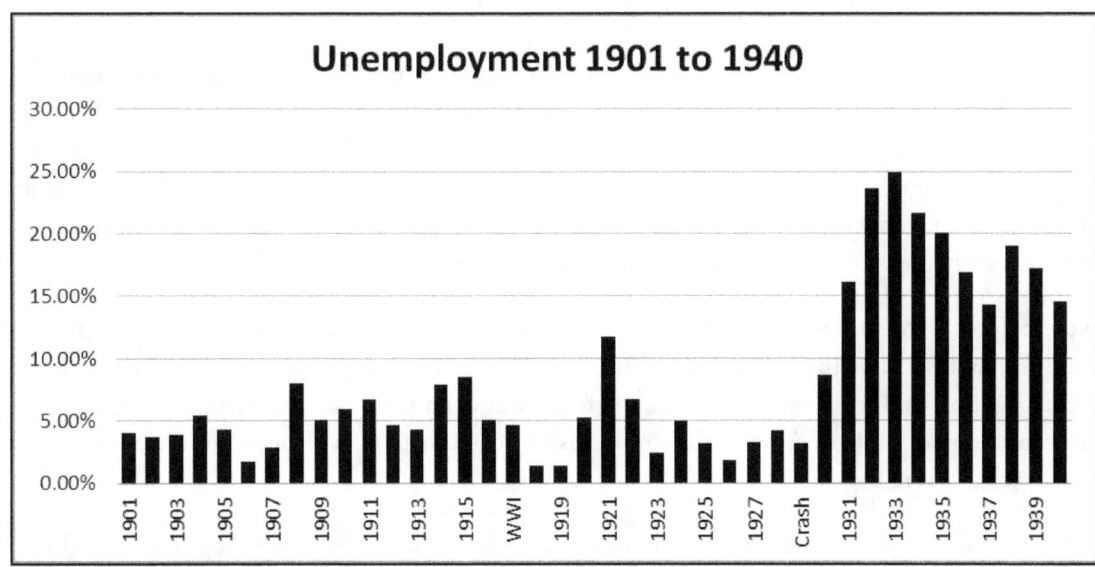

So let's make a plan and fix the darn banking system.

That ought to do it!

Well, maybe or not.

In 1933 the National Bank system and its supporting Federal Reserve System were considered the backbone of the United States' banking especially in terms of protecting 'the peoples' deposits' (money). As the Crash of 1929 and the current depression and the resulting bank failures had raped 'the peoples' deposits' it was felt safeguards were required.

The Pecora Investigation findings were important in determining that separation of commercial and investment banking was necessary in protecting the country from further suffering caused by financial collapse, especially collapse from 'speculation' and 'unethical practices' by members of the financial industry.

Those opposed to Glass-Steagall cited the evidence in the Pecora Investigation as not supporting Glass-Steagall regulations.

Looks like spin city was working overtime or in the words of John Kenneth Galbraith **"...the only function of economic forecasting is to make astrology look respectable."** Seriously though, the same evidence with different interpretations each in opposition to the other.

The Banking Act of 1933 a.k.a. **Glass-Steagall**, officially titled, An Act to provide for the safer and more effective use of the assets of banks, to regulate interbank control, to prevent the undue diversion of funds into speculative operations, and for other purposes.

Over time the sections 16, 20, 21 & 32 of the Banking Act of 1933 that separated commercial banking from investment banking came to be known as Glass-Steagall. It also established the Federal Deposit Insurance Corporation (FDIC). All FDIC insured banks were required to be, or to apply to become, members of the Federal Reserve System by July 1, 1936. In 1939 legislation repealed the requirement that FDIC-insured banks join the Federal Reserve System thus ensuring a strong dual banking system and a weaken National Bank System.

Even before Glass-Steagall most commercial banks had already fled the horribly depressed securities markets. For those that hadn't run from the securities markets screaming in terror the Banking Act of 1933 reduced their time frame to get out from five years to one year. By get out of the securities markets I mean sever their relationships or affiliations with securities firms or acting as though they were a securities firm.

Today we refer to Glass-Steagall as the following sections that deal with separating commercial and investment banking, securities and insurance underwriting.

Section 16 - Prohibited National Banks from purchasing or selling securities except for a customer's account, as the customer's agent, unless the securities were purchased for the bank's account as 'investment securities'. These 'investment securities' were to be determined by the Office of the Comptroller of the Currency as, permitted national bank investments. National Banks were also forbidden to participate in the underwriting or distributing of securities.

This effectively eliminated the McFadden Acts permission for national banks to act as "dealers" in buying and selling debt securities.

National Banks were able to buy, sell, underwrite, and distribute United States government and general obligation state and local government securities. These securities became known as 'bank-eligible securities'. The Comptroller interpreted this to mean marketable securities rated 'investment grade' by the rating agencies. If they were not rated then the 'credit equivalent' was permissible. *This would lead to sever problems later.*

In short no bank could buy, sell, underwrite, or distribute any security except as specifically permitted by Section 16.

Section 20 - Prohibited any member bank of the Federal Reserve System , a state chartered or national bank, from being affiliated with a company that "engaged principally" in "the issue, flotation, underwriting, public sale, or distribution" of securities.

This is where it starts to breakdown. The term 'engaged principally' leaves the barn door wide open to interpretation! Meaning affiliates are not really affected by the Glass-Steagall provisions thus creating a 'loophole'.

Then there is the Office of the Comptroller of the Currency who gets to decide what securities are 'bank-eligible'! That is a person! This the aforementioned 'later' part that develops problems after WWII.

Section 21 - Prohibited any company or person from taking deposits if it was in the business of "issuing, underwriting, selling, or distributing" securities. This applied to all banks. Securities organizations were not prevented from owning separate subsidiaries/affiliates such as thrifts/Savings & Loans at were thrifts or state chartered, non-Federal Reserve System member banks. This will become important later

Even at the time of Glass-Steagall those who supported the separation of commercial and investment banking were concerned with the differences between what a bank, could and couldn't do under Glass-Steagall and the ambiguity implied with what a subsidiary or affiliate of said bank engaged in securities could or couldn't do.

Section 32 - Prohibited any Federal Reserve System member bank from having any officer or director in common with a company "engaged primarily" in the business of "purchasing, selling, or negotiating" securities, unless the Federal Reserve Board granted an exemption.

This was later amended under the Banking Act of 1935 to include employees. I'll bet somebody tried to create a new title to sneak someone under the radar on this one.

A couple more significant sections…

Section 5(c) applied Section 16's rules to Federal Reserve System member state chartered banks.

Section 23

23a regulated extensions of credit between a bank and any nonbank affiliate.

23b - Required all transactions between a bank and its nonbank affiliates to be on "arms-length" market terms. What the hell does that really mean!

And a regulation

Regulation Q - Prohibited banks from paying interest on demand deposits, checking accounts. Up until 1986 it also imposed maximum rates of interest on other types of bank deposits.

> The above prohibitions were not without detractors even at the time. Some folks thought the securities markets would be harmed if commercial banks could not engage in the securities markets. (Commercial banks take deposits. Those deposits are 'the peoples' money'.)
>
> In other words the securities markets would not go as high as some would desire because 'the peoples deposits' could contribute to higher prices and make more money for the private investors. Seriously, the more money there is going into a price environment means there is greater demand and the prices go higher. So without 'the peoples' money' stock prices would not go as high as they would if 'the peoples' money' was participating in the market and participating in the inherent risks involved in securities.

Other Interesting provisions

Section3(a) mandated that each Federal Reserve Bank had to monitor local Federal Reserve System member banks' lending and investment to ensure there was no "undue use" of bank credit for "speculative trading or carrying" of securities, commodities or real estate.

Section 7 put limits on the total amount of loans a member bank could make 'secured' by stocks or bonds and permitted the Federal Reserve Board to impose tighter restrictions and to limit the total amount of such loans that could be made by member banks in any Federal Reserve district.

Section 22 eliminated personal liability for new shareholders of national banks. This was considered a 'double liability' as those new shareholders had not taken on the risks of the actions of prior activities of the bank.

Sections 5(c) with Section 27 required state member banks to provide the Federal Reserve Board and national banks to provide the Comptroller of the Currency reports concerning their affiliations. (Who are you playing with and to what extent?)

Section 13 Governed transactions between Federal Reserve member banks and their nonbank affiliates.

Section 11(a) Federal Reserve System banks were not allowed to act as agents for nonbanks in the placing loans to brokers or dealers.

Sections 19 with Section 30 defined criminal penalties for misconduct by officers or directors of Federal Reserve System member banks and authorized the Federal Reserve to remove such officers or directors.

So what do we have?

We have commercial banks in the Federal Reserve System regulated as to what they can and cannot do with deposits, ambiguity as to what their affiliates can and cannot do, a person, the Office of the Comptroller of the Currency, deciding what are bank-eligible securities and hordes of investment bankers wanting to get at 'the peoples' money', regulation of the extending of credit between a bank and its' non-bank, whatever that is, affiliate and those transactions at 'arms-length', whatever the hell that means and banks cannot pay interest on checking accounts.

Sounds pretty good until we come to the part where FDIC insured banks are not required to be part of the Federal Reserve System and thereby not subject to the oversight and regulations of the Federal Reserve meaning Sections; 16, 20, 21 & 32. The result is that we have State Chartered investment banks and State Chartered Commercial banks outside the Federal Reserve guidelines with Investment banks, who do not take deposits, still involved in the securities industry. Loophole derived here.

Alert! Except for Section 21, Glass–Steagall applies only to Federal Reserve member commercial banks!

In short there is still a separate banking system without 'deposits' that wants those 'deposits' to generate income from.

The rest of this story is how that separate banking system worked to get their hands on those 'deposits' and much, much more. As this adventure continues this separate banking system will be referred to as 'shadow banking system', 'capital markets' or 'nonbank banks'. These other banking systems incursion into the commercial banking market will erode the ability of the commercial banking system, protected and regulated under Glass-Steagall, to provide a safe haven for 'the peoples' deposits' until the commercial banking system nearly comes apart. Nearly hell! It ceases to exist at all.

Max Warburg serves under Hjalmar Schacht on the board of the Reichsbank in Germany immigrates to the United States in 1938.

1934

Global trade has decreased from 1929 figures by over 60%.

The Reciprocal Trade Agreements Act of 1934 gave the president incredible power to negotiate tariffs bilaterally with the power of legislation as a simple majority instead of two thirds vote as a treaty required.

America goes off the Gold Standard, establishes the price of gold at $35 per once and at the same time allowing for expansion of the money supply.

"I rob banks for a living, what do you do?" **John Dillinger**

> "Flash Gordon" comic strip debuts, Apollo Theater reopens in Harlem, far right leagues rally in front of the Palais Bourbon in an attempted coup against the French Third Republic, creating a political crisis in France, Austrian Civil War begins, Casey Stengel becomes manager of Brooklyn Dodgers, John Dillinger breaks out of jail, Edwin Hubble photo shows as many galaxies as Milky Way has stars, 1st Masters golf championship began in Augusta, GA, US Auto-Lite Strike begins, culminating in a five-day melee between Ohio National Guard troops and 6,000 strikers and picketers, Securities & Exchange Commission established, Donald Duck made his 1st screen appearance, All-American Soap Box Derby is held in Dayton, Ohio, Mao Tse-tung & 25,000 troops begin 6,000 mile Long March,

The Federal Credit Union Act was to make credit available and promote thrift through a national system of nonprofit, cooperative credit unions. These too would have huge problems later.

"Before the arrival of the Credit Union, people who were from the poor background or a working class background couldn't borrow from banks." **John Hume**

J.P. Morgan & Co. dropped investment banking choosing to operate as a commercial bank. During the Depression commercial banking was more lucrative and besides this will all blow over and start doing both later. They would later slide back in to investment banking.

There is much discussion out there concerning FDR and his relationship to international bankers.

1935

On to Ottawa Trek – In April thousands of men walked out to strike and protest the horrible conditions in Canadian work camps and went to Vancouver. Two months later the men boarded box cars to go to Ottawa where they hoped the pleas would be heard. Most stopped in Regina while their representatives went to a meeting in Ottawa. The meeting did not go well and the workers representatives were escorted from the building and returned to Regina. The Royal Canadian Mounted Police (RCMP) had the town cut off by road blocks and would not let the protestors leave.

The representatives called a meeting in a town square to update all interested public persons on the progress of the protest. Well the RCMP decide to break up the meeting and start lobbing tear gas, shooting pistols in to the crowd and generally caused a real mess. Then put up a stockade around the protestors location.

The long and short is the protestors were able to go home and the government was so vilified in the press they were voted out in the next election.

1st Sugar Bowl & 1st Orange Bowl, Bob Hope 1st heard on network radio as part of "The Intimate Revue", Iceland becomes 1st country to legalize abortion, "Monopoly" board game goes on sale for 1st time, Jesse Owens equals or breaks 6 world records in one hour, Supreme Court declares FDR's Nat'l Recovery Act unconstitutional, US Congress accepts FDR's "New Deal", Floods at Yangtzee Jiang & Hoangh, kills 200,000, FDR signs an act prohibiting export of US arms to belligerents, Italy invades Ethiopia, Anti-fascist People front forms in Brussels, Anti-British riots in Egypt, FDR proclaims Philippine Islands a free commonwealth and Nazi's deprive German Jews of their citizenship.

Banking Act of 1935

Section 21 does not prevent a deposit taking enterprise from participating in any of the securities underwriting and dealing activities permitted in **Section 16** and allowed under Section 16 a bank to buy stocks and debt securities for a customer's account.

Section 32 is amended to include an employee also.

The players, as we proceed, are the Federal Reserve Board, the Office of the Comptroller of the Currency, the Supreme Court, the Secretary of the Treasury, the House of Representatives, the Senate, the office of the President, the Federal Deposit Insurance Corporation and the citizens.

Let's go back to Section 16 for a bit and look at bank-ineligible securities recalling that Section 5c makes Section 16 rules apply to state-chartered banks that are a member of the Federal Reserve System.

From Investment Company Institute v Camp 1970 prohibitions that apply to dealing in and underwriting or distributing securities.

> Section 16 of the Glass-Steagall Act as amended, 12 U.S.C. 24, Seventh, provides that the 'business of dealing in securities and stock (by a national bank) shall be limited to purchasing and selling such securities and stock without recourse, solely upon the order, and for the account of, customers, and in no case for its own account * * *. Except as hereinafter provided or otherwise permitted by law, nothing herein contained shall authorize the purchase by (a national bank) for its own account of any shares of stock of any corporation.

> Section 16 also provides that a national bank 'shall not underwrite any issue of securities or stock.'

> And § 21 of the same Act, 12 U.S.C. 378(a), provides that 'it shall be unlawful—(1) For any person, firm, corporation, association, business trust, or other similar organization, engaged in the business of issuing, underwriting, selling, or distributing, at wholesale or retail, or through syndicate participation, stocks, bonds, debentures, notes, or other securities, to engage at the same time to any extent whatever in the business of (deposit banking).'

What we have is a question of intent! The intent of the framers of the law based upon their experiences and the intent of regulators in the future. As in the past the future will bring the issue of competition into question and the 'loopholes' of Glass-Steagall or failure of a comprehensive structure to mitigate the effects of competition in the banking and financial, securities, market places.

Morgan Stanley started with assets from JP Morgan. Operating partners are Harold Stanley and Henry S. Morgan, grandson of J. Pierpont Morgan.

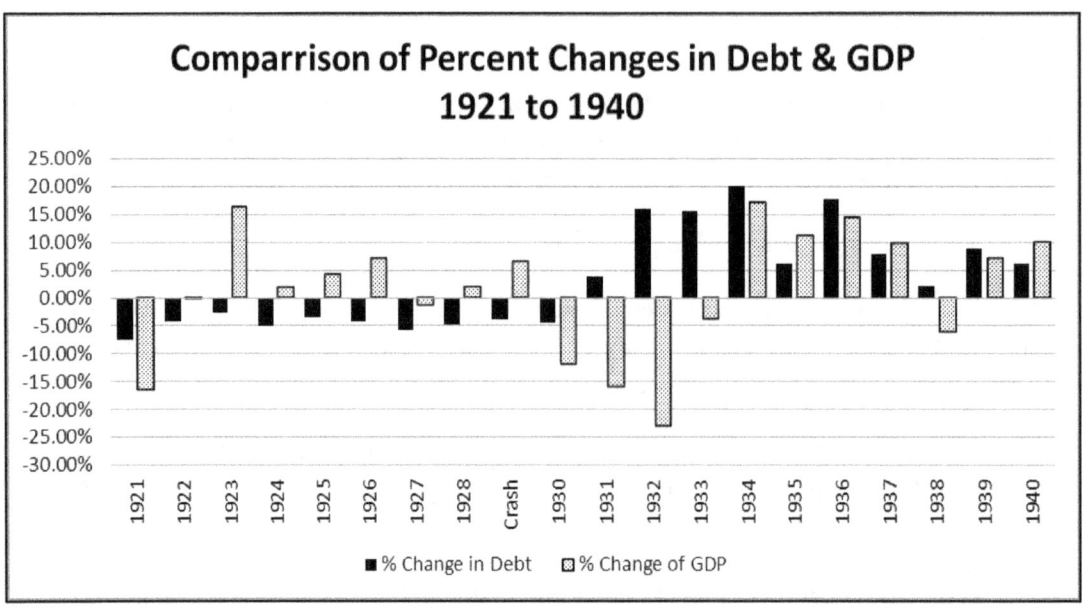

1936

"A good leader can't get too far ahead of his followers." **Franklin Delano Roosevelt**

Commodity Exchange Act replaced the Grain Futures Act of 1922 and provided federal regulation of all commodities and futures trading activities and requires all futures and commodity options to be traded on organized exchanges.

Billboard magazine publishes its 1st music hit parade, "Green Hornet" radio show is 1st heard on WXYZ Radio in Detroit, 1st radioactive substance produced synthetically (radium E), The Phantom, makes his appearance in comics, Military coup in Japan, Hitler breaks Treaty of Versailles, sends troops to Rhineland, Anti-Jewish riots break out in Palestine, Joe DiMaggio makes his major-league debut, "Gone With the Wind" by Margaret Mitchell, published, several state records of temperatures of over 110 degrees and some to 120 degrees, Nazi-Germany & Japan sign Anti-Komintern pact, First edition of Life Magazine, United Auto Workers stage 1st sit-down strike,

Dust Bowl ends.

1937

The Recession of 1937 was one of the worst recessions of the century at least percentage wise or something like that. The event seems to be still widely debated giving cause for pause that anybody has any idea what was or is going on. The debate is around fiscal policy of the government to balance the budget, reduction in investment because of declining profits and the tightened monetary policy of the Federal Reserve. In any event a lot of people got it stuck to them again and hard.

"Prince Valiant" comic strip appears, Cartoon characters Daffy Duck, Elmer J Fudd & Petunia Pig, debut, Dirigible Hindenburg explodes in flames at Lakehurst, NJ (36 die), Golden Gate Bridge, SF, dedicated, Memorial Day Massacre - Chicago police shoot on union marchers, 10 die, Marx Brothers' "A Day At The Races" opens, Senate rejects FDR proposal to enlarge Supreme Court, Politburo enables Operative Order 00447: execute 193,000 Russians, The Marihuana Tax Act of 1937 is passed in America, essentially rendering marijuana and all its by-products illegal, George E T Eyston sets world auto speed record at 345.49 MPH, George E T Eyston sets world auto speed record at 345.49 MPH, J. R. R. Tolkien's "The Hobbit" is published, "To Have & Have Not" published, Japan recognizes Franco government, Red Sox acquire the contract of 19-year-old Ted Williams, 1st feature-length color & sound cartoon premieres (Snow White), Mae West performs Adam & Eve skit that gets her banned from NBC radio.

1938

Federal National Mortgage Association, Fannie Mae is created as part of the New Deal program. Fannie Mae purchases VA and FHA loans from Mortgage lenders so they can have additional funds to generate more loans.

March of Dimes established to fight polio, 1st jazz concert was held at Carnegie Hall (Benny Goodman), German troops entered Austria, US Federal Crop Insurance program authorized, Mexico takes control of foreign-owned oil properties, Teflon invented by Roy J Plunkett, NY makes syphilis test mandatory in order to get a marriage license, Headless Mad Butcher victim found in Cleveland, Ella Fitzgerald records "A-Tisket, A-Tasket", Sandoz Labs manufactures LSD, Superman 1st appears in DC Comics' Action Comics Series issue #1, Comic strip "Dennis the Menace," 1st appears, George E T Eyston sets world auto speed record at 357.5 MPH, The Great Hurricane of 1938 makes landfall on Long Island in New York. The death toll is estimated at 500-700 people, Archbishop of Dubuque, Francis J. L. Beckman, denounces Swing music as "a degenerate musical system... turned loose to gnaw away at the moral fiber of young people", warning that it leads down a "primrose path to hell"., US forbids child labor in factories, DuPont announces its new synthetic fiber will be called "nylon", Orson Welles panics a nation with broadcast of "War of the Worlds", Groundbreaking begins for Jefferson Memorial in Wash DC and Dutch national debt hits ƒ3,986,629,805.70.

The last three economic incidents seem to have the **Federal Reserve somewhere in there screwing things up** or maybe they really didn't a clue.

Siegmund's second cousin, Eric Warburg, founded Warburg Pincus in New York in 1938.

1939

Banks in the Federal Deposit Insurance Corporation no longer are required to be in the Federal Reserve System. *Really!*

> Black Friday bush fires burn 20,000 square kilometers of land in Australia, claiming the lives of 71 people, Uranium atom 1st split, Columbia University, 30,000 killed by earthquake in Concepcion Chile, Earthquake hits Chillan Chile, 10,000 killed, Belgian Spaak government falls, Belgian government of Pierlot forms and falls, Supreme Court outlaws sit-down strikes, Guy Lombardo & Royal Canadians 1st record "Auld Lang Syne", Germany occupies Czechoslovakia, Lithuania state, forced to give Memel territory to, Spanish Civil War ends, Madrid falls to Francisco Franco, membership in Hitler Youth becomes obligatory, Italy invades Albania, India, the Hindustani Lal Sena (Indian Red Army) is formed and vows to engage in armed struggle against the British, "The Grapes of Wrath" published, Batman comics hit street, Germany & Italy announced an alliance known as the Rome-Berlin Axis, food stamps are 1st issued, "3 Little Fishies," by Kay Kyser hits #1, Frank Sinatra made his recording debut, 5th Dutch government of Colijn falls, 1st broadcast of "Dinah Shore Show", "Wizard of Oz" premieres at Grauman's Chinese Theater, Russian offensive under General Zjoekov against Japanese invasion in Mongolia, Belgium mobilizes, Hitler orders extermination of mentally ill, Switzerland proclaims neutrality, German U-boat sinks British passenger ship Athenia, Britain declares war on Germany. France follows 6 hours later quickly joined by Australia, NZ, South Africa & Canada, FDR declares "limited national emergency" due to war in Europe, Iraq & Saudi Arabia declare war on Nazi-Germany, Churchill calls Soviets "riddle wrapped in a mystery inside an enigma", Albert Einstein informs FDR of possibilities of atomic bomb, NAACP organized Legal Defense & Education Fund, US allows "cash & carry" arms sales during WW II and Kate Smith 1st sings Irving Berlin's "God Bless America".

1940

COLORADO NAT. BANK OF DENVER v. BEDFORD, Treasurer of State of Colorado

The state of Colorado required the Colorado National Bank to collect and remit taxes imposed by the state on the users of safety deposit boxes. Colorado National bank refused.

The court ruled in favor of the state of Colorado.

The tax being a permissible tax on customers of the bank, it is settled by our prior decisions that the statutory provisions requiring collection and remission of the taxes do not impose an unconstitutional burden on a federal instrumentality. Especially is this true since the bank under the Colorado act is allowed three per cent of the tax for the financial burden put upon it by the obligation to collect.

FCC hears 1st transmission of FM radio with clear, static-free signal, Britain's 1st WW II rationing (bacon, butter & sugar), "In The Mood" by Glenn Miller hits #1, Tom & Jerry created by Hanna & Barbera debut by MGM, Walt Disney's animated movie "Pinocchio," released, Russo-Finnish Winter War ends, 1st electron microscope demonstrated, Himmler orders establishment of Auschwitz Concentration Camp, Nazi armies attack Netherlands, Belgium & Luxembourg, Winston Churchill succeeds Neville Chamberlain as British Prime Minister, The first German bombs of the war fall on England, Netherlands surrender to Germany, German armor division moves into Northern France, McDonald's opens its first restaurant, Italy declares war on allies, Gen. Charles de Gaulle on BBC tells French to defy Nazi occupiers, US passes Alien Registration Act requiring Aliens to register, diplomatic relations broken between Britain & Vichy government in France, Bugs Bunny debuts in "Wild Hare", 49 die & 200 injured when Hercules Powder Co plant explodes, Willys unveiled its General Purpose vehicle ("Jeep") and Woody Woodpecker debuts.

Franklin Delano Roosevelt defeats **Wendell Willkie** a controversial Republican candidate.

1941 to 1960 WWII, American Pie, the World Changes and So Does Banking (but who's looking)

World War II starts and government spending goes through the roof as the nation goes to war.

Canada & US acquire air bases in Newfoundland (99 yr. lease), Joe Louis KOs Red Burman in 5, Supreme Court upheld Federal Wage & Hour law, sets min wages & max hrs., Plutonium was produced and isolated, "Captain America" appears in a comic book, Grand Coulee Dam in Washington goes into operation, Greece Army surrenders to German Nazis RAF brings Greek king George II to Egypt, "Citizen Kane," directed & starring Orson Welles, premieres in NY, General Mills introduces Cheerios, California's March Field, Bob Hope performs his USO show, Joe DiMaggio 56-game hitting streak, FDR declares state of emergency due to Germany's sinking of Robin Moor, English & French troop overthrow pro-German Syria, President Franklin Roosevelt signs "GI Bill of Rights", Florey & Heatley present freeze dried mold cultures (Penicillin), NY Yankee Lefty Gomez walks most (11) in a shutout (Yanks 9, St L 0) (go figure), US President Franklin Roosevelt and British Prime Minister Winston Churchill issue the joint declaration that later becomes known as the Atlantic Charter, Brooklyn Dodgers win their 1st pennant in 21 years, Ted Williams ended the baseball season with .406 batting avg., coup in Panama declares Ricardo Adolfo de la Guardia Arango the new president, Japan Tojo regime forms, Walt Disney's "Dumbo" released, US savings bonds go on sale, Mount Rushmore is completed, Japanese attack Pearl Harbor (a date that will live in infamy), US Office of Censorship created to control info pertaining to WW II and battle of the American Volunteer Group, better known as the "Flying Tigers" in Kunming, China.

1942

Bob Feller, enlists in Navy & reports for duty to Norfolk Virginia, Bronx magistrate rules all pinball machines illegal, "Woman of the Year," starring Hepburn & Tracy opens at Radio City, Daylight Savings War Time goes into effect in US, "Archie" comic book debuts, About 150 Japanese warplanes attacked the Australian city of Darwin, FDR orders detention & internment of all west-coast Japanese-Americans, The "Battle of Los Angeles", Food rationed in US, Red Sox star Ted Williams enlists as a Navy aviator, Anne Frank begins her diary, FBI captures 8 Nazi saboteurs from a sub off NY's Long Island, Carlson's Raiders land on Makin, Gilbert islands, bombing on continental US soil, Mount Emily Oregon (WW II), self-sustaining nuclear chain reaction demonstrated, Chicago, Tweety Bird, aka Tweety Pie, debuts in "Tale of Two Kitties", "Casablanca" premieres at Hollywood Theatre, NYC, Potatoes rationed in Holland.

1943

President Franklin Roosevelt, in an attempt to check inflation associated with war effort spending, freezes wages and prices, prohibits workers from changing jobs unless the war effort would be aided thereby, and bars rate increases to common carriers and public utilities.

William H Hastie, civilian aide to secretary of war, resigns to protest segregation in armed forces, Frankfurters replaced by Victory Sausages (mix of meat & soy meal), Hitler declares "Total War" (*well he sure got that*), World's largest office building, Pentagon, completed, Pre sliced bread sale banned to reduce bakery demand for metal parts (*both rationed*), Chile breaks contact with Germany & Japan, shoe rationing begins in US, new volcano Paracutin erupts in farmer's corn patch (Mexico), Anti-fascist strikes in Italy, Jimmy Durante & Garry Moore premiere on radio, US forbid racial discrimination in war industry, mob of 60 from the Los Angeles Naval Reserve Armory beat up everyone perceived to be Hispanic, starting the week-long Zoot Suit Riots, Argentina taken over by Gen. Rawson & Col. Juan Peron, FDR signs withholding tax bill into law, Federal troops put down racial riot in Detroit, RAF bombs Hamburg (*20,000 dead, total war*), Gen. Eisenhower announced unconditional surrender of Italy, Streptomycin, the antibiotic remedy for tuberculosis, is isolated, American bombers strike a hydro-electric power facility and heavy water factory in German-controlled Vemork, Norway and a military coup in Bolivia.

1944

The Bretton Woods International Monetary Agreement creates the International Monetary Fund to facilitate international settlements as many countries fix their currency to the dollar as a standard.

Bing Crosby records "Swinging on a Star" for Decca Records, 1st black reporter accredited to White House, Harry McAlpin, Batman & Robin comic strip premieres in newspapers, 16th Academy Awards - "Casablanca,", 2,500 women trample guards & floorwalkers to purchase 1,500 alarm clocks announced for sale in a Chicago Illinois dept. store, Mount Vesuvius, Italy explodes, Supreme Court (Smith v Allwright) "white primaries" unconstitutional, South Carolina rejects black suffrage, Messerschmitt Me 262 Sturmvogel, 1st jet bomber, makes 1st flight, 14,000 Jews of Munkacs Hungary deported to Auschwitz, **D-Day, June 6**, Iceland declares independence from Denmark, IBM dedicates the program-controlled calculator, the Automatic Sequence Controlled Calculator, race riots in Athens Alabama, Jackie Gleason-Les Tremayne show premieres on NBC radio, Hitler orders Paris to be destroyed (*read "Is Paris Burning"*), suffrage is extended to women in France, "Adventures of Ozzie & Harriet" debut on CBS radio, Navy says black women can join WAVES, Mary Coyle Chase's "Harvey," premieres in NYC, Civil War breaks out in a newly-liberated Greece, between communists and royalists, bandleader, Major Glenn Miller, lost over English Channel and Leonard Bernstein's musical "On the Town," premieres in NYC.

1945

Harry S Truman becomes President as FDR dies if office 1945 to 1953

"You cannot stop the spread of an idea by passing a law against it." **Harry S. Truman**

Arab League forms, Princess Elizabeth, later to become Queen Elizabeth II, joins the British Army as a driver, Billboard publishes its 1st album chart (King Cole Trio is #1), Ella Fitzgerald & Delta Rhythm Boys record "It's Only a Paper Moon", "Arthur Godfrey Time" begins a 27 year run on CBS, Branch Rickey announces formation of the US Negro Baseball League, UN Charter signed by 50 nations, US Communist Party forms, Atom Bomb dropped on Hiroshima (Aug 6), Hank Greenberg's final day HR wins pennant for Tigers, "Meet the Press" premieres on radio, Chinese civil war begins, Chiang Kai-Shek vs. Mao Tse-Tung, JPL WAC Corporal Launch (1st Man-Made Object to escape Atmosphere), Nazi war crime trial opens in Nuremberg, World Bank was created with the signing of an agreement by 28 nations, International Monetary Fund established,

Diners Club card introduced.

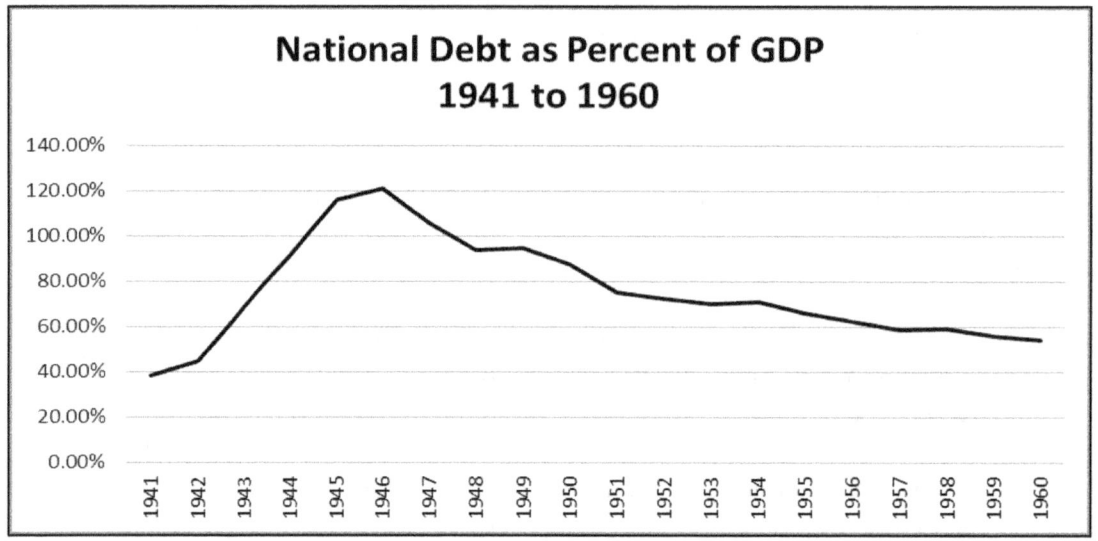

1946

There was a brief recession of several months while the nation retooled for a peace time economy. This is widely considered an 'after war' recession and was mild.

"Show Boat" opens at Ziegfeld Theater NYC, US president sets up CIA, Central Intelligence Agency, Bank of England nationalized, race riot in Columbia Tenn., Winston Churchill's "Iron Curtain" speech, 1st US rocket to leave the Earth's atmosphere, 400,000 US mine workers strike, Tsunamis generated by a quake in Aleutian Trench strike Hilo

Hawaii, Jackie Robinson debuts as 2nd baseman for the Montreal Royals, Press Harry Truman seizes control of nation's railroads to delay a strike, Patent filed in US for H-Bomb, 1st bikini bathing suit displayed (Paris), US Supreme court rules race separation on buses, unconstitutional, "Annie Get Your Gun" opens at Imperial Theater NYC, Philippines gains independence from US, President Harry Truman orders desegregation of all US forces, Great Calcutta blood bath - Moslem/Hindu riot (3-4,000 die), 1st mobile long-distance car-to-car telephone conversation, John F Kennedy (D-Mass) elected to House of Representatives, Hank Williams begins to record on Sterling label, Tide detergent introduced, 4th French republic established and Flamingo Hotel in Las Vegas opens.

Board of Governors v. Agnew

A 'few fellows' were directors of the Patterson National Bank that was member of the national banking association and the Federal Reserve while they were employed by Eastman, Dillon & Co., a partnership, that touted itself as being 'Underwriters, Distributors, Dealers and Brokers in Industrial, Railroad, Public Utility and Municipal Securities.'

The Board of Governors of the Federal Reserve had warned them against this relationship and had eventually sought to force their separation from the bank.

The 'few fellows' took issue and went to the District Court of the District of Columbia seeking relief from the Boards decision. The District Court says sure 'few fellows' that stupid Board has it all wrong, keep your seats on the Banks Board of Directors and work for that securities underwriting firm.

The Board of Governors of the Federal Reserve ain't done yet. They go to the Supreme Court of these United States of America looking for support for their position.

The Supreme Court says sure that's a securities firm no matter how that dim witted District Court says so fire the dirty conniving twits and let's get on with better things.

World war two was over and the United States was the only fully intact industrial nation in the world. For the next couple of decades unemployment was low, the economy was good and people were enjoying the 'American Dream'. Vast tracts of single family homes were going up, the national interstate highway system was being built, **Dinah Shore was singing 'See the USA in a Chevrolet...' and people were**. Air travel was becoming affordable, science and technology were making tremendous strides, televisions were selling well and so were cars.

Coming home wasn't so great for some.

Battle of Athens a.k.a. The McMinn County War

When veterans returned from World War Two they found their county run by corrupt government officials and found their only viable avenue of redress to be force of arms and some dynamite to bring democratic order back to their home.

Sigmund George Warburg founds S. G. Warburg & Company, investment bank, in London.

1947

Britain nationalizes its coal industry.

"Finian's Rainbow" opens at 46th St Theater NYC, 1st commercial TV station west of Mississippi opens in Hollywood CA, Arabs & Jews reject British proposal to split Palestine, Press Harry Truman introduces Truman-doctrine to fight communism, "Kraft Television Theater" premieres on NBC, Tennis shoe introduced, India declares independence from UK, Islamic part becomes Pakistan, "Kukla, Fran & Ollie" premieres, Chuck Yeager in Bell XS-1 makes 1st supersonic flight (Mach 1.015), "You Bet Your Life," with Groucho Marx, premieres on ABC radio, Day after UN decree for Israel, Jewish settlements attacked and 1st "Howdy Doody Show," (Puppet Playhouse), telecast on NBC.

1948

Britain nationalizes its railways.

Netherlands & Indonesia agree to a cease fire, Mahatma Gandhi assassinated by Nathuram Godse, NASCAR is incorporated, Communist Party seizes complete control of Czechoslovakia, Supreme Court rules religious instructions in public schools unconstitutional, Organization of American States charter signed at Bogota, Colombia, North Korean proclaims itself People's Democratic Republic of Korea, Rhodes conference on Israeli-Arab war opens, Soviet Union begins Berlin Blockade, Allen Funt's "Candid Camera" TV debut on ABC and 20 die & 6,000 made ill by smog in Donora Pennsylvania.

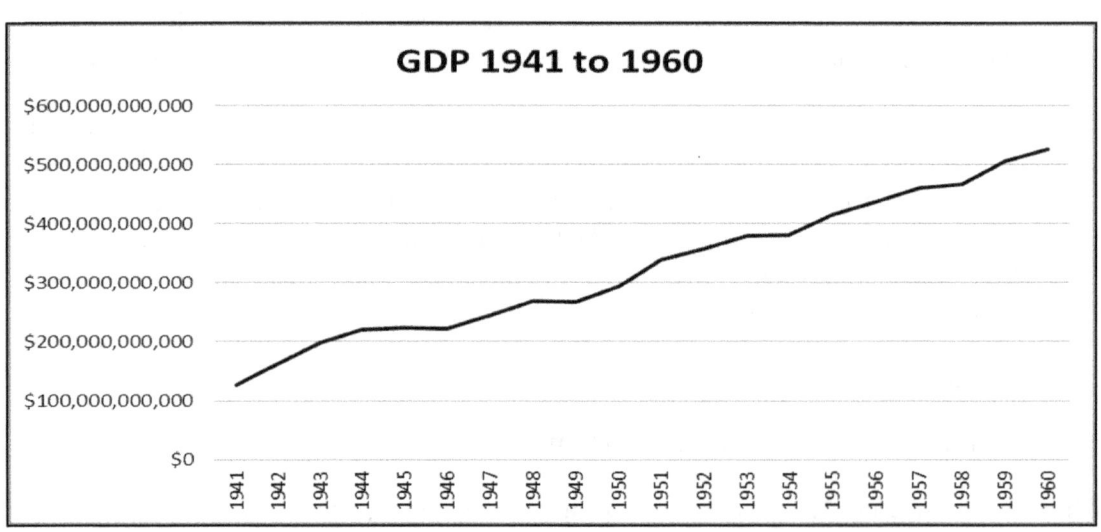

1949

Britain nationalizes its steel & iron industry.

> RCA introduces 45 RPM record, Joe DiMaggio becomes 1st $100,000/year baseball player, Mass arrests of communists in India, Bollingen Prize for poetry awarded to Ezra Pound, Israel & Egypt sign an armistice agreement, NATO (North Atlantic Treaty Org) ratified, Harry Truman signs bill establishing a rocket test range at Cape Canaveral, "Hop along Cassidy" becomes 1st network western, USSR explodes their 1st atom bomb, Dutch Guilder devalued 30.3%, People's Rep of China proclaimed by Mao Tse-tung (National Day), Republic of China (Taiwan) forms on island of Formosa, 14 US Communist Party leaders convicted of sedition and the Greeks civil war ends.

The 1949 Recession was short lived and mild that was likely generated by **tightening of the money supply**. That it followed President Truman's' Fair Deal may have been simply coincidence or a confidence backlash.

The United States sends Nelson Rockefeller, John Foster Dulles, John McCloy, Harry Dexter White, Owen Lattimore, and Alger Hiss to the **United Nations formation meeting.**

1950s - Car loans were developed during the 1950's, 24 month term.

1950

Commercial banks have about 52% of the assets of the United States financial institutions. Investment Banks and such seem to be doing OK.

> Ho Chi Minh begins offensive against French troops in Indo China, Hank Snow's 1st appearance on "Grand Ole Opry", The Great Brinks Robbery, NY jury finds former State Dept. official Alger Hiss guilty of perjury, India becomes a republic ceasing to be a British dominion, Sen. Joe McCarthy finds "communists" in US Ministry of Foreign Affairs, Walt Disney's "Cinderella" released, "Your Show of Shows" with Sid Caesar & Imogene Coca premieres on NBC Writers include Mel Brooks, Neil Simon & Woody Allen, Silly Putty invented, "Peter Pan" opens at Imperial Theater NYC, Diner's Club issues its 1st credit cards, US Supreme Court undermines legal foundations of segregation, Korean conflict begins; N Korea invades S Korea, Pres. Harry Truman orders army to seize control of RR to avert a strike, Peanuts by Charles M. Schulz published, Mother Teresa founds Missionaries of Charity in Calcutta, India, "Guys & Dolls" opens, Paul Harvey begins his national radio broadcast.

The Federal Deposit Insurance Act of 1950 provided federal bank regulators the option of aiding a troubled institution with loans or buy the assets of the bank until such time as the bank could recover sufficiently to buy the assets back. Before this, federal regulators could only close the bank, liquidate the assets and pay insured depositors or look for another bank to purchase the troubles bank.

1951

Persia nationalizes Anglo-Iranian Oil Company.

Thought extinct since 1615, a Cahow is rediscovered in Bermuda, Life After Tomorrow, 1st film to receive an "X" rating, Supreme Court rule "clear & present danger" of incitement to riot is not protected speech & can be a cause for arrest, Liz Taylor's 1st divorce (Conrad Hilton Jr.), "King & I" opens at St James Theater NYC, Julius & Ethel Rosenberg are convicted of spying, Pres. Harry Truman fires Gen Douglas McArthur, Jay Forrester patents computer core memory, Racial segregation in Wash DC restaurants ruled illegal, Mantle and Mays begin baseball careers, King Abdullah I of Jordan is assassinated, Walt Disney's "Alice In Wonderland" released, Bill Veeck (Cleveland Indians) sends Eddie Gaedel, a 3'7" midget, to pinch-hit, "Search for Tomorrow" debuts on CBS, Swiss males vote against female suffrage, "Paint Your Wagon" opens at Shubert Theater NYC and a military coup under Col Adib el-Shishakli in Syria.

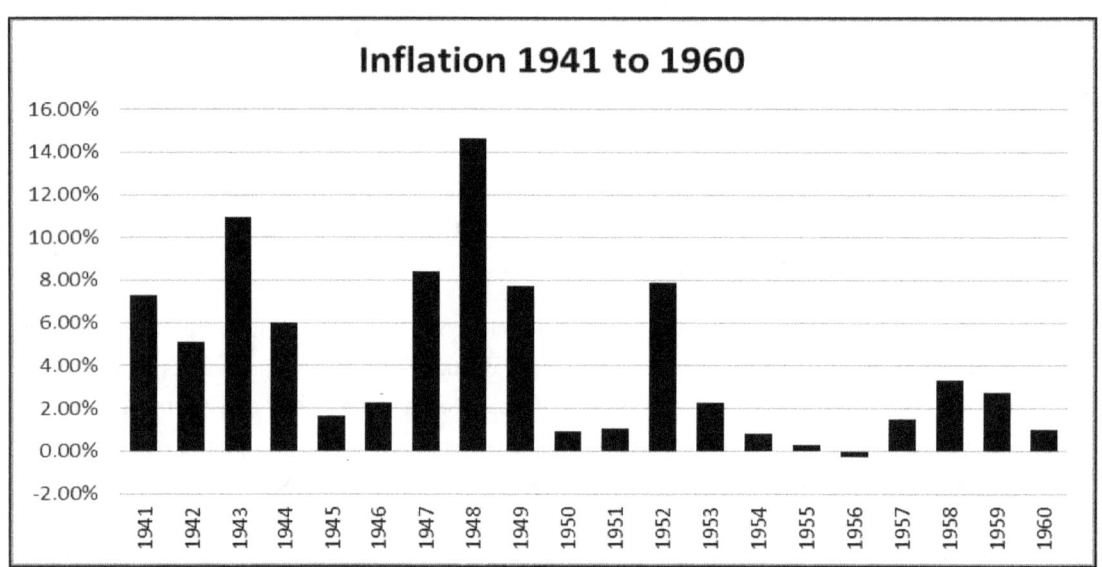

1952

Press Harry Truman seizes steel mills to avert a strike.

French Plevin government falls, Belgian Pholien government resigns, "Today Show" premieres with Dave Garroway & Jack Lescoulie on NBC-TV, Elizabeth II is proclaimed Queen of the UK, Dick Button performs 1st figure skating triple jump in competition, demonstrations against apartheid in South-Africa, Big Bang theory proposed in Physical Review by Alpher, Bethe & Gamow, Popular uprising in Bolivia, Mr. Potato Head is 1st toy advertised on television, women of Greece are given the right to vote, 1st "Bandstand" broadcast in Philadelphia on WFIL-TV (Dick Clark joins in 1955 as a substitute-host),

French troops shoot on demonstrators at Casablanca and 1st transistorized hearing aid offered for sale.

1953

Dwight David Eisenhower becomes President 1953 to 1961 Republican

"There is nothing wrong with America that the faith, love of freedom, intelligence and energy of her citizens cannot cure." **Dwight David Eisenhower**

Census indicates 239,000 farmers gave up farming in last 2 years. European agriculture has picked up reducing demand for American crops.

> Flooding in Netherlands, kills 1,835, "Peter Pan" by Walt Disney opens, "Adventures of Superman" TV series premieres in syndication, Georgia approves US 1st literature censorship board, US Court of Appeals rules that Organized Baseball is a sport & not a business, affirming the 25-year-old Supreme Court ruling, **Dr. Jonas Salk announces vaccine to prevent polio,** "TV Guide" publishes 1st issue, Warner Brothers premieres the first 3-D film, entitled House of Wax, Scientists identify DNA, President Eisenhower signs Offshore Oil Bill, Fidel Castro begins rebellion, California introduces sales tax, Swanson sells its' 1st "TV dinner", "Make Room for Daddy," starring Danny Thomas, premieres, Milton Berle Show premieres, TV broadcasting begins in Belgium, Chuck Yeager reaches Mach 2.43 in Bell X-1A rocket plane.

Norman Dodd, investigator for the **Reece Committee** begins looking into tax-free foundations activities. The committee's investigation is suddenly halted.

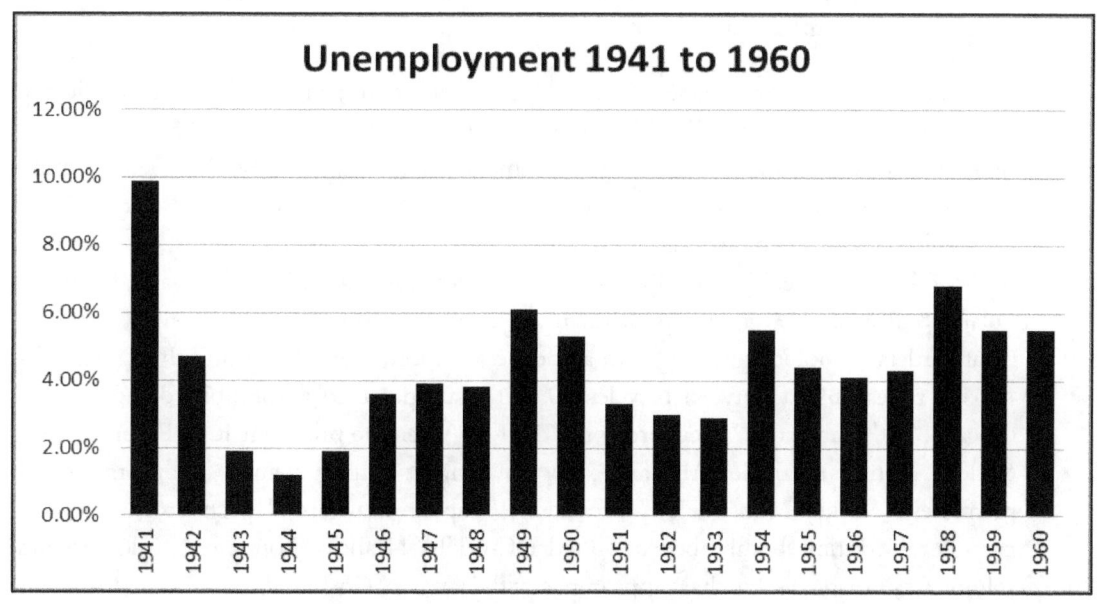

1954

The Dow Jones Industrial Average closes above the peak it reached just before the 1929 crash.

"The death of democracy is not likely to be an assassination from ambush. It will be a slow extinction from apathy, indifference, and undernourishment." **Robert M. Hutchins**

Jacques Cousteau's 1st network telecast airs on "Omnibus" (CBS), Eisenhower warns against US intervention in Vietnam, closed since 1939, the London bullion market reopens, Elvis Presley records his debut single, "That's All Right", Colonel Nasser seizes power & becomes PM of Egypt, Senate Army-McCarthy televised hearings began, Bell labs announces 1st solar battery, British raid Nairobi Kenya (Mau Mau suspects arrested), Supreme Court unanimously rules on Brown v Topeka Board of Education reversed 1896 "separate but equal" Plessy V Ferguson decision, IBM announces vacuum tube "electronic" brain that could perform 10 million operations an hour, France agrees to independence of North & South Vietnam, Nautilus, 1st atomic-powered vessel (sub), commissioned by the Navy, and Burger King is opened in Miami, Florida.

Chemical Bank of New York merges with Corn Exchange Bank

The Recession of 1954 was a result of the Feds' reaction to inflation after the end of the Korean War. They tightened money again.

1955

Chase National (3rd largest bank) & Bank of the Manhattan Company (15th largest bank) merge to form Chase Manhattan.

US & Panama sign canal treaty, "Scrabble" debuts on board game market, 1st presidential news conference filmed for TV (Eisenhower), Israel acquires 4 of 7 Dead Sea scrolls, 1st seagoing oil drill rig placed in service, , Yemen: failed coup by Abdullah Seif el-Islam, Congress orders all US coins bear motto "In God We Trust", Imperial Bank of India nationalized, West Germany granted full sovereignty by 3 occupying powers, Warsaw Pact is signed by the Soviet Union, Albania, Bulgaria, Czechoslovakia, East Germany, Hungary, Poland & Romania, Argentine parliament accepts separation of church & state, Supreme Court orders school integration "with all deliberate speed", "Rock Around the Clock" hits #1, US raises import duty on bicycles 50%, 1st sun-powered automobile demonstrated, Chicago, Ill, "Gunsmoke" premieres on CBS TV, Argentine president Juan Peron, resigns & flees, Detroit outfielder Al Kaline, 20, is youngest batting champ, "Honeymooners" premieres, "Mickey Mouse Club" premieres, "Captain Kangaroo" premieres, Argentine peso devalued, time bomb aboard United DC-6 kills 44 above Longmont Colorado and Johnny Cash made his 1st chart appearance with "Cry Cry Cry".

1956

The Bank Holding Company Act only limited nonbanking activities of companies that owned two or more commercial banks, "one bank holding companies" could own interests in any type of company other than securities firms covered by Glass–Steagall Section 20. **"Loophole"!** They are also forbidden from buying banks in another state.

> Sudan (Anglo-Egyptian Sudan) declares independence from Egypt & UK, Abigail Van Buren's "Dear Abby" column 1st appears in newspapers, Martin Luther King Jr.'s home bombed, Britain abolishes death penalty, Khrushchev denounces Stalin at 20th Soviet Party Conference, Morocco tears up the Treaty of Fez, declares independence from France, General strike in Cyprus protesting exile of archbishop Makarios, Spain relinquishes her protectorate in Morocco, A doctor in Japan reports an "epidemic of an unknown disease of the central nervous system", marking the official discovery of Minamata disease, Golda Meir begins her term as Israel's foreign minister, Anti-protons detected in the atmosphere, Federal interstate highway system act signed, British government sends 3 aircraft carriers to Egypt after Egypt seizes Suez Canal, Thousands of Hungarians protest against the government and Soviet occupation. (The Hungarian Revolution is crushed on November 4), Largest observed iceberg, 208 by 60 miles, 1st sighted, "The Price Is Right" debuts on NBC, Guy Mitchell's "Singing the Blues," single goes #1 for 10 weeks.

Goldman Sachs & Company handled the IPO for Ford Motor Company

1957

Richie Ashburn fouls hits fan Alice Roth twice in same at bat 1st one breaks her nose, 2nd one hits her while she is on the stretcher. *This doesn't have anything to do with economics. Just a real 'aw shit' day for Alice. Richie probably didn't feel so good about it either.*

> An Irish Republican Army (IRA) unit attacks Brookeborough RUC barracks in one of the most famous incidents of the IRA's Operation, Wham-O Company produces the 1st Frisbee, Israeli forces withdraw from Sinai Peninsula, India annexes Kashmir, Suez Canal cleared for all shipping, Britain agrees to Singaporean self-rule, Due to lack of funds, Saturday mail delivery in US is temp halted, Larry King's 1st radio broadcast, Pulitzer prize awarded to John F Kennedy (Profiles in Courage), "I Love Lucy," last airs on CBS-TV, USSR announces successful test of intercontinental ballistic missile, Malaysia (formerly Malaya) gains independence from Britain, Pres. Eisenhower signs 1st civil rights bill since Reconstruction, Thailand military coup under marshal Sarit Thanarat, "Perry Mason" with Raymond Burr premieres on CBS-TV, Pres. Eisenhower apologizes to finance minister of Ghana, Komla Agbeli Gbdemah, after he is refused service in a Dover, Del, restaurant, French author Albert Camus awarded Nobel Prize in Literature, world longest suspension bridge opens (Mackinac Straits Mich.), 2nd Soviet Earth-satellite launched, Celtic Bill Russell sets NBA record of 49 rebounds and Indonesia begins nationalizing Dutch possessions.

1958

Credit cards started becoming commonly used. The first credit card was from **Bank of America as the BankAmericard** and later became known as **Visa**. Gee, living in Oregon and using my credit card to buy something while on vacation in Florida is a pretty good thing. That it might be used to destroy states usury laws later seems not to have occurred to anybody, yet.

Treaties establish European Economic Community (Common Market), 9,000 scientists of 43 nations petition UN for nuclear test ban, Dictator Marcos Perez Jiménez flees Venezuela, Larrazabal takes power, 1st man-made nuclear fusion, US launches their 1st artificial satellite, Explorer 1, Comic strip "BC" 1st appears, Indonesian air force bombs Padang, Sumatra, Greek Clandestine Radio (communist), Voice of Truth 1st transmission, Nikita Khrushchev becomes Soviet premier & 1st sect of Communist Party, "Great leap forward" movement in China, Ceylon emergency crisis proclaimed, British parachutists lands on Cyprus, Anti-Chinese uprising in Tibet, Atomic sub USS Nautilus completes 1st trip under North Pole, Guinea votes for independence from France, 5th French republic forms, USSR lends Egypt 400 million rubles to build Aswan Dam, Boris Pasternak refuses Nobel prize for literature, French franc devalued.

1958 Recession as the money supply is tightened again. I guess those bankers really do not like inflation.

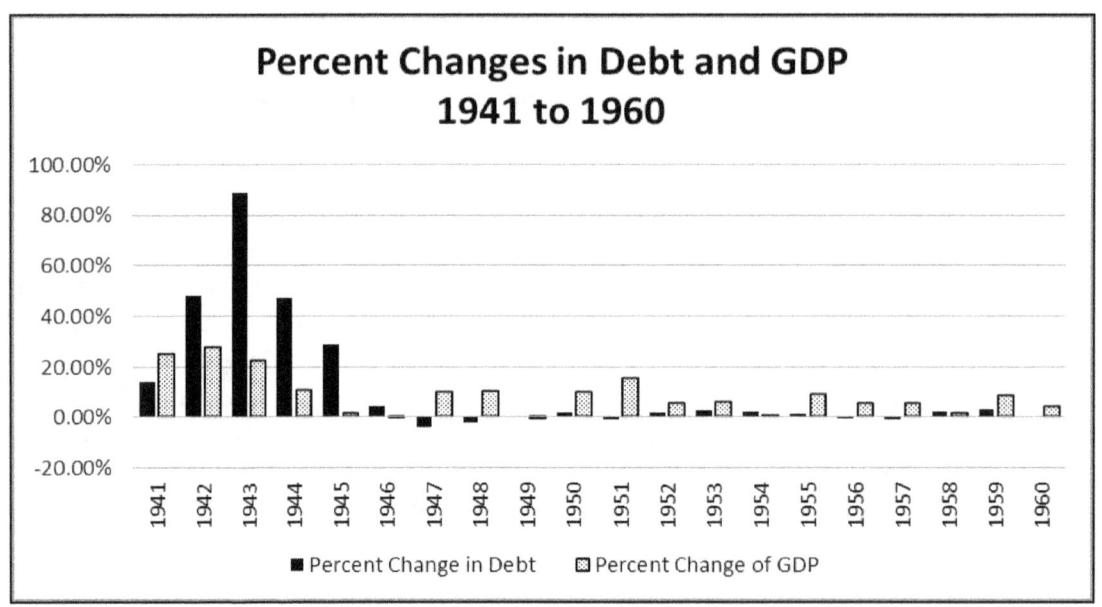

1959

Iran & United States sign economic & military treaty.

Steel strike of 1959 leads to significant importation of foreign steel for the first time in United States history.

> Castro takes Cuba, Charles de Gaulle inaugurated as President of France's 5th Republic and grants amnesty to 130 to Algerian death row convicts, King Boudouin promises Belgian Congo independence, Italy government of Fanfani resigns, "Sleeping Beauty" released, Texas Instruments requests patent of IC (Integrated Circuit), Barbie doll goes on sale, $3.6 million heroin seizure in NYC, 1st Daytona 500 auto race-Lee Petty wins, Iran & US sign economic & military treaty, Groucho, Chico & Harpo's final TV appearance together, Pro-Egyptian coup fails in Mosul Iraq, Oklahoma ends prohibition, after 51 years, St Lawrence Seaway linking Atlantic and Great Lakes opens to shipping, Cuba invades Panama, 1st Grammy Awards: Perry Como & Ella Fitzgerald win, Iceland gunboats shoot at British fishing ships, Soviet forces arrive in Afghanistan, Presbyterian church accepts women preachers, Postmaster General bans D H Lawrence's book, Lady Chatterley's Lover (overruled by US Court of Appeals in Mar 1960), Cayman Islands separated from Jamaica, steel strike of 1959 begins, leading to significant importation of foreign steel for the first time in United States history, Soviet Union's Luna-2 is 1st spacecraft to land on the Moon, Sandy Koufax breaks Dizzy Dean's NL mark of 18 strikeouts in a game, Sultan of Brunei promulgates a constitution, Chinese troops move into India, 1st episode of "Rocky & His Friends" (Moose and Squirrel; Boris and Natasha; Fractured Fairy Tales...), 12 nations sign treaty for scientific peaceful use of Antarctica, Dom Mintoff demands independence for Malta,

J.P. Morgan merges with the Guaranty Trust Company of New York becoming the **Morgan Guaranty Trust Company**

Commercial banks now have only about **38% of the assets** of United States financial institutions and are becoming rather frustrated by the restrictions of Glass-Steagall. *I bet you thought this was a recent thing.*

So what do the commercial banks start doing but forming one bank holding companies? *Loophole intact and fully functioning*

Alaska and Hawaii Statehood

1960

Recession of 1960 The Fed tightened the money supply again bringing about the recession. This is accomplished by raising interest rates. We will see some dramatic effects of this policy in the late 70s and early 80s.

> The Bank of France issues new franc, worth 100 times the value of existing francs (*Brazil uses this method later*), Cameroon (French Cameroon) gains independence from France, Chad declares independence from France, Bathysphere "Trieste" reach bottom of Pacific (10,900 m), Protest strike in Poznan Poland, Miracle on Ice, Pres. Eisenhower signs Civil Rights Act of 1960, US is 1st country to use the birth control pill legally, Israeli soldiers

capture Adolf Eichmann in Buenos Aires, Military coup overthrows democratic government of Turkey, British Somaliland (now Somalia) gains independence from Britain, Zaire (formerly Belgian Congo) declares independence from Belgium, Ghana becomes a republic, Italian Somaliland gains independence, unites with Somali Republic, Ivory Coast, Dahomey, Upper Volta & Niger declare independence, Moise Tsjombe declares Congolese county Katanga independence, Elijah Muhammad, leader of Nation of Islam, calls for a black state, Francis Gary Powers U-2 spy trial opens in Moscow, Jordan premier Hazza-el-Madjali receives deadly injury from bomb attack, Iraq, Iran, Kuwait, Saudi-Arabia & Venezuela form OPEC, Cuba nationalizes US banks, Flintstones premieres (1st prime time animation show), Belgium threatens to leave UN due to criticism on its' Congo-policy, Ray Charles' "Georgia On My Mind" reaches #1 and Adventures of Huckleberry Finn released August. *(The following summer my brother and I built a raft of logs at the river and were later found several miles downriver. Great fun! How many parents bemoaned ever having taken their kids to see that one?)*

1961 to 1988 Hippies, Riots, War, Oil, No More Gold, An Actor is President and Deregulate the Crud out of Every Thing
John F. Kennedy becomes President 1961 to 1963 Assassinated Democratic

"The American, by nature, is optimistic. He is experimental, an inventor and a builder who builds best when called upon to build greatly." **John F. Kennedy**

> **Russia introduces a new ruble worth $1.11 (*they will do the new Ruble thing again in 1998*),** UN genocide pact goes into effect, Supremes signed with Motown Records, President Dwight D. Eisenhower delivers a televised farewell address to the nation three days before leaving office, in which he warns against the accumulation of power by the "military-industrial complex", Portuguese rebels seize cruise ship Santa Maria, military coup in El Salvador, Peace Corp established, failed assassination attempt on King Saif al-Islam Achmad of Yemen, 1,400 Cuban exiles land in Bay of Pigs attempt to overthrow Castro, uprising of French parachutist of Gen Salan/Challe in Algeria, bus with 1st group of Freedom Riders bombed & burned in Alabama, last trip (Paris to Bucharest) on Orient Express (after 78 years), Soviet ballet dancer Rudolf Nureyev defects to West, Kuwait declares independence from UK, Iraq announces that Kuwait is a part of Iraq (***Kuwait disagrees and this issue is revisited later***), Cosmonaut Gherman Titov circles Earth for a full day in Vostok 2, construction of the Berlin Wall begins in East Germany, Francis the Talking Mule is mystery guest on "What's My Line", Bob Dylan's 1st NY performance, Roger Maris sets record of 61 HRs (*no performance enhancing issues here*), 75,000 Flemings demand equal rights & Flemish language in Belgium, JFK sends 18,000 military advisors to South Vietnam, India seizes Goa & 2 other Portuguese colonies, Beatles and Beach Boys are making the scene.

John F. Kennedy appoints **James J. Saxon to the Office of the Comptroller of the Currency** which incidentally makes him the regulator of the National Banks. Mr. Saxon gets all up in arms because this nifty national bank system is losing market share to the non-banking/shadow banking system that is outside the Federal Reserve.

First National 'City Bank' of New York establishes "negotiable certificates of deposit" in 1961. *OK, so this isn't really a deposit as understood in 1933 and is therefore not construed to be regulated as such. This is a 'work-around' to avoid Glass-Steagall. Really it is quite innovative in its own right and made them a ton of money.*

1962

Cuban missile crisis begins as John F. Kennedy becomes aware of missiles in Cuba.

> United States Navy SEALs established, Dutch & Indonesian navy encounter in Etna Bay New Guinea, US begins spraying foliage in Vietnam to reveal Viet Cong guerrillas (? Agent Orange?), UN General Assembly censures Portugal (because of Angola), President Kennedy begins blockade of Cuba, John Glenn is 1st American to orbit Earth (Friendship 7), K-Mart opens, Supreme Court backs 1-man-1-vote apportionment of seats in state leg,

Military coup in Syria, 1st US satellite to reach the moon launched, Continental Airlines Flight 11 crashes after bombs explode on board, Ross Perot begins Electronic Data Systems, Rolling Stones 1st performance (Marquee Club, London) and Peter, Paul & Mary release their 1st hit "If I Had a Hammer".

1963

Lyndon Baines Johnson becomes president as Kennedy is assassinated 1963 to 1969

"For this is what America is all about. It is the uncrossed desert and the unclimbed ridge. It is the star that is not reached and the harvest sleeping in the unplowed ground. . ." **Lyndon Baines Johnson**

The safety net breaks

Mr. Saxon, Office of the Comptroller of the Currency a.k.a. OCC starts issuing regulations permitting national banks to offer their customers something called **'comingled accounts'**, basically these are mutual funds and that national banks could 'underwrite, municipal revenue bonds. This was done to help the banks under Glass-Steagall compete with the non-banking/shadow banking system that is outside the Federal Reserve and quit losing market share. The Supreme Court shoots these down. See Investment Company Institute v Camp for the 'mutual fund' issue 1970.

1st discotheque opens, Whiskey-a-go-go in LA, "Dr. No" premieres in US, Equal Pay Act enacted, Yugoslavia proclaimed a Socialistic Republic, State of siege proclaimed in Iran, Ayatollah Khomeini arrested, Supreme Court rules against Bible reading/prayer in public schools, ZIP Codes are introduced for United States mail, US, Russia & England sign nuclear Test ban treaty, Allan Sherman releases "Hello Mudda, Hello Fadda", Martin Luther King Jr.'s "I Have a Dream Speech" at Lincoln Memorial, 1st US TV appearance of Beatles, "Tennessee Tuxedo," cartoon debuts, Dam bursts in Italy, 3,000+ die, Jim Brown sets NFL single-season rushing record, 1,863 yds., Bell Telephone introduces push button telephone, President John F. Kennedy assassinated and Jerry Garcia & Bob Weir played music together for the 1st time.

Chairman of the House Banking and Currency Committee Wright Patman [D Texas], said in a speech dedicating the new FDIC building.

"I think we should have more bank failures. The record of the last several years of almost no bank failures . . . is to me a danger signal that we have gone too far in the direction of bank safety."

1964

President Lyndon B Johnson declares "War on Poverty".

From the end of WWII to 1963 the number of bank closures a year never exceeded 5 and averaged about 2.5 per year. From 1964 to 1970 bank closures averaged 6 per year.

> Bahamas becomes self-governing, President Lyndon B Johnson declares "War on Poverty", Anti-US rioting broke out in Panama Canal Zone, Teamsters negotiate 1st national labor contract, GI Joe, debuts, France & Great-Britain sign accord over building channel tunnel, Greeks & Turks begin fighting in Limassol, Cyprus, Malcolm X leaves Black Muslim Movement, Military coup in Brazil by Gen Castello Branco, Sandy Koufax is 1st to strike out the side on 9 pitches, Separatists riot in Quebec, Jan & Dean release "Little Old Lady From Pasadena", North Vietnam fires on a US destroyer in Gulf of Tonkin (*ah crud, here we go*), "Man from U.N.C.L.E," premieres on NBC-TV and for the 1st time since 1800, residents of Wash DC permitted to vote.

"That this House considers that the continued issue of all the means of exchange be they coin, bank-notes or credit, largely passed on by cheques by private firms as an interest-bearing debt against the public should cease forthwith; that the Sovereign power and duty of issuing money in all forms should be returned to the Crown, then to be put into circulation free of all debt and interest obligations…" **Captain Henry Kerby British MP**

1965

The **Coinage Act of 1965** eliminated silver from dimes and quarters and reduced the silver content of the half dollar from 90% to 40%. Don't see much silver in your pocket change anymore.

> Riots: Watts, Chicago , France announces it will convert $150 million of its currency to gold, State funeral of Winston Churchill, Dutch government of Marijnen falls, Temptations' "My Girl" reaches #1, Cosmonaut Aleksei Leonov, leaving his spacecraft Voskhod 2 for 12 minutes, becomes the person to walk in space, India & Pakistan engage in border fight, Duncan patents "Pampers", Several Arab nations break ties with West Germany after it established diplomatic relations with Israel, Supreme Court of the United States decides on Griswold v. Connecticut, effectively legalizing the use of contraception by married couples (*I really don't know what to say about this, Really*), Israeli/Jordanian border fights, Several U.S. states and parts of Canada are hit by a series of blackouts lasting up to 13 hours, Congo military coup under Gen Mobutu, Press Kasavubu overthrown, "A Charlie Brown Christmas," premieres, Pope Paul VI & Orthodox Patriarch Athenagoras I simultaneously lift mutual excommunications that led to split of 2 churches in 1054, Borman & Lovell Splash down in Atlantic ends 2 week Gemini VII mission.

1966

First National Bank of Logan v. Walker Bank and Trust Co. the court held that state law concerning the branching of banks was to be upheld as the National Banking Act made such a provision. It is worth noting here that this decision overrode the Comptroller of the Currency who had issued the 'certificate' to allow the branching of these banks. Historically the Comptroller of the Currency has favored the branching of National Banks irrespective of state law.

> Military coup by Col. Jean-Bédell Bokassa in Central African Republic, LBJ says US should stay in South Vietnam until communist aggression ends, 1st soft landing on Moon (Soviet Luna 9), Military coup in Syria, Premier Obote grabs power in Uganda, Coup ousts Pres. Kwame Nkrumah of Ghana, anti-war demonstrators march in NYC, Medicare goes into effect, "Star Trek" premieres, UN deprives South Africa of Namibia and a coup in Burundi overthrows monarchy and more riots in the US.

The Federal Tax Lien Act of 1966 "The entire taxing and monetary systems are now under the Uniform Commercial Code"

1967

"I hate banks. They do nothing positive for anybody except take care of themselves. They're first in with their fees and first out when there's trouble." **Earl Warren Chief Justice of the Supreme Court**

> Grenada gains partial independence from Britain, Sonny & Cher release "Beat Goes On", "Smothers Brothers Comedy Hour" premieres, East Europeans attending World Amateur hockey championships in Vienna, ask for political asylum, Aretha Franklin records "Respect", Stalin's daughter Svetlana Allilujeva asks for political asylum in US, Harlem (NYC) voters defy Congress & reelect Adam Clayton Powell Jr., Military coup in Greece, Silver hits record $1.60 an ounce in London, Arab-Israeli Six Day War, Race riots all over the place, Congo uprising, Silver hits record $2.17 an ounce in New York, Gold pool nations pledge support of $35 per ounce gold price, People's Rep of South Yemen (Aden) gains independence from Britain, 1st human heart transplant performed (Dr. Christian Barnard, South Africa) and an unsuccessful coup against Greek King Constantine II.

Fannie Mae begins purchasing 'conventional' mortgages also!

1968

US Mint stops buying & selling gold.

2-tiered gold price negotiated in Wash DC by US & 6 European nations.

Congress repeals requirement for a gold reserve.

Truth in Lending Act requires banks to disclose loan terms & fees. *Imagine the heck out of that! Whatever were they thinking?*

> Martin Luther King and Bobby Kennedy Assassinations, Chicago Democratic National Convention Riots, US Surveyor 7 lands near lunar crater Tycho, "Rowan & Martin's Laugh-In" premieres on NBC (I love that show), Spy ship USS Pueblo & 83-man crew seized in Sea of Japan by N Korea, Israeli-Jordan border fight, 1st pulsar announced (CP

1919 by Jocelyn Burnell at Cambridge), Uprising in South Yemen, , lots of riots, Pres. Johnson signs 1968 Civil Rights Act, Gold reaches then record high ($39.35 per ounce) in London, USS Scorpion sinks with 99 men lost, Canada announces it will replace silver with nickel in coins, Revolt in Iraq, 650,000 Warsaw Pact troops invade Czechoslovakia, Swaziland gains independence from Britain, Detroit Tigers' Denny McLain's 30th victory of season, revolt in Panama and Mali military coup.

Fannie Mae spins off Ginnie Mae as a standalone.

1969

Richard Millhouse Nixon becomes President 1969 to 1974 Resigned from office Republican

"What kind of nation we will be, what kind of world we will live in, whether we shape the future in the image of our hopes, is ours to determine by our actions and our choices." **Richard Millhouse Nixon**

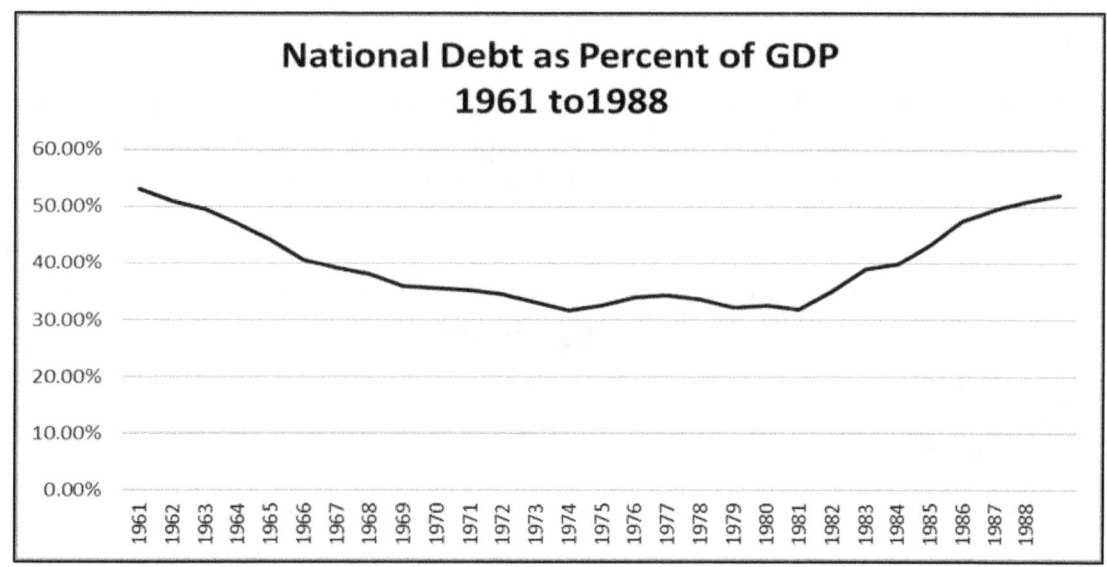

Peru nationalizes US oil interests.

Gold reaches then record high ($47 per ounce) in Paris.

More race and war riots, France begins arms embargo against Israel, **Beatles perform last live gig (42-min concert on roof of Apples HQ),** Al-Fatah-leader Yasser Arafat becomes president of PLO, military coup in Syria, Chinese-Russian border dispute leaves 100s dead, British invade Anguilla, Civil unrest in Rosario, Argentina, Who release rock opera "Tommy", Riots on the Caribbean island of Curaçao, 1st men on Moon, Neil

Armstrong and Edwin Aldrin Jr. from Apollo 11, Edward Kennedy pleads guilty to leaving scene of an accident a week after the Chappaquiddick car accident that killed Mary Jo Kopechne, Woodstock rock festival, revolution in Libya brings Col. Muammar al-Gaddafi to power, massacre of civilians at Mylai South Vietnam, by US is 1st reported and a bomb attack on a bank in Milan.

"Most Americans have no real understanding of the operation of the international money lenders. The accounts of the Federal Reserve System have never been audited. It operates outside the control of Congress and manipulates the credit of the United States." **Senator Barry Goldwater**

Recession of 1969 More **tightening of the monetary policy** as the Federal Reserve raises interest rates.

Social Security over-withholding, funds not issued to held as part of the 'trust fund' concept, are transferred thereby creating 'intra-governmental debt that is frequently not counted as part of the annual deficit.

Gus Levy takes over at **Goldman Sachs & Company**.

1970

Bank Holding Company Act Amendments allowed commercial banks, via holding companies, to take deposits and make commercial loans. Start saying goodbye to Glass-Steagall; while the Federal Reserve Board was responsible for determining what was a banking activity.

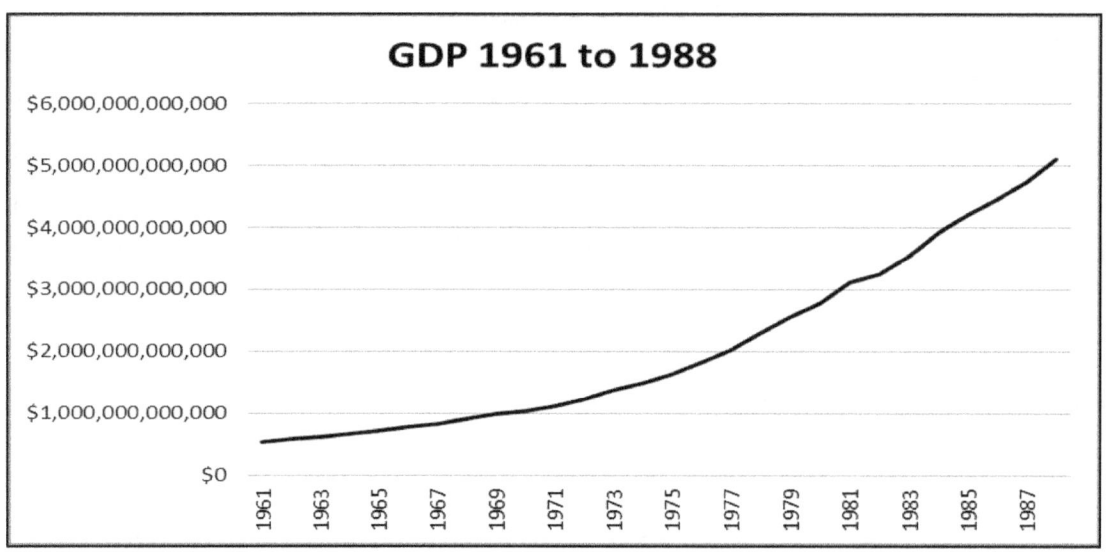

Federal Home Loan Mortgage Corporation (Freddie Mac) is created as a government sponsored enterprise to by mortgages from Savings & Loans.

Fannie Mae and Freddie Mac, their debt from buying mortgages does not show on federal governments balance sheets even though it is widely believed the government will come to their aid should they have trouble.

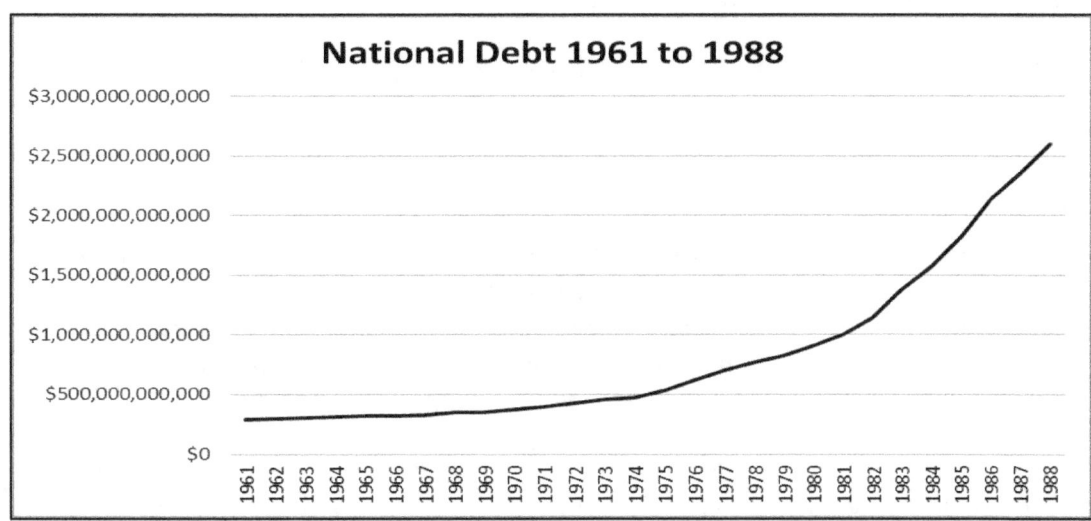

Ginnie Mae, a spin-off of Fannie Mae, makes up the first mortgage-backed securities, using VA & FHA mortgages and backs them up with a guarantee.

The Bank Secrecy Act of 1970 a.k.a. The Currency and Foreign Transactions Reporting Act. The act requires financial institutions to keep records of cash purchases of negotiable instruments, report daily cash transactions of $10,000 or more and to report transactions that might indicate money laundering, tax evasion, or any other type of criminal enterprise.

Marxist government takes over in Congo, Japan becomes 4th nation to put a satellite (Osumi) in orbit, US lowers voting age from 21 to 18, Cambodia military coup, Concorde makes its 1st supersonic flight, Qatar gains independence from Britain, Apollo 13 announces "Houston, we've got a problem!", Thor Heyerdahl crosses Atlantic on reed raft Ra, Tonga (formerly Friendly Islands) declares independence from UK, more riots in US, failed assassination attempt on Jordanian king Hussain, Palestinians seize 3 jetliners, riot to buy Rolling Stone tickets in Milano Italy, cyclone kills estimated 300,000 in Chittagong Bangladesh, flooding ravages Ganges delta, 200,000-1 million killed, Russia lands self-propelled rover on Moon, Pope Paul VI wounded in chest during a visit to Philippines, Soviet Venera 7 is 1st spacecraft to land on another planet (Venus) and Polish uprising fails.

UNITED STATES v. PHILLIPSBURG NATIONAL BANK AND TRUST COMPANY
et al In this case the court held that the merging of two banks in a town with three banks would

create an unfair advantage and reduce competition and thereby the community would suffer. Justice Brennan wrote the opinion and Justice Harlan wrote the dissenting opinion.

Remember the actions of Saxon a few years ago? Well here it the consequence.

Lots of people talk about this next Supreme Court case.

INVESTMENT COMPANY INSTITUTE v CAMP

During the 1960s regulators had already been giving banks greater leeway concerning securities.

First National City Bank wanted to and was in fact operating a collective investment fund. (*That's like a Mutual Fund*) The Bank sought and received the approval of the Office of the Comptroller of the Currency (*here we go again with OCC*) as required by law. This ticked off a bunch of people operating Mutual Funds in the area and they went to court. The District Court decided the bank could not operate a Mutual fund, the Court of Appeals said sure they can and the Supreme Court said no way. Also the Securities and Exchange Commission thought it was alright.

The opinion of the court was written by Justice Stewart and is included here because I believe it clearly covers the issues and circumstances that got us into mess. Additionally it provides some historical perspective. The opinion is in legalese and may take a little effort to wade through but I believe the effort is time well spent and will add clarity to the events that follow.

There were two dissenting opinions by Justices Harlan and Blackmun that are not included. You may conclude that those opinions rationalize the methods by which we came to our current state.

I

These companion cases involve a double-barreled assault upon the efforts of a national bank to go into the business of operating a mutual investment fund. The petitioners in No. 61 are an association of open-end investment companies and several individual such companies. They brought an action in the United States District Court for the District of Columbia, attacking portions of Regulation 9 issued by the Comptroller of the Currency,[1] on the ground that this Regulation, in purporting to authorize banks to establish and operate collective investment funds, sought to permit activities prohibited to national banks or their affiliates by various provisions of the Glass-Steagall Banking Act of 1933, 48 Stat. 162.[2] The petitioners also specifically attacked the Comptroller's approval of the application of First National City Bank of New York for permission to establish and operate a collective investment fund. In No. 59 the National Association of Securities Dealers filed a petition in the United States Court of Appeals for the District of Columbia Circuit seeking review of an order of the Securities and Exchange Commission that partially exempted the collective investment fund of First National City Bank of New York from various provisions of the Investment Company Act of 1940.[3]

In No. 61 the District Court concluded that the challenged provisions of Regulation 9 were invalid under the Glass-Steagall Act.[4] The Comptroller and First National City Bank appealed from this decision, and the appeal was consolidated with the petition for review in No. 59. The Court of

Appeals held that the actions taken by the Securities and Exchange Commission and the Comptroller were fully consonant with the statutes committed to their regulatory supervision. Accordingly, it affirmed the order of the Commission and reversed the judgment of the District Court.5 We granted certiorari to consider important questions presented under federal regulatory statutes.6 For the reasons that follow, we hold Regulation 9 invalid insofar as it authorizes the sale of interests in an investment fund of the type established by First National City Bank pursuant to the Comptroller's approval. This disposition makes it unnecessary to consider the propriety of the action of the Securities and Exchange Commission in affording this fund exemption from certain of the provisions of the Investment Company Act of 1940.

* In No. 61 it is urged at the outset that petitioners lack standing to question whether national banks may legally enter a field in competition with them. This contention is foreclosed by Association of Data Processing Service v. Camp, 397 U.S. 150, 90 S.Ct. 827, 25 L.Ed.2d 184. There we held that companies that offered data processing services to the general business community had standing to seek judicial review of a ruling by the Comptroller that national banks could make data processing services available to other banks and to bank customers. We held that data processing companies were sufficiently injured by the competition that the Comptroller had authorized to create a case or controversy. The injury to the petitioners in the instant case is indistinguishable. We also concluded that Congress did not intend 'to preclude judicial review of administrative rulings by the Comptroller as to the legitimate scope of activities available to national banks under (the National Bank Act).' 397 U.S., at 157, 90 S.Ct., at 832. This is precisely the review that the petitioners have sought in this case. Finally, we concluded that Congress had arguably legislated against the competition that the petitioners sought to challenge, and from which flowed their injury. We noted that whether Congress had indeed prohibited such competition was a question for the merits. In the discussion that follows in the balance of this opinion we deal with the merits of the petitioners' contentions and conclude that Congress did legislate against the competition that the petitioners challenge. There can be no real question, therefore, of the petitioners' standing in the light of the Data Processing case. See also Arnold Tours v. Camp, 400 U.S. 45, 91 S.Ct. 158, 27 L.Ed.2d 179.

II

The issue before us is whether the Comptroller of the Currency may, consistently with the banking laws, authorize a national bank to offer its customers the opportunity to invest in a stock fund created and maintained by the bank. Before 1963 national banks were prohibited by administrative regulation from offering this service. The Board of Governors of the Federal Reserve System which until 1962 had regulatory jurisdiction over all the trust activities of national banks, allowed the collective investment of trust assets only for 'the investment of funds held for true fiduciary purposes.' The applicable regulation, Regulation F, specified that 'the operation of such Common Trust Funds as investment trusts for other than strictly fiduciary purposes is hereby prohibited.' The Board consistently ruled that it was improper for a bank to use 'a Common Trust Fund' as an investment trust attracting money seeking investment alone and to embark upon what would be in effect the sale of participations in a Common Trust Fund to the public as investments.' 26 Fed.Reserve Bull. 393 (1940); see also 42 Fed.Reserve Bull. 228 (1956); 41 Fed.Reserve Bull. 142 (1955).

In 1962 Congress transferred jurisdiction over most of the trust activities of national banks from the Board of Governors of the Federal Reserve System to the Comptroller of the Currency, without modifying any provision of substantive law. Pub.L. 87—722, 76 Stat. 668, 12 U.S.C. 92a. The Comptroller thereupon solicited suggestions for improving the regulations applicable to trust activities. Subsequently, new regulations were proposed which expressly authorized the collective investment of monies delivered to the bank for investment management, so-called managing agency accounts. These proposed regulations were officially promulgated in 1963 with changes not material here.7 In 1965 the First National City Bank of New York submitted for the Comptroller's approval a plan for the collective investment of managing agency accounts. The Comptroller promptly approved the plan, and it is now in operation. This plan, which departs in some respects from the plan envisaged by the Comptroller's Regulation, is expected, the briefs tell us, to be a model for other banks which decide to offer their customers a collective investment service.

III

Under the plan the bank customer tenders between $10,000 and $50,000 to the bank, together with an authorization making the bank the customer's managing agent. The customer's investment is added to the fund, and a written evidence of participation is issued which expresses in 'units of participation' the customer's proportionate interest in fund assets. Units of participation are freely redeemable, and transferable to anyone who has executed a managing agency agreement with the bank. The fund is registered as an investment company under the Investment Company Act of 1940. The bank is the underwriter of the fund's units of participation within the meaning of that Act. The fund has filed a registration statement pursuant to the Securities Act of 1933. The fund is supervised by a five-member committee elected annually by the participants pursuant to the Investment Company Act of 1940. The Securities and Exchange Commission has exempted the fund from the Investment Company Act to the extent that a majority of this committee may be affiliated with the bank, and it is expected that a majority always will be officers in the bank's trust and investment division.9 The actual custody and investment of fund assets is carried out by the bank as investment advisor pursuant to a management agreement. Although the Investment Company Act requires that this management agreement be approved annually by the committee, including a majority of the unaffiliated members, or by the participants, it is expected that the bank will continue to be investment advisor.

Section 16 of the Glass-Steagall Act as amended, 12 U.S.C. 24, Seventh, provides that the 'business of dealing in securities and stock (by a national bank) shall be limited to purchasing and selling such securities and stock without recourse, solely upon the order, and for the account of, customers, and in no case for its own account * * *. Except as hereinafter provided or otherwise permitted by law, nothing herein contained shall authorize the purchase by (a national bank) for its own account of any shares of stock of any corporation.'10 The petitioners contend that a purchase of stock by a bank's investment fund is a purchase of stock by a bank for its own account in violation of this section.

Section 16 also provides that a national bank 'shall not underwrite any issue of securities or stock.' And § 21 of the same Act, 12 U.S.C. 378(a), provides that 'it shall be unlawful—(1) For any person, firm, corporation, association, business trust, or other similar organization, engaged in the business of issuing, underwriting, selling, or distributing, at wholesale or retail, or through syndicate participation, stocks, bonds, debentures, notes, or other securities, to engage at the same time to any extent whatever in the business of (deposit banking).' The petitioners contend that the creation and operation of an investment fund by a bank which offers to its customers the opportunity to purchase an interest in the fund's assets constitutes the issuing, underwriting, selling or distributing of securities or stocks in violation of these sections.

IV

The questions raised by the petitioners are novel and substantial. National banks were granted trust powers in 1913. Federal Reserve Act § 11, 38 Stat. 261. The first common trust fund was organized in 1927, and such funds were expressly authorized by the Federal Reserve Board by Regulation F promulgated in 1937. Report on Commingled or Common Trust Funds Administered by Banks and Trust Companies, H.R.Doc.No.476, 76th Cong., 2d Sess., 4—5 (1939). For at least a generation, therefore, there has been no reason to doubt that a national bank can, consistently with the banking laws, commingle trust funds on the one hand, and act as a managing agent on the other. No provision of the banking law suggests that it is improper for a national bank to pool trust assets, or to act as a managing agent for individual customers, or to purchase stock for the account of its customers. But the union of these powers gives birth to an investment fund whose activities are of a different character. The differences between the investment fund that the Comptroller has authorized and a conventional open-end mutual fund are subtle at best, and it is undisputed that this bank investment fund finds itself in direct competition with the mutual fund industry. One would suppose that the business of a mutual fund consists of buying stock 'for its own account' and of 'issuing' and 'selling' 'stock' or 'other securities' evidencing an undivided and redeemable interest in the assets of the fund.11 On their face, §§ 16 and 21 of the Glass-Steagall Act appear clearly to prohibit this activity by national banks.

But we cannot come lightly to the conclusion that the Comptroller has authorized activity that violates the banking laws. It is settled that courts should give great weight to any reasonable construction of a regulatory statute adopted by the agency charged with the enforcement of that statute. The Comptroller of the Currency is charged with the enforcement of the banking laws to an extent that warrants the invocation of this principle with respect to his deliberative conclusions as to the meaning of these laws. See First National Bank v. Missouri, 263 U.S. 640, 658, 44 S.Ct. 213, 215, 68 L.Ed. 486, 493.

The difficulty here is that the Comptroller adopted no expressly articulated position at the administrative level as to the meaning and impact of the provisions of §§ 16 and 21 as they affect bank investment funds. The Comptroller promulgated Regulation 9 without opinion or accompanying statement. His subsequent report to Congress did not advert to the prohibitions of the Glass-Steagall Act. Comptroller of the Currency, 101st Annual Report 14—15 (1963).13 **To be sure, counsel for the Comptroller in the course of this litigation and specifically in his briefs and oral argument in this Court, has rationalized the basis of Regulation 9 with great professional competence. But this is hardly tantamount to an administrative interpretation of §§ 16 and 21.** In Burlington Truck Lines v. United States, 371 U.S. 156, 83 S.Ct. 239, 9 L.Ed.2d 207, we said, 'The courts may not accept appellate counsel's post hoc rationalizations for agency action * * *. For the courts to substitute their or counsel's discretion for that of the (agency) is incompatible with the orderly functioning of the process of judicial review.' Id., at 168—169, 83 S.Ct. at 246. Congress has delegated to the administrative official and not to appellate counsel the responsibility for elaborating and enforcing statutory commands. It is the administrative official and not appellate counsel who possesses the expertise that can enlighten and rationalize the search for the meaning and intent of Congress. Quite obviously the Comptroller should not grant new authority to national banks until he is satisfied that the exercise of this authority will not violate the intent of the banking laws. If he faces such questions only after he has acted, there is substantial danger that the momentum generated by initial approval may seriously impair the enforcement of the banking laws that Congress enacted.

There is no dispute that one of the objectives of the Glass-Steagall Act was to prohibit commercial banks, banks that receive deposits subject to repayment, lend money, discount and negotiate promissory notes and the like, from going into the investment banking business. Many commercial banks were indirectly engaged in the investment banking business when the Act was passed in 1933. Even before the passage of the Act it was generally believed that it was improper for a commercial bank to engage in investment banking directly.[14] But in 1908 banks began the practice of establishing security affiliates that engaged in, inter alia, and business of floating bond issues and, less frequently, underwriting stock issues.[15] The Glass-Steagall Act confirmed that national banks could not engage in investment banking directly, and in addition made affiliation with an organization so engaged illegal. One effect of the Act was to abolish the security affiliates of commercial banks.[16]

It is apparent from the legislative history of the Act why Congress felt that this drastic step was necessary. The failure of the Bank of United States in 1930 was widely attributed to that bank's activities with respect to its numerous securities affiliates.[17] Moreover, Congress was concerned that commercial banks in general and member banks of the Federal Reserve System in particular had both aggravated and been damaged by stock market decline partly because of their direct and indirect involvement in the trading and ownership of speculative securities.[18] The Glass-Steagall Act reflected a determination that policies of competition, convenience, or expertise which might otherwise support the entry of commercial banks into the investment banking business were outweighed by the 'hazards' and 'financial dangers' that arise when commercial banks engage in the activities proscribed by the Act.[19]

The hazards that Congress had in mind were not limited to the obvious danger that a bank might invest its own assets in frozen or otherwise imprudent stock or security investments. For often securities affiliates had operated without direct access to the assets of the bank. This was because securities affiliates had frequently been established with capital paid in by the bank's stockholders, or by the public, or through the allocation of a legal dividend on bank stock for this purpose.[20] The legislative history of the Glass-Steagall Act shows that Congress also had in mind and repeatedly focused on the more subtle hazards that arise when a commercial bank goes beyond the business of acting as fiduciary or managing agent and enters the investment banking business either directly or by establishing an affiliate to hold and sell particular investments. This course places new promotional and other pressures on the bank which in turn create new temptations. For example, pressures are created because the bank and the affiliate are closely associated in the public mind, and should the affiliate fare badly, public confidence in the bank might be impaired. And since public confidence is essential to the solvency of a bank, there might exist a natural temptation to shore up the affiliate through unsound loans or other aid.21 Moreover, the pressure to sell a particular investment and to make the affiliate successful might create a risk that the bank would make its credit facilities more freely available to those companies in whose stock or securities the affiliate has invested or become otherwise involved. Congress feared that banks might even go so far as to make unsound loans to such companies.22 In any event; it was thought that the bank's salesman's interest might impair its ability to function as an impartial source of credit.23

Congress was also concerned that bank depositors might suffer losses on investments that they purchased in reliance on the relationship between the bank and its affiliate.24 This loss of customer good will might 'become an important handicap to a bank during a major period of security market deflation.'25 More broadly, Congress feared that the promotional needs of investment banking might lead commercial banks to lend their reputation for prudence and restraint to the enterprise of selling particular stocks and securities, and that this could not be done without that reputation being undercut by the risks necessarily incident to the investment banking business.26 There was also perceived the danger that when commercial banks were subject to the promotional demands of investment banking, they might be tempted to make loans to customers with the expectation that the loan would facilitate the purchase of stocks and securities.27 There was evidence before Congress that loans for investment written by commercial banks had done much to feed the speculative fever of the late 1920's.28 Senator Glass made it plain that it was 'the fixed purpose of Congress' not to see the facilities of commercial banking diverted into speculative operations by the aggressive and promotional character of the investment banking business.29

Another potential hazard that very much concerned Congress arose from the plain conflict between the promotional interest of the investment banker and the obligation of the commercial banker to render disinterested investment advice. Senator Bulkley stated:

'Obviously, the banker who has nothing to sell to his depositors is much better qualified to advice disinterestedly and to regard diligently the safety of depositors than the banker who uses the list of depositors in his savings department to distribute circulars concerning the advantages of this, that, or the other investment on which the bank is to receive an originating profit or an underwriting profit or a distribution profit or a trading profit or any combination of such profits.'30

Congress had before it evidence that security affiliates might be driven to unload excessive holdings through the trust department of the sponsor bank.31 Some witnesses at the hearings expressed the view that this practice constituted self-dealing in violation of the trustee's obligation of loyalty, and indeed that it would be improper for a bank's trust department to purchase anything from the bank's securities affiliate.32

In sum, Congress acted to keep commercial banks out of the investment banking business largely because it believed that the promotional incentives of investment banking and the investment banker's pecuniary stake in the success of particular investment opportunities was destructive of prudent and disinterested commercial banking and of public confidence in the commercial banking system. As Senator Bulkley put it: 'If we want banking service to be strictly banking service, without the expectation of additional profits in selling something to customers, we must keep the banks out of the investment security business.'33

V

The language that Congress chose to achieve this purpose includes the prohibitions of § 16 that a national bank 'shall not underwrite any issue of securities or stock' and shall not purchase 'for its own account * * * any shares of stock of any corporation,' and the prohibition of § 21 against engaging in 'the business of issuing, underwriting, selling, or distributing * * * stocks, bonds, debentures, notes, or other securities.' In this litigation the Comptroller takes the position that the operation of a bank investment fund is consistent with these provisions, because participating interests in such a fund are not 'securities' within the meaning of the Act. It is argued that a bank investment fund simply makes available to the small investor the benefit of investment management by a bank trust department which would otherwise be available only to large investors, and that the operation of an investment fund creates no problems that are not present whenever a bank invests in securities for the account of customers.

But there is nothing in the phrasing of either § 16 or § 21 that suggests a narrow reading of the word 'securities.' To the contrary, the breadth of the term is implicit in the fact that the antecedent statutory language encompasses not only equity securities but also securities representing debt. And certainly there is nothing in the language of these provisions to suggest that the sale of an interest in the business of buying, holding, and selling stocks for investment is to be distinguished from the sale of an interest in a commercial or industrial enterprise.

Indeed, there is direct evidence that Congress specifically contemplated that the word 'security' includes an interest in an investment fund. The Glass-Steagall Act was the product of hearings conducted pursuant to Senate Resolution 71 which included among the topics to be investigated the impact on the banking system of the formation of investment and security trusts.34 The subcommittee found that one of the activities in which bank security affiliates engaged was that of an investment trust: 'buying and selling securities acquired purely for investment or speculative purposes.'35 Since Congress generally intended to divorce commercial banking from the kinds of activities in which bank security affiliates engaged, there is reason to believe that Congress explicitly intended to prohibit a national bank from operating an investment trust.36

But, in any event, we are persuaded that the purposes for which Congress enacted the Glass-Steagall Act leave no room for the conclusion that a participation in a bank investment fund is not a 'security' within the meaning of the Act. From the perspective of competition, convenience, and expertise, there are arguments to be made in support of allowing commercial banks to enter the investment banking business. But Congress determined that the hazards outlined above made it necessary to prohibit this activity to commercial banks. Those same hazards are clearly present when a bank undertakes to operate an investment fund.

A bank that operates an investment fund has a particular investment to sell. It is not a matter of indifference to the bank whether the customer buys an interest in the fund or makes some other investment. If its customers cannot be persuaded to invest in the bank's investment fund, the bank will lose their investment business and the fee which that business would have brought in. Even as to accounts large enough to qualify for individual investment management, there might be a potential for a greater profit if the investment were placed in the fund rather than in individually selected securities, because of fixed costs and economies of scale. The mechanics of operating an investment fund might also create promotional pressure. When interests in the fund were redeemed, the bank would be effectively faced with the choice of selling stocks from the fund's portfolio or of selling new participations to cover redemptions. The bank might have a pecuniary incentive to choose the latter course in order to avoid the cost of stock transactions undertaken solely for redemption purposes.

Promotional incentives might also be created by the circumstance that the bank's fund would be in direct competition with mutual funds that, from the point of view of the investor, offered an investment opportunity comparable to that offered by the bank. The bank would want to be in a position to show to the prospective customer that its fund was more attractive than the mutual funds offered by others. The bank would have a salesman's stake in the performance of the fund, for if fund were less successful than the competition the bank would lose business and the resulting fees.

A bank that operated an investment fund would necessarily put its reputation and facilities squarely behind that fund and the investment opportunity that the fund offered. The investments of the fund might be conservative or speculative, but in any event the success or failure of the fund would be a matter of public record. Imprudent or unsuccessful management of the bank's investment fund could bring about a perhaps unjustified loss of public confidence in the bank itself. If imprudent management should place the fund in distress, a bank might find itself under pressure to rescue the fund through measures inconsistent with sound banking.

The promotional and other pressures incidental to the operation of an investment fund, in other words, involve the same kinds of potential abuses that Congress intended to guard against when it legislated against bank security affiliates. It is not the slightest reflection on the integrity of the mutual fund industry to say that the traditions of that industry are not necessarily the conservative traditions of commercial banking. The needs and interests of a mutual fund enterprise more nearly approximate those of securities underwriting, the activity in which bank security affiliates were primarily engaged. When a bank puts itself in competition with mutual funds, the bank must make an accommodation to the kind of ground rules that Congress firmly concluded could not be prudently mixed with the business of commercial banking.

And there are other potential hazards of the kind Congress sought to eliminate with the passage of the Glass-Steagall Act. The bank's stake in the investment fund might distort its credit decisions or lead to unsound loans to the companies in which the fund had invested. The bank might exploit its confidential relationship with its commercial and industrial creditors for the benefit of the fund. The bank might undertake, directly or indirectly, to make its credit facilities available to the fund or to render other aid to the fund inconsistent with the best interests of the bank's depositors. The bank might make loans to facilitate the purchase of interests in the fund. The bank might divert talent and resources from its commercial banking operation to the promotion of the fund. Moreover, because the bank would have a stake in a customer's making a particular investment decision—the decision to invest in the bank's investment fund—the customer might doubt the motivation behind the bank's recommendation that he make such an investment. If the fund investment should turn out badly there would be a danger that the bank would lose the good will of those customers who had invested in the fund. It might be unlikely that disenchantment would go so far as to threaten the solvency of the bank. But because banks are dependent on the confidence of their customers, the risk would not be unreal.

These are all hazards that are not present when a bank undertakes to purchase stock for the account of its individual customers or to commingle assets which it has received for a true fiduciary purpose rather than for investment. These activities, unlike the operation of an investment fund, do not give rise to a promotional or salesman's stake in a particular investment; they do not involve an enterprise in direct competition with aggressively promoted funds offered by other investment companies; they do not entail a threat to public confidence in the bank itself; and they do not impair the bank's ability to give disinterested service as a fiduciary or managing agent. In short, there is a plain difference between the sale of fiduciary services and the sale of investments.37

The Glass-Steagall Act was a prophylactic measure directed against conditions that the experience of the 1920's showed to be great potentials for abuse. The literal terms of that Act clearly prevent what the Comptroller has sought to authorize here. Because the potential hazards and abuses that flow from a bank's entry into the mutual investment business are the same basic hazards and abuses that Congress intended to eliminate almost 40 years ago, we cannot but apply the terms of the federal statute as they were written. We conclude that the operation of an investment fund of the kind approved by the Comptroller involves a bank in the underwriting, issuing, selling, and distributing of securities in violation of §§ 16 and 21 of the Glass-Steagall Act. Accordingly, we reverse the judgment in No. 61 and vacate the judgment in No. 59.

It is so ordered.

When the Supreme Court publishes the decision everybody and their third cousins' ex-mother-in-law get all excited.

> The all excited aforementioned third cousins' ex-mother-in-law runs to the phone and calls her 2nd daughter Gracie (a 32 year old plastic bombshell going on 14 who happens to be married to Big Bank Guy).
>
> Mother-in-law says, "Gracie get off the chaise lounge by the large kidney shaped pool attended by a cute cabana boy and tell 'Big Bank Guy' he's got to get some lawyers together to start writing new banking regulations."
>
> Gracie responds, "Aw Ma, cabana boy is cleaning the pool."
>
> "Listen Gracie if you want that place in Barbados you gotta tell 'Big Bank Guy' the Supreme Court just gave Bankers permission to get just about whatever they want if they can get Mr. Comptroller of the Currency to justify it upfront," rightfully frustrated aforementioned third cousins ex-mother-in-law says.

Gracie rolls over on the chaise giving the cute cabana boy a better view, poutingly saying, "Ma you know he hates it when I start telling him what to do. I'll never get that Tiffany necklace if I tick him off now." *Apparently it is Ma that wants the place in Barbados what with Gracie having a cute cabana boy already.*

Aforementioned third cousins' ex-mother-in-law tells Gracie the 32 year old plastic bombshell going on 14, "Just tell him you got a line on a gold mine and he'll perk right up."

Gracie the 32 year old plastic bombshell going on 14 cringes, "Ok Ma but he perked up last night, I'll give it a try" and hangs up wondering if she should roll over again because cute cabana boy seems to have attention deficit disorder. Gracie can't imagine he might be 'gay'.

Aforementioned third cousins' ex-mother-in-law shrugs telling herself 'there is only so much she can do with a 32 year old plastic bombshell going on 14'.

The bold lines in the decision basically tells regulators to explain fully when making rulings and not after. Hence regulators have greater success in getting past the Supreme Court in the future.

Goldman Sachs & Company gets hit with several law suits over the failure of the Penn Central Transportation Company. Seems the loss was around $80 million of which the greatest percentage was issued thru the Company. The Company also opens its first International office in London.

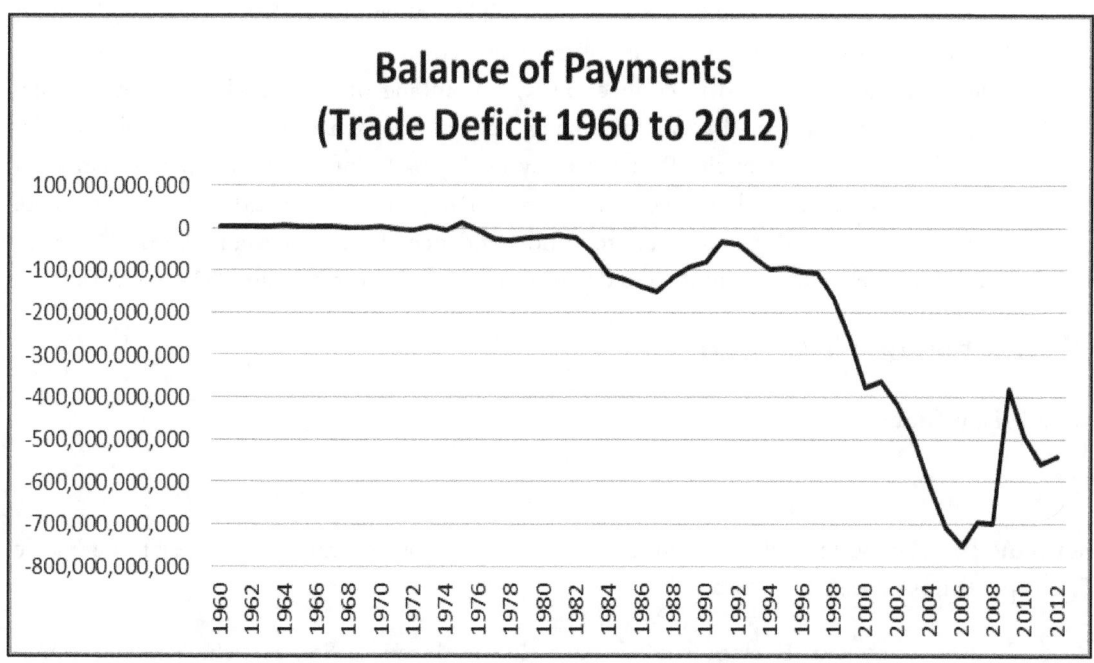

1971

President Nixon takes the United States off the gold standard because too many people were demanding gold and it was leaving the country and the treasury, **'Nixon Shock'**. This is similar to the problem Jefferson had with silver in 1806 but is attached to the **Bretton Woods System**.

> *Just a thought here: that maintaining a gold or silver standard has a down side to it. When that metal leaves the treasury the amount of gold or silver supporting the currency is diminished theoretically becoming zero. Many will argue against this notion and talk about currency and valuations and much more. The bottom line is that a nation still needs currency to operate internally to the extent that transactions must continue for the economy to thrive. Recall the situation in Ohio, way back when, when they decided to have their banks issue notes because there was too little federal currency available. Additionally with a deficit in the balance of payments between countries more gold and/or silver would be leaving the country especially as Richard Nixon decides to open China and we all know where so much is imported from these days.*

> *Another issue with a metallic standard it that there is a limited supply of precious metals on the planet but apparently not a limited supply of people. Just cipher on it a bit.*

Freddie Mac issues its first Mortgage Participation Certificate security, an MBS (Mortgage Backed Security) of ordinary/regular mortgages.

> Cigarette advertisements banned on TV, Idi Amin ousts Milton Obote to become dictator of Uganda, Swiss men accept female suffrage, after 1,200 years Britain abandons 12-shilling system for decimal, Chile president Allende nationalizes banks/copper mines, United Kingdom lifts all restrictions on gold ownership, Sri Lanka insurrection, more riots in US, Samuel Lee Gravely Jr. becomes 1st black admiral in US Navy, NY Times began publishing "Pentagon Papers", more riots, failed attempt on King Hassan II Shirat Morocco, Sudan military coup, the dollar is allowed to float against the yen for the first time, 6 Klansmen arrested in connection with bombing of 10 school buses, 90 Russian diplomats expelled from Britain for spying, Indian troops partly aided by Mukti Bahini (Bengali guerrillas) defeat the Pakistan army in the Battle of Garibpur, Cambodian Civil War: Khmer Rouge rebels, The Libertarian Party of the United States is formed, Bangladesh (East Pakistan) declares independence from Pakistan, Don McLean's "American Pie" released and the US dollar is devalued 7.9% in Holland ($1=Ÿ3,245).

US ends ban on China trade.

Attica Prison Riots

1972

"Supreme Excellence in warfare lies in the destruction of your enemy's will to resist in advance of perceptible hostilities." **Sun Tzu**

> NASA announces development of space shuttle, Japanese Sgt. Shoichi Yokoi is found hiding in a Guam jungle, where he had been since the end of World War II, Bloody Sunday: British soldiers shoot on Catholics in Londonderry, Military coup ousts civilian

government of Ghana, 1st scientific hand-held calculator (HP-35) introduced ($395), US airlines begin mandatory inspection of passengers & baggage, slag heap dam collapses above Buffalo Creek WV, baseball players' strike ends after 13 days, five White House plumbers apprehended after second burglary of Democratic National. HQ, Watergate, Bloody Friday: 22 IRA-bombs explode in Belfast, Gold hits record $70 an ounce in London, thieves steal 18 paintings from the Montreal Museum of Fine Arts, Palestinian terrorists kill 11 Israelis at 1972 Munich Olympics, Tanzania troops march in to Uganda and Nolan Bushnell (co-founder of Atari) releases Pong (the commercially successful video game).

1973

1973–75 Recession Because of spending for the Viet Nam War and OPECs huge increases on oil prices we got stagflation, a Stock Market Crash, higher unemployment and a recession

Wounded Knee Incident , Mali & Niger break diplomatic relations with Israel, West African Economic Community formed (Benin, Ivory Coast, Mali, Mauritania, Niger, Senegal, Upper Volta), Roe v. Wade: US Supreme Court legalizes some abortions, jury finds Watergate defendants Liddy & McCord guilty on all counts, Comic strip "Hagar The Horrible" debuted, US dollar devalues 10%, gold goes up $10 overnight to record $95 an ounce in London, Japan allows its citizens to own gold, terrorist bombings in Cyprus, Gold hits record $102.50 an ounce in London, President Nixon confesses his role in Watergate cover-up and is forced to resign (*darn straight*), President of Uruguay dissolves Parliament and heads a coup d'état, Israel at War, VP Spiro T Agnew pleads no contest to tax evasion & resigns, 5 month oil embargo by Arab states against US & Netherlands, Bosporus Bridge in Istanbul, Turkey is completed and Greek regime attacks students with tanks.

1974

Gerald Ford becomes President as Nixon resigns 1974 to 1977 Republican

Equal Credit Opportunity Act basically it provides for significant sanctions on financial institutions if they are found guilty of discrimination on the basis of race, color, religion, national origin, sex, marital status, or age.

Franklin National Bank collapses due to fraud and mismanagement; at the time it was the largest bank failure in the history of the United States.

Silver hits record $3.40 an ounce in New York, gold hits record $161.31/silver hits record $3.97 an ounce in London, silver futures hit record $4.81½ an ounce in London, gold hits record $188 an ounce in Paris, military coup in Niger, India becomes 6th nation to explode an atomic bomb, US & Saudi Arabia sign military-economic contract, military coup in Ethiopia, Turkey invades Cyprus, Richard, "I am not a crook", Nixon resigns presidency, VP Gerald Ford becomes 38th Pres., Coup in East-Timor, gold becomes legal to own in the US and Franklin Mint strikes Panama's Gold 100 balboa coin.

Household debt is 60% of disposable personal income.

1975

Pres. Gerald Ford signs $2.3 Billion loan-authorization for New York City.

Bomb explodes at annex of Amsterdam metro station, Portugal military coup under general Spinola fails, Kurds end fight against Iraqi army, Cambodia President Lon Nol flees before Red Khmer, last US helicopter leaves US embassy grounds, Saigon surrenders, hail stones as large as tennis balls hit Wernerville Tenn., India annexes Principality of Sikkim, 1st oil pumped from North Sea oilfield, Italy's Communist party PCI wins, Jimmy Hoffa disappears in suburban Detroit, Pakistani military coup, star in constellation Cygnus goes nova becoming 4th brightest in sky, Czech tennis star Martina Navratilova asks for US political asylum in New York City during the US Open and Papua New Guinea gains independence from Australia.

Admiral Chester Ward publishes **"Kissinger ON THE COUCH."** In it he asserts about the Council on Foreign Relations. "The most powerful cliques in these elitist groups have one objective in common: they want to bring about the surrender of the sovereignty and national independence of the United States."

From Money Magazine

"The study of money, above all other fields in economics, is one in which complexity is used to disguise truth or to evade truth, not to reveal it. The process by which banks create money is so simple the mind is repelled. With something so important, a deeper mystery seems only decent."
John Kenneth Galbraith

Home Mortgage Disclosure Act (HMDA) creates requirements for financial institutions to collect loan information, and report the information to the government and make it publicly available.

1976

Venezuela nationalizes oil fields.

The Federal Land Policy and Management Act of 1976 ended homesteading. The federal government would retain control of western public lands. The exception was in Alaska, the law allowed homesteading until 1986.

> Military coup in Ecuador, Morocco-Algeria battles in Westerly Sahara, British pound falls below $2 for 1st time, Conrail takes over operations from six bankrupt railroads in the northeastern U.S., The Apple I is created, gold ownership legalized in Australia, Teton Dam in Idaho bursts, raid on Entebbe-Israel rescues 229 Air France passengers, Hank Aaron hits 755th & last home, 8.2 Tangshan earthquake kills estimated 240,000 Chinese, flash flood in Big Thompson Canyon Colo. on Route 34, kills 139 (*I drove out of that Canyon a few minutes before the road in the narrows was covered with water*), Mexican peso devalued, Supreme Court lifts 1972 ban on death penalty for convicted murderers, Syrian army

conquerors Beirut, Mozambique closes border with Rhodesia, Morocco & Mauretania break diplomatic relations with Algeria and 8 Ohio National Guardsmen indicted for shooting 4 Kent State students.

From here on out the United States imports more than it exports. This represents manufacturing jobs that are gone and likely to stay gone.

The United States government moves to a totally 'fiat' system when any references to gold are removed from the definition of the dollar.

John L. Weinberg and John C. Whitehead become co-senior partners of **Goldman Sachs.**

1977

Jimmy Carter becomes President 1977 to 1981 Democratic

"The best way to enhance freedom in other lands is to demonstrate here that our democratic system is worthy of emulation." **Jimmy Carter**

Community Reinvestment Act was meant to ensure that those who had limited means, were living in less than desirable geographic areas, or were minorities had better chances of receiving loans for homes stopping the process of 'red-lining'.

CRA would be blamed by many as the root cause of the sub-prime mess. Maybe this is simply a case of good and proper intentions gone awry. Awry, because it became a political tool used to get votes instead of a planned and structured effort for the 'general welfare' of the nation.

I also found it interesting that this act came the year after the United States became a net exporting nation.

Salomon Brothers tries to market a "private label" mortgage backed security (doesn't have GSE mortgages). It flops.

> Snow falls in Miami, Florida this is the only time in the history of the city that snowfall has occurred. It also fell in the Bahamas, Fleetwood Mac's "Rumors" released, massacre of Atocha in Madrid, Bank of America adopts the name VISA for their credit cards, members of Baader-Meinhoff jailed for life after a trial lasting nearly 2 years in Stuttgart, Germany, Moluccan extremists hold 105 schoolchildren & 50 others hostage on a hijacked train in Netherlands, Trans Alaska oil pipeline completed, Coup in Seychelles, Pakistan's army, led by Gen Mohammad Zia ul-Haq, seizes power, Libyan-Egyptian border fights, Radio Shack issues a press release introducing TRS-80 computer 25 existed, within weeks thousands were ordered, Ethiopia drops diplomatic relations with Somalia and West German commandos liberate Boeing 737, 86 hostages at Mogadishu,.

Deregulation is the buzz word because of the need for profits that were inhibited by the OPEC/oil thing and a general slowdown.

President Carter puts a **stimulus package** into play.

According to the Financial Crisis Inquiry Commission report of Jan 2011 the Financial Sector held $3 trillion in debt and the US GDP is about $2.3 trillion, 1.3 times GDP. See 2007 for how that changed.

Larry Fink of First Boston and Lewis Ranieri of Salomon develop **securitization**. Mortgages are pooled together then the 'pool' is sliced into what are called tranches and sold off to investors. This eventually becomes huge business and becomes a large part of the 2008 crash.

Time out

The Shadow Banking system, investment banks and hedge funds etc., soon start becoming more and more important to the economy by providing credit or 'credit opportunities'. As we saw during the 1950s commercial banking was losing market share to the non-regulated banking system already. By becoming of increasing importance in that their ability to evolve products in an unregulated market place allowed for exorbitant amounts of money to support the growth of the economy. We will see those 'financial products' develop further over the next thirty years and we will see the efforts made to be sure this newly evolving market avoid regulation.

Often the literature states a belief the reason the 'Shadow Banking' system could grow so rapidly was it 'did not have to endure the 'costs of regulation'. While there are 'associated paper work costs' with being a regulated bank this could also mean a cost as not having access to additional funds because of regulation thereby being regulated costing the regulated banking system money.

Furthermore, 'deregulation' reduced the direct costs related to policing regulation adherence but it also severely hampered the ability to see and understand what was happening, all in the name of a free market philosophy. Please don't get me wrong, I am an old Yankee trader at heart and thoroughly believe in the values of competition, but only to a point. That point would come under the idea that your freedom stops at my nose and my freedom stops at your nose. We have already seen the damage too much unregulated freedom in the financial segment of our society can cause, 1893, 1907 and 1929 so why take the risks again. It seems all too painfully obvious at this point there was something running-a-muck in the world of finance. Why not stop and address the issue. I have come to think that the 1933 establishment of a banking structure was believed/understood/faithfully adhered to without any idea of completing the regulation of banking. In a time of deregulation there was likely little thought of addressing any notion of regulating anything thus opening financial markets to abuses.

Here comes another real screwing of the people.

Supreme Court's Marquette decision gives banks the right to make loans in states other than the state where they are headquartered and at the interest rates allowed where they are head quartered Delaware and South Dakota rush to change their usury laws and welcome banks to relocate and take advantage of the new rates they can charge.

Boy did these guys stick it to us here.

Were banks so poor they needed to do this? Help….help!

To date there is no national **usury** law?

MARQUETTE NATIONAL BANK OF MINNEAPOLIS v. FIRST OF OMAHA SERVICE CORPORATION

Justice Brennan writes the opinion.

First National Bank of Omaha is of course chartered in Nebraska. It is part of the Bank Americard plan and acquires credit card business in Minnesota. First National Bank of Omaha Bank charges its Minnesota cardholders interest as allowed by Nebraska law. That interest is higher than what Minnesota law allows. The Marquette National Bank of Minneapolis who also does the Bank Americard plan gets PO'd and takes First National Bank of Omaha to court saying they can't charge those rates because it violates a Minnesota usury law and the National Bank Act

The state court said that's a 'no no' can't do it.

The Minnesota Supreme Court reversed the state trial court saying it's ok to charge the higher interest rate because they ain't located in Minnesota.

The US Supreme Court agreed and follows part of the decision.

> (a) As a national bank, Omaha Bank is a federal instrumentality whose interest rate for its BankAmericard program is governed by federal law, and under § 85 a national bank may charge interest "on any loan" at the rate allowed by the laws of the State where the bank is "located."

> (b) Apart from its BankAmericard program, Omaha Bank is located in Nebraska, where it is chartered.

> (c) Omaha Bank cannot be deprived of its Nebraska location merely because under the BankAmericard program it extends credit to residents of another State, for it is in Nebraska that credit is extended by the Bank's honoring sales drafts of Minnesota customers, unpaid-balance finance charges are assessed, payments are received, and credit cards are issued

> (d) Nor does the statutory location of the bank change because the credit cards can be used to purchase goods and services outside Nebraska

> (e) Congress in enacting the National Bank Act of 1864 intended to facilitate a "national banking system," whose interstate nature was fully recognized, and there was no intention to exempt interstate loans from the reach of the predecessor of 12 U.S.C. 85

> (f) Though the "exportation" of interest rates, such as occurred here, may impair the ability of States to maintain effective usury laws, such impairment has always been implicit in the National Bank Act and any correction of that situation would have to be achieved legislatively.

So what happened? **North Dakota and Delaware** changed their usury laws as stated to accommodate the banking industry and draw employment to their states. It really grips my gizzard that some folks praise these states for creating jobs for their citizens.

Don't want to pay these high credit card rates pass a law! Actually there have been efforts to pass a federal usury law to no effect at this point. Another possibility would be to force banks to charge the interest rate allowed in the state of residence of the card holder. Either way the banks are going to put tons of 'our' cash into stopping either of these measures that stick it us.

This appears to be a situation the founders could not have anticipated. After all who would have envisioned a plastic card you can carry around and buy things on credit back in the old days?   The world changed and the country had to deal with it.

"Swipe fees have increased steadily since the introduction of debit cards 20 years ago, when there were no swipe fees at all. Merchants can't negotiate or control them. They've tried, but they have no leverage against the big banks and issuers. So they get ignored." **Peter Welch**

Cleveland, Ohio becomes the first post-Depression era city to default on its loans.

> Sweden bans aerosol sprays, China lifts a ban on Aristotle, Shakespeare, & Dickens, 50,000 demonstrate in Amsterdam against neutron bomb, South Africa military goes into Angola, US launches Pioneer Venus 1; produces 1st global radar map of Venus, General strike in Peru, military coup in Mauritania, Bolivia military coup, bomb attack in Beirut, Gunmen open fire on an Israeli El Al Airline bus in London, Irani army shoots on Khomeini followers in Teheran, gold hits record $223.50 an ounce in London, President Carter signs Hawkins-Humphrey full employment bill and Uganda troops attack Tanzania.

Salomon: John Gutfreund became managing partner. The company goes public and he is the CEO. Getting all innovative they start to sell the **first mortgage-backed securities** they bought from banking institutions and then sold them as packages to various investors in the US and abroad. These investors may or may not have had much experience with mortgages.

International Banking Act causes new foreign bank branches to come under Glass-Steagall but **grandfathers existing branches out of Glass-Steagall restrictions.** *This 'grandfather' thing was totally stupid!*

Late in the year inflation starts a steep rise.

1979

Household credit card debt has risen from under **$1,000 in 1979 to over $8,000 in 2007** per household at this printing. This seems to have accounted for some expansion of the GDP, or not. Maybe it's just more purchasing of cheap imported goods.

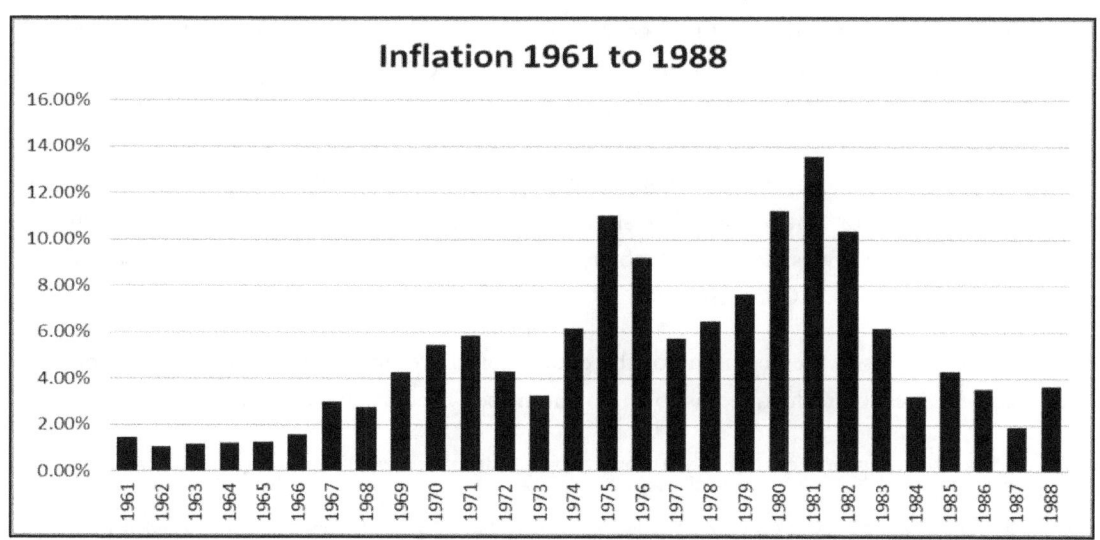

Inflation 1961 to 1988

Inflation soars to double digits as oil prices rise.

US & China (Peoples Republic) begin diplomatic relations, price of gold increases to record $875 troy oz., "YMCA" by Village People peaks at #2, Sino-Vietnamese War begins, war between North & South Yemen, battles between Kurds & Iranians, Elton John becomes 1st western rocker to perform live in USSR, European Market accepts Greece as member, Sioux nation receives $100 million in compensation for Black Hills SD, **OPEC raises oil prices 24%,** Sony introduces the Walkman, Nicaraguan dictator Anastasio Somoza flees to Miami, coup in Afghanistan, coup in Central African Republic, 100,000 demonstrate in Bonn against nuclear energy, military coup in El Salvador, Bolivia military coup, Americans taken hostage at US Embassy (Teheran, Iran) and the USSR airlifts invasion army to Afghanistan.

As inflation is getting out of hand because of the rise in oil prices Paul Volcker, head of the Federal Reserve, raised interest rates and caused a sharp recession in the first half of 1980. Carter introduces his own policies to reduce inflation. The Federal Reserve reduces interest rates to work with Carters' ideas.

What I still don't get is if the inflation was caused significantly because of rising oil prices why raise interest rates and slow everything down instead of allowing the economy to adjust to the additional costs incurred by the higher oil prices. Maybe the inflation wasn't because of higher oil prices.

1980

"Before 1980, it was basically illegal for U.S. banks to invent new products." **Scott Cook**

International Decade of Water & Sanitation begins, gold reaches $1,000 an oz., 175,000 pay to hear FRANK SINATRA sing in Rio de Janeiro, FBI releases details of Abscam, a sting operation that targeted 31 elected & public officials for bribes for political favors,

Miracle on Ice, Cubans of the Mariel boatlift sail to Florida, Pete Rose, 39, steals second, third, & home in one inning, some more riots, Mount St. Helens blows its top, fascist bomb attack on Bologna Italy train station, Libyan invasion in Chad, Iraqi President Saddam Hussein declares holy war against Iran, 4,800 die in series of earthquakes that devastated southern Italy, Georgia tanker at Pilottown La., spills 1.3 million gallons of oil after an anchor chain caused a ship to leak and the Comprehensive Environmental Response, Compensation, and Liability Act (known as either CERCLA or Superfund) is enacted by the U.S. Congress.

Anyway you cut it this is the beginning of the end. From here on the National Debt as a percent of the Gross Domestic Product begins to climb and nobody seems able to do anything about it.

What follows is more pointed history with more crass comments and a few thoughts.

This roller coaster doesn't just go up, down and around, it also passes thru the house of mirrors and thru that tent your parents wouldn't let you near.

What does this mean?

By lowering the reserves kept at the Federal Reserve banks the law decreased the safety net of funds kept on hand to pay the insured savings that are now increased from $40,000 to $100,000. The Interest rate ceilings are removed from the states that give a crud about their citizens and they appoint a paid board to makes sure it happens. Seems I recall it was the Fed that raised rates in the first place. Makes a lot of darned sense to me, **NOT!** *It also means the bone they gave the people was, a little more insurance and made the rest sound like a good thing because of the interest rate problems the Fed. created in the late 1970s. Seems like somebody saw an opportunity and took it.*

Seems to me this also made it more difficult to prosecute lenders! Holy cow!

Railroads and trucking are de-regulated. De-reg fever. Could this be an epidemic? I need a shot! Nurse! Nurse!

Gerald A. LEWIS, Comptroller of the State of Florida v. BT INVESTMENT MANAGERS, INC.,

An out-of-state bank holding company wanted to start an investment management operation in the state of Florida. The application was rejected by the Board of Governors of the Federal Reserve System on the grounds that it was prohibited by the Bank Holding Company Act of 1956 because the laws of the state of Florida forbid out-of-state bank holding companies from such activities as well as other activities. The court ruled the statutes violated the Commerce Clause of the Constitution and as such discriminatory and "parochial legislation" and therefore unconstitutional and the Bank Holding Company Act of 1956 didn't allow this kind of discrimination against out-of-state bank holding companies.

Wasn't there something about the Hunt brothers trying to corner the silver market? Didn't this also drive up gold?

Early 1980s recession sometimes called a "double-dip" or "W-shaped"

The Revolution in Iran and the inconsistent Iranian oil shipments drove oil prices up around the world leading to the 1979 energy crisis. Throw in the Fed's tightening of the money supply and we have a recession

The Depository Institutions Deregulation and Monetary Control Act The Act establishes reserve requirements for all banks including ones not in the Federal Reserve System. It also begins getting rid of Regulation Q that established interest rates that banks can pay on deposits. Allowed savings and loans associations to issue credit cards among other rights. It exempted installment plan companies, federally chartered banks and other loan companies from state usury laws. *Get that last one! MORTGAGE and OTHER types of LOANS are EXEMPTED from state USURY LAWS! Let's try that again.* **MORTGAGE and OTHER types of LOANS are EXEMPTED from state USURY LAWS!**

Seems this usury exemption has to do with the **Federal Reserve** raising rates to fight inflation. This makes me go HUMMMMM. Then it sets up the Depository Institutions Deregulation Committee to ensure the federal interest rate ceilings are all gone in six years.

Seriously, oil costs certainly contributed to inflation as businesses fought to keep going by pushing the costs into the business market passing it on to the consumer. Things are tough for people already so why constrict the economy by raising interest rates adding an additional difficulty. Ah, I remember, banks do not like inflation because the dollars the loans are paid back with are worth less than the ones they loaned out.

Volker started driving up interest rates and we see in the chart above 1981 has inflation dropping along with GDP as expected. But lo, the national debt starts a steep rise as federal income falls because of the declining economy and the unemployment rise sharpens. This is supposed to be good for the country and the economy and therefore the people? I just don't see it.

"Few men have virtue to withstand the highest bidder." George Washington

1981

Ronald Reagan becomes President 1981 to 1989 Republican

"We are a nation that has a government—not the other way around. And that makes us special among the nations of the earth." **Ronald Reagan**

"Christmas is the time when kids tell Santa what they want and adults pay for it. Deficits are when adults tell government what they want and their kids pay for it." **Richard Lamm**

All **12 Federal Reserve** banks established a Community Affairs Office. This was meant to provide public and private guidance to keep aligned with the Community Reinvestment Act.

Salomon Brother's become the first of the Wall Street investment banks to go public. Looks like the risk is somewhat mitigated for the partners.

David Maxwell becomes CEO of Fannie Mae. More than ever mortgage securities are marketed. By increasing the marketing effort of these mortgage securities more of them are placed into the private sector as investment quality securities. The problem is that as they originated with the government they are assumed to be still covered by the government and therefore 'safe'. This action also increasing the funds available for new government backed home loans. The 'safe' notion kinda works as long as the increases in sales do not out outrun the housing market or a strong recession doesn't come along. Another event that can cause instability is when a large increase of money into this 'securities market' comes along increasing demand to the point fervent demand and rapid sales of the security and then multiple resale of the same security.

So why does David Maxwell want to sell of these home loans? Probably because Fannie Mae is a profit enterprise and more action means more money coming thru and therefore more profits and more profits mean more bonus money.

> French government accord sends 60 Mirage fighter jets to Iraq, Peoples Republic of China throws out Netherlands ambassador due to submarine sale to Taiwan, Bobby Sands, IRA member, begins 65-day hunger strike (*he dies*), Colombia drops diplomatic relations with Cuba, race riots in London, 10,000 copper workers in Chile strike, West German metal workers strike, Bangladesh Pres. Ziaur Rahman is shot by group of rebel officers, Israeli F-15/F-16 destroys alleged Iraqi plutonium production facility, AIDS epidemic is formally recognized, riots at Casablanca, Belize (British Honduras) gains independence from UK, citing official misconduct in the investigation and trial, Amnesty International charges the U.S. government with holding Richard Marshall of the American Indian Movement as a political prisoner and a bomb attack on Antwerp Belgium synagogue.

Board of Governors v. Investment Company Institute, 450 U.S. 46 (1981), allowed banks to act as investment advisors concerning closed-end investment companies as it is closely related to banking activities.

Donald T. Regan, a former **Merrill Lynch CEO**, becomes the **Treasury Secretary** and chairman of the **Depository Institutions Deregulation Committee**. *There seems to be something just plain wrong here.*

Senator Garn becomes chair of Senate Banking, Housing, and Urban Affairs Committee.

M. Danny Wall becomes majority staff director. Big time deregulation fan and advocate him. *I'll bet the boys in the finance arena were having galas and partying like rock stars.*

The Bank of England completely does away with required Liquidity Reserves for banks. That's right banks in England are no longer required to hold any reserves against deposits or liabilities. This means banks' ability to expand the money supply becomes infinite. At the time of the financial crisis the ratio between money supply and Central Bank Reserves had become 80 to 1.

Understand that what you deposit is a credit advance to the bank. Your deposits are an IOU the bank presents to you, a promise to pay. Except that the deposit is guaranteed by the government eliminating risk except that the money does come from the government which means we owe we owe.

1982

Commission on Housing recommends the GSEs (Government Sponsored Enterprises) be moved off the federal governments' books. This makes me go hum especially as Fannie Mae has just started aggressive marketing of securities of their home loans.

The **Garn-St. Germain Depository Institutions Act** sponsored by, Congressman Fernand St. Germain, **Democrat** of Rhode Island, and Senator Jake Garn, **Republican** of Utah and the **Alternative Mortgage Transaction Parity Act of** 1982 which was contained in title VIII of the aforementioned can be considered at the root of the failure of hundreds or even thousands of banks.

Here are a few of the ways they stuck it to us. They made it possible for savings and loans to have loans on, corporate, business, agricultural or commercial loans of up to 10% of the assets they held. Worse yet it raised the limit on direct investments by savings institutions in nonresidential real estate to 40% of their assets from 20%.

Then there was the Net worth Certificate Program. Under this program the FDIC and the FSLIC would buy things called Net Worth Certificates from troubled *savings institutions* and sell them back when things got better. *What better?*

More good stuff These acts also allowed for new types of mortgages: **Adjustable-rate mortgages, where the interest rate always goes up (it has to go up so they can sell the loan), interest-only mortgages (the buyer pays the interest only for the first few years** – *(Does this make a thirty year loan a thirty-five year loan or make it a twenty-five year loan after the?)* and balloon payment mortgages *(These have a large payment waiting when the loan comes due) and preempted state laws in the process.*

Further it allowed people to take a loan on a property and give the property to somebody else and not have to create a new loan. *Looks good for trust purposes Do you have a trust? I don't!*

I wonder how Merrill Lynch and the others felt about how this might help protect the *brokered discount* business, which they made tons of bucks on.

Oh, by the way, the vote was 272-91

Deregulation of interstate buses. *Let's just de-reg. the crud out of everything*

Final episode of "The Lawrence Welk Show" airs, United States places an embargo on Libyan petroleum imports because of their support of terrorist groups, Argentinian forces land on South Georgia Island, precipitating war with the U.K., 30,000 Israeli troops invade Lebanon to drive out PLO, Supreme Court rules all children, regardless of citizenship, are entitled to a public education, US imposes sanctions against Poland for banning Solidarity trade union, the Federal Reserve announces that the operating capacity of factories has gone down to 67.8% and the early 80's recession is under way.

1983

48 Banks fail. *Oops.*

The first collateralized mortgage obligation (CMO) made up of Freddie Mac mortgages is created at First Boston.

> Nazi war criminal Klaus Barbie arrested in Bolivia, US president Ronald Reagan introduces "Star Wars"-plan (SDI), King Hussein of Jordan ceases negotiations with PLO, suicide bomber kills 63 at US Embassy in Lebanon, Armenian extremists bomb at Orly, France, US mint strikes 1st gold coin in 50 years (Olympic Eagle) and the last 80 US combat soldiers in Grenada withdraw.

1984

FDIC starts paying out more than it brings in as 79 banks fail. *What did happen to those extra premiums?*

Chemical Bank of New York starts Chemical Venture Partners getting into the private equities business.

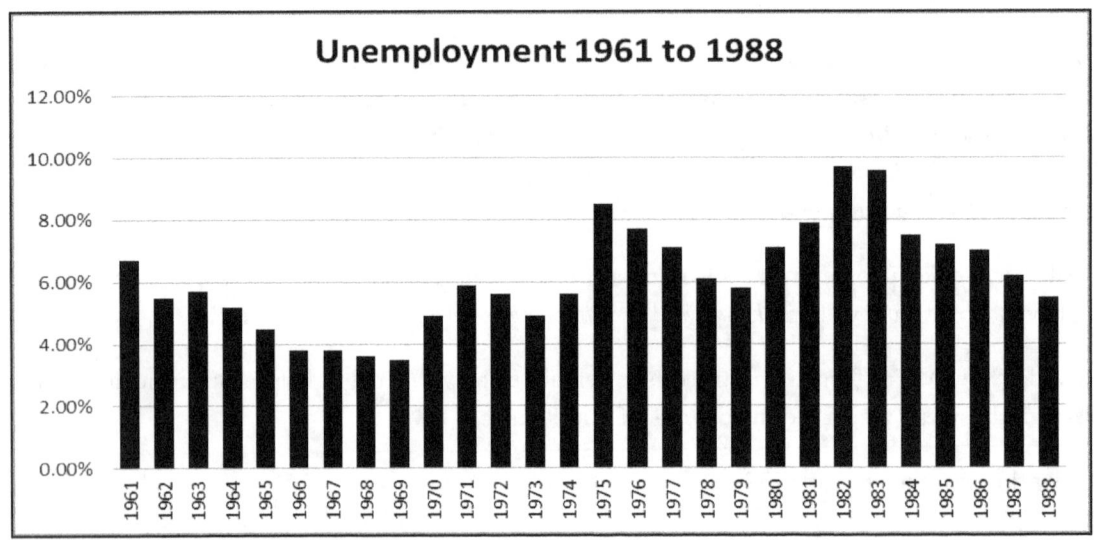

The **Secondary Market Enhancement Act (SMMEA)** is an effort to allow private mortgage-securities companies to compete with the GSEs, Fannie and Freddie. By limiting pension funds to purchasing mortgage related products that are 'highly rated' the credit rating agencies importance in the economy is magnified. These agencies are paid by the vendors of the products they are rating. What did Washington say….."Few men have virtue to withstand the highest bidder."

> Supreme Court reinstated $10M award to Karen Silkwood's family, Pete Rose becomes 1st NL player to get 4,000 hits in a career, Springsteen releases "Born in the USA", Sikh "Golden Temple" uprising India, failed coup by cocaine growers in Bolivia, "Cosby Show" premieres on NBC-TV, suicide car bomb attacks US Embassy annex in Beirut, Walter Payton passes Jim Brown as NFL's career rushing leader, Monterey Bay Aquarium opens and a Creosote bush determined to be 11,700 years old.

Securities Industry Association v. Board of Governors of the Federal Reserve System

The Supreme Court held that Bank of America Corporation could, under the Bank Holding Company Act and not in violation of Section 20 of the Glass-Steagall Act, acquire and operate a non-banking affiliate engaged in primarily in retail securities brokerage because that affiliates activities were "so closely related to banking . . . as to be a proper incident thereto."

From the decision

> The Board's determination that a bank holding company's acquisition of such a brokerage business as Schwab's is not prohibited by § 20 of the Glass-Steagall Act, is reasonable and supported by the statute's plain language and legislative history, and deserves the deference normally accorded the Board's construction of the banking laws. The term "public sale" in § 20 should be read to refer to the underwriting activity described by the terms that surround it, and to exclude the type of retail brokerage business in which Schwab principally was engaged. This reading of the statute is further supported by the Board's similar long-standing interpretation of identical language found in another provision of the Glass-Steagall Act. Moreover, the legislative history demonstrates that Congress enacted § 20 to prohibit the affiliation of commercial banks with entities that are engaged principally in activities such as underwriting. None of the hazards of underwriting is implicated by Schwab's brokerage activities.

The Senate passes bills to get rid of much of Glass-Stegall. The House of Representatives says no.

J.P. Morgan & Co. purchased the Purdue National Corporation.

Here comes 'too big to fail'.

Continental Illinois National Bank and Trust Company, the 7th largest bank in the United States at the time, was going belly up when the Federal Reserve let the bank have over $8 billion via the discount window in an effort to stop a run on the bank. Long story short more money gets pumped in and at a Senate hearing later the Comptroller of the Currency C. T. Conover defended his position by admitting that regulators will not let the largest 11 banks fail.

If smaller banks can fail why would, big investors use the smaller banks if their uninsured large deposits are virtually guaranteed in the biggest banks.

Yeah Team! Let's perpetuate the problem and encourage big banks to take more risks, they know 'Uncle Sugar' will fix things up if they get in trouble.

Maybe too big to fail is too big?

1985

125 banks fail. Where are those premiums? What is up with all these very smart people getting their banks in to trouble?

THE SAVINGS AND LOAN SCANDAL

By now, lots of Savings and Loans were going down the tubes from the effects of the last few years and runs started happening in Maryland and Ohio and as the Texas as oil boom peters out more than 1,000 thrifts, a.k.a. Savings & Loans, nationwide will fail between 1986 and 1995; the debacle will cost $500 billion, including $124 billion in taxpayer money.. Since good old Uncle Sam insured individual deposits the collapse was going to be expensive. Uncle Sam got the Resolution Trust Company to take over and liquidate S&L assets thereby taking over the bankrupt institutions. Those billions would be trillions today.

> British pound (£) sinks to record low $US1.11, bomb attack on Borobudur temple in Java, cold wave damages 90% of Florida's citrus crop, Iraqi air raid on Iran oil-island Kharg, Libya throws out 1000s Tunisian/Egyptian gas workers, Pres. Reagan bans importation of South African Krugerrands, Nevado del Ruiz volcano erupts in Colombia, kills 25,000 and Microsoft Windows 1.0 is released.

NORTHEAST BANCORP, INC v. BOARD OF GOVERNORS OF the FEDERAL RESERVE SYSTEM

A bank holding company from Massachusetts wants to buy a bank in Connecticut. They are required to obtain permission from the Federal Reserve Board under the Bank Holding Company Act (BHCA) of 1956 to buy a bank in another state. The BHCA, Section 3,d, a.k.a. the Douglas Amendment, says the Board cannot make such an approval unless the purchase "is specifically authorized by the statute laws of the State in which such bank is located, by language to that effect and not merely by implication." Connecticut and Massachusetts have such provisions on their books with the criteria that there must be a reciprocal laws in the state of the purchasing bank and they further stipulate the bank must be in New England.

Potential competitors went before the Federal Reserve Board in opposition saying the Douglas Amendment didn't really say they could do this. Also if it did this went against the Equal Protection Clause and the Commerce and Compact clause of the constitution because the state laws allowing such purchases discriminated against non -New England banks and bank holding companies.

The Federal Reserve Board of Governors approved the purchase and Court of Appeals said sure it's ok go ahead.

The Supreme Court decided that no part of the constitution was being violated and told the folks against the purchase to go suck eggs.

1986

138 banks fail. *Ouch! Where will the money come from? The percent national debt to GDP is around 45% up from around 32% in 1980. Where the hell is all the money and why are these banks failing.*

Chemical Bank of New York merges with Texas Commerce Bank

The Tax Reform Act of 1986 (TRA) gets rid of deductions on interest on consumer loans i.e., credit cards and car loans but continues deductions for interest on mortgage loans. TRA gets rid of that part of Regulation Q that placed limits on interest rates paid on deposit accounts like saving and NOWs.

The Real Estate Mortgage Investment Conduit (REMIC) becomes law. It prevents double-taxation of mortgage securities. The secondary market on mortgages goes thru the roof.

> US begins economic sanctions against Libya, Spain recognizes Israel, military coup in Lesotho, rebel army conquerors Kampala Uganda, Haiti's President-for-Life Jean-Claude Duvalier flees to France, French air force bombs Ouadi Doum airport in Chad, Corazon Aquino becomes president of Philippines as Marcos flees, West Berlin disco bombing, US air raids Libya, nuclear disaster, 4th reactor at Chernobyl USSR, 7,000,000 Americans form "Hands Across America", Tip O'Neill refuses to let Reagan address House of Representatives , Supreme Court struck down Gramm-Rudman deficit-reduction law in the case of Bowsher v. Synar, 10 killed & 60 injured at ETA-bomb attack in Madrid, House of Representatives impeaches Judge Harry E Claiborne on tax evasion, Volcanic eruption in Cameroon releases poison gas, killing 2,000, US Navy officer Jerry A Whitworth sentenced to 365 years for spying, failed assassination attempt on Chilean dictator Pinochet, bomb attacks in Paris and Seoul, assassination attempt on India premier, **The United Kingdom government suddenly deregulates financial markets, leading to a total restructuring of the way in which they operate in the country, in an event now referred to as the Big Bang,** *SEC imposes a record $100 million penalty against Ivan Boesky*, **Iran-Contra affair erupts** and race riot in Karach.

Deregulation became global and many countries deregulated their financial institutions during the 1980s. *That Europe and other banks had fewer restrictions than US banks was used as an excuse to deregulate US banks. So, I have to wonder who started this. Guess it doesn't matter who just that it happened.*

The 'Big Bang' in London or Something Wicked this Way Comes Again. Since London had become enamored with being the financial center of the world dramatic changes were made to British banking laws basically opening ways for banks to generate funds in new and imaginative ways. *That really was a bit snippy on my part don't you think.*

This also got the ball rolling for traditional banks to become universal banks, retail and investment banking and stock brokers all under one roof, the bane of our existence. *This really ought to be sounding familiar.* Incidentally this wasn't just going on in England. Countries all over the world, especially in Europe, were following this trend.

What does the USA do? We followed the parade to greater glory.

This didn't even require a new act of congress or a presidential signature. The Federal Reserve Board, in December, decide that good old **Glass-Steagall' Section 20 needed to be reinterpreted to allow banks to have up to 5% of gross revenues in investment banking business.**

Along with this, the **Federal Reserve allows Bankers Trust** to start doing some unsecured credit business.

A banner year for **Goldman Sachs & Company** as they underwrote the IPO of Microsoft, were involved with General Electric buying RCA, joined two foreign stock exchanges London and Tokyo and were the first United States bank to rank in the top 10 of mergers and acquisitions in the UK.

1987

Real Estate Mortgage Investment Conduits become an issue for Fannie Mae. Seems Mr. Maxwell wants to use them but congress and Wall Street ain't so happy about the notion.

> Astronomers at University of California see 1st sight of birth of a galaxy, Pres. Reagan's veto of Clean Water Act is overridden by Congress, no-smoking rules take effect in federal buildings, Syrian army marches into Beirut, Vincent van Gogh's "Sunflowers" sells for record 22.5M pounds ($39.7 million), last wild condor captured on California wildlife reserve, Tamil bomb attack in Colombo Sri Lanka and Sri Lanka Air Force bomb Tamil, The Loughgall ambush: The SAS kill 8 IRA members and 1 civilian, in Loughgall, Northern Ireland, Military coup in Fiji Island, Supreme Court rules school teaching evolution need not teach creation, Nazi Klaus Barbie, sentenced to life in France, Battle between Iranian pilgrims & Saudi-Arabian troops, France & Great-Britain send minesweepers to Persian Gulf, Coup in Burundi suspends constitution, Kirby Puckett goes 6-for-6 with 2 HRs in Minn. 10-6 win, 200,000 gays march for civil rights in Washington, Great Storm of 1987 hits France and England, "Black Monday" Dow Jones down 508.32 points, iceberg twice size of Rhode Island sighted in Antarctic and Palestine uprising begins in Israeli-occupied West Bank.

CLARKE, Comptroller of the Currency v. SECURITIES INDUSTRY ASSOCIATION & SECURITY PACIFIC NATIONAL BANK v. SECURITIES INDUSTRY ASSOCIATION

Security Pacific National Bank wants to start securities under an affiliate called Discount Brokerage which it wants to establish. Security Pacific National Bank wants Discount Brokerage offices inside its home state, outside its home state and in Security Pacific branches. Security Pacific National Bank applies to the Office of the Comptroller of the Currency (OCC) for permission.

The **Office of the Comptroller of the Currency** says sure enough go right on ahead, saying the discount brokerage offices aren't branches under the **McFadden Act**. Also as banks have non-branch offices for purposes why not.

The Securities Industry Association takes issue with this decision and proceeds legally. They figure these are branches and should be treated as such under law

The Supreme Court says it's ok because **the McFadden Act** only refers to the **core functions** of the bank.

The root of all evil

Mortgage Backed Securities (MBS) and Credit Default Obligations (CDO).

The Federal Reserve Board is subject to Congressional review and wished they'd review the dickens out of this.

Citicorp, Bankers Trust and J.P. Morgan go to the Federal Reserve Board asking to have Glass-Steagall restrictions lifted so they can start underwriting in various like, hold on to your hats here, *mortgage backed securities*, did you get that, ***mortgage backed securities***, commercial paper and municipal revenue bonds etc..

These financial institutions try making their case saying, investors are smarter now, **rating agencies are real good** and regulations on corporations are more than adequate now.

Paul Volker, the Chairman of the Federal Reserve Board, figures these guys are just trying to grab more money and will just lower the standards to generate security business and sell bad paper to John Public. *Talk about foresight.* Anyway he gets out voted by Alan Greenspan and a couple of other guys.

The next month Chase Manhattan comes along wanting to start underwriting. The Fed says sure but we are concerned about mixing underwriting and commercial banking but what the heck Glass-Steagall says "principally engaged" so why not just a little and goes from a 5% limit to a 10% limit on this underwriting business. The Fed Board says this will be good because there will be better efficiency and more competition.

Drexel Burnham Lambert creates **"collateralized debt obligations" (CDOs).** These are securities made up of varied loans and bonds that have many different levels of rick associated. These CDOs have to receive a credit soundness rating form one agency or another. I wonder if those that had a reputation for high ratings got more work than others. Didn't they have a guy named Milliken working for them?

August - Alan Greenspan becomes chairman of the Federal Reserve Board. Mr. Greenspan had been a director of J.P. Morgan and likes deregulation so US banks can compete with foreign financial institutions apparently both here and abroad.

I have to figure multi-national corporations can get financing from anywhere they want and are not restricted to their own country. After all foreign investment helped build America. Since financial institutions around the world either have or are expanding the way they do business our guys figure they need to expand their business base to compete which might seem reasonable until this mess comes along. Then I figure it might really have just been to see who gets the biggest toys.

Securities Industry Association v. Board of Governors of the Federal Reserve System

The Court agreed with the Federal Reserve Board that Bank America Corp. (a Bank Holding Company) could buy Charles Schwab a Stock Brokerage who was principally engage in the simple buying and selling of stocks. It was determined that this simple buying and selling did not violate Section 20 of Glass-Steagall because that section was meant to apply to underwriting which Schwab did not do.

Senator John McCain gets with federal regulators to talk about the investigation of Lincoln Savings and Loan. Charles Keating who owned Lincoln was the senator's business partner. *Just a little side note*

THE CRASH OF 1987 or the BIG Computer Glitch dump

October 19 stock markets in the United States experienced one of their biggest falls like ever, down 22%. World markets dropped right after, the next trading day.

Interesting set-up here

Concerns about the dollars' recent decline, that excessive borrowing was being used for company takeovers and insider trading and Germany boosts the value of the mark

With a little bit of help from programmed trading algorithms that automatically created sell orders the market crashed. Asia and Europe fell as the sun rose and their markets opened. *Seems it is a global market and there might actually be a butterfly somewhere causing the storm.*

These losses spurred the reduction in interest rates in the United States and abroad so the business of doing business could continue.

This might have been the first step in the housing bubble. Concerns that major banks might go bust led the Fed and other major central banks to lower interest rates sharply. Alternative mortgages were allowed in 1982 and money is easier now. Really, this might be the spot where the formula first came into play.

Wasn't there a housing bubble in England a couple of years after this? Yeah we borrowed the idea from the British or did they 'give' it to us. *Maybe they're still pissed about that "shot heard around the world" thing?*

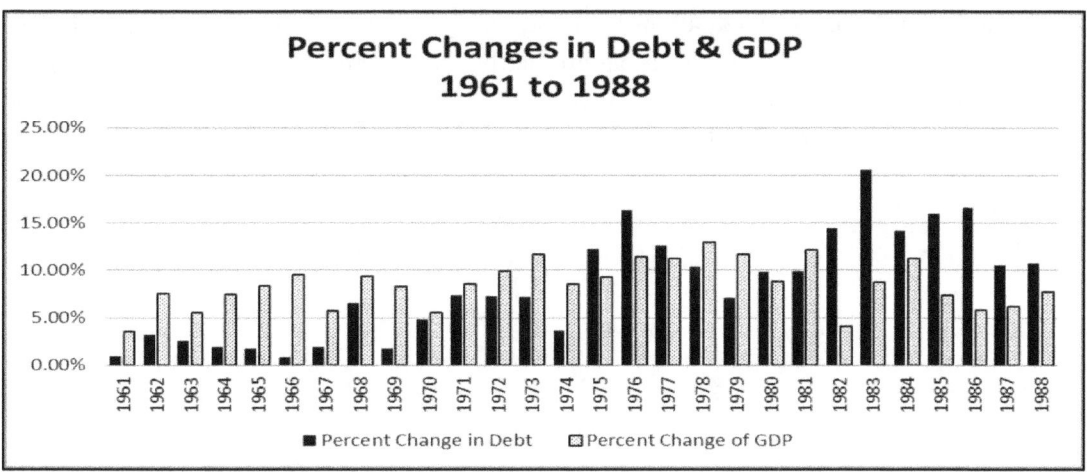

Percent Changes in Debt & GDP 1961 to 1988

■ Percent Change in Debt   ▢ Percent Change of GDP

1988

Wendy Gramm, a.k.a. Mrs. U.S. Sen. Phil Gramm, R-Tex. becomes chairperson of the **U.S. Commodities Futures Trading Commission**. *By the way she was able to exempt derivatives and swaps from regulation.*

December Silverado Savings &Loan goes under sticking us with over a billion dollar mess. Seems Neil Bush was on the board and came under scrutiny about loans to friends. *Let us see; loans to friends and the place goes belly up. How does that work anyway?*

1st Republic Bank, Dallas gets bailed out to the tune of $4 billion.

The Senate tries to get rid of much of Glass-Steagall and the House of Representatives still says no. *Maybe that two term thing has some benefits.*

The market shrinks for tranched mortgage securities as many groups lose tons of money on them.

Guardian Savings and Loan issues the first 'subprime'-backed mortgage security.

Long Beach Mortgage starts to enter the subprime securitization market.

> Ashland Oil storage tank spills 3.8 million gallons, Canada-US free trade agreement, Panamanian General Manuel Noriega indicted by US grand jury for drugs, British pound note ceases to be legal tender, replaced by one pound coin, Eritrean War of Independence, US imposes economic sanctions on Panama, USSR, US, Pakistan & Afghanistan sign Afghanistan treaty, Coup in Haiti, rioting in New York City's Tompkins Square Park, 5-day power blackout of downtown Seattle, IBM announces shipment of 3 millionth PS/2 personal computer, Israel's supreme court upholds ban on Kahane`s Kach Party as racist, US-Soviet effort free 2 grey whales from frozen Arctic, Barrow, AK, Reagan signs credit-card disclosure-bill, *Drexel agrees guilty to security felonies, pays a $650 million fine* and Pan AM Flight 103 was destroyed by a bomb killing 243 passengers and 16 crew (also known as the Lockerbie bombing).

The dynamics of the Glass-Steagall issue. Who are the players? Seems like there are the big and small banks, small banks don't want big brother big bank (*who wants to play with lots of money*) taking the toys away, insurance companies are regulated separately and seem to like it that way, for now, and security firms just want all the money.

1989 to 2008 Banking Innovation Runs-A-Muck, 911, the New Barons, Politicians & 2008 Crisis

George H. W. Bush becomes President 1989 to 1993

"The United States is the best and fairest and most decent nation on the face of the earth." **George H W Bush**

"Friday the 13th" virus strikes hundreds of IBM computers in Britain, Pres. Reagan pardons George Steinbrenner for illegal funds for Nixon, military coup in Paraguay, 24 satellites of the Global Positioning System are placed into orbit, US bust Chinese ring, capture record 820 lbs. heroin ($1B value), largest art robbery in the history (Isabella Stewart Gardner Museum in Boston), where 12 paintings valued at $100 million are stolen, Beijing students take over Tiananmen Square in China, Kenya announces worldwide ban on ivory to preserve its elephant herds, President Bush orders nearly 2,000 troops to Panama, a solar flare from the Sun creates a geomagnetic storm that affects microchips, leading to a halt of all trading on Toronto's stock market, Hungary proclaims itself a republic & declares communist rule ended, Bulgarians demonstrate in Sofia for democratic rights, Jesuit priests are killed by El Salvadorian troops, Communist Party resigns in Czechoslovakia and Larry Bird sets 71 game free throw record. Over at the U.S. Commodities Futures Trading Commission **derivatives and swaps are kept from the burdens of regulation.** *Don't need to deregulate what isn't regulated already. I'd bet those folks made a lot of campaign contributions.*

Jeb Bush has an office building in Miami the government has to cover the $5 million **second mortgage** on.

What with Savings and Loans falling like October leaves in a gale **Congress passes the Financial Institutions Reform, Recovery, and Enforcement Act (FIRREA).** Now we get the Resolution Trust Corporation and the Savings Association Insurance Fund that replaces the Federal Savings and Loan Insurance Corporation. It also puts regulatory authority to the Office of Thrift Supervision (OTS). *Bail! Bail you fools before we all sink!*

Speaking of bailing the RTC sells off the iffy real estate it had sitting around using securitization and over collateralization, get good enough ratings and dang, investors buy them right up.

Michael Milken gets himself kinda out of his mess by taking a plea for reporting and securities violations receiving 10 years in the big house and $600 million fine. Then he goes and rolls on some other dudes and is out in two years. The SEC still won't let him play. Maybe he doesn't really care because the man is still really well off.

1990

Here are those premiums!

The **Federal Deposit Insurance Corporation** begins to raise its premium rate for the first time in its history. Banks have to pay more to stay insured with the FDIC.

There are several references saying **Paul Volcker** comes to believe Fannie Mae needs less capital on hand than banks!

> Panama's leader Gen. Manuel Noriega surrenders to US authorities, Tower Of Pisa closed to the public after leaning too far, 200,000 demand return of Lithuania's independence, crackdown of Azerbaijani pro-independence demonstrations by Soviet army in Baku, Nelson Mandela (political prisoner-27 years) freed in South Africa, Lithuania declares its Independence, riots in London over the new poll tax laws, <u>Michael Milken pleads innocent to security law violations</u>, wrecking cranes began tearing down Berlin Wall at Brandenburg Gate, European court rules pension rights for both men & women, Hubble Space Telescope sends 1st photograph's from space, Ukraine declares independence, Iraq invades & occupies Kuwait, Emir flees to Saudi Arabia, Armenia declares independence, Uganda RPF rebels move into Rwanda, Lech Walesa sworn in as Poland's 1st popularly elected president and United Somali Congress seizes Presidential Palace.

Perhaps that CRA was used by some to influence the decisions of others. I am coming to believe the modifications to CRA and the timing thereof is germane to the entirety of the situation. I believe the CRA was used in a back-handed way by some regulators to encourage subprime loans and the use of alternative mortgages was not restricted to in any way to subprime markets but was aggressively introduced into investment and vacation home markets.

During the 1990s, the national debt increased by 75%, GDP rose by 69%, and the S&P 500 grew more than threefold. What is wrong with this picture?

By the way there were corporate scandals all over the place giving us all warm fuzzies. **Not!** These scandals were likely an additional factor in the fall of the US markets and in investor confidence.

Early 1990s Recession

Inflation starts creeping up in the late 1980s so the Fed starts raising interest rate to slow things down some in 1990

1991

Chemical Bank of New York merges with Manufacturers Hanover Trust Company

> Soviets storm buildings in Vilnius to block Lithuania independence, Operation Desert Storm begins (of course it is about the oil), Sudan's government imposes Islamic law nationwide, LA Police severely beat Rodney King, captured on amateur video, Exxon pays $1-billion in fines & cleanup of Valdez oil spill, Croatia declares independence, Apple releases Macintosh System 7.0, failed military coup in Mali, 400,000 demonstrate for democracy in Madagascar, communist coup is crushed in USSR, Macedonia votes for independence from Yugoslavia and experimental Biosphere 2 in Oracle Arizona begins.

Federal Deposit Insurance Corporation Improvement Act of 1991 becomes law.

Let the FDIC to dip deeper into U. S. Treasury funds to recover to its required reserve levels. FDIC to determine premiums for banks were to now become based on risk levels. Failing banks were to be closed in the best cost-effective manner. The FDIC could now only reimburse insured and insured depositors only, depositors to the maximum guaranteed by law.

The FDICI Act seems to have been meant to get rid of the **'too big to fail'** notion. Looks good until you get to the part about how two-thirds of the FDIC Board of Directors, the Federal Reserve Board of Governors, and approval of the Treasury Secretary could kick in an exception in **'cases of systemic risk'**. I believe that refers to a domino effect in the financial sector. Kinda looks like it do anyway.

The **Federal Reserve System** could no longer lend to banks in financial trouble

The **RTC** closed with its duties sent back to the **FDIC**.

The Bush administration tries to get rid of Glass-Steagall but the House of Representatives stays the course and says no.

Bank of Credit & Commerce International gets raided in seven countries. (BCCI is worth looking up)

Price Waterhouse and Ernst & Young, the banks auditors get sued over their......what would you call it ....complacency.....collusion......ineptitude.....anyway they screwed the pooch and got caught.

One Paul Mozer of Salomon Brothers was caught manipulating the Treasury bond market by finding clever was to buy more bonds than allowed by law. Result Salomon is fined $290,000,000 and CEO Gutfreund leaves the company and takes a SEC fine of $100,000.

The Cold War Ends as the Union of Soviet Socialist Republics dissolves. The Cold War really didn't end it just changed. They still got nukes pointed at us and we still got nukes pointed at them. What did happen was the genie was let out of the bottle as borders became insignificant to International Organizations whether they multi-national corporations, political or religious organizations or what the heck ever.

1992

<u>Lewis v United States</u> The 9th Circuit Court determines that "The regional Federal Reserve banks are not government agencies. ...but are independent, privately owned and locally controlled corporations."

Noteworthy Presidential Election

William Clinton (D), George H W Bush (R) and Ross Perot (Reform Party) all run for President. Perot received 19,741,065 votes but no Electoral College votes. Some folks feel Perot's draw of votes gave the election to Clinton. The demographics do not strongly support that position. It does demonstrate that the two major parties are not fulfilling the needs of the people adequately.

> Europe breaks down trade barriers, ethics committee votes to reveal congressmen who bounced checks, truck bombing of Israeli embassy in Buenos Aires, Arg., USS Missouri decommissioned (*while in the Navy I was able to see this magnificent ship*), Peru's Pres. Alberto Fujimori suspend constitution & dissolved Congress, Serbian troops begin siege of Sarajevo, court throws out Apple's lawsuit against Microsoft, Supreme Court rules fund soliciting can be banned at airports (*so that's what happen to those folks in orange*), Canada, Mexico, and the United States announce NAFTA, Ruby Ridge, Idaho (*poor lady shot dead while holding her baby*) and Somali Civil War: President George H. W. Bush orders 28,000 US troops to Somalia in Northeast Africa and 300,000 destroy mosque of Babri India.

Rodney King Riots

Federal Housing Enterprises Financial Safety and Soundness Act of 1992 Fannie Mae and Freddie Mac are now required to devote a percentage of their lending in support of affordable housing. (they first credit ramp up their 'pools' of such, securitize them and sell 'em off to make room for more). Fannie and Freddie even get to have an oversight group to help them make sure it happens.

Fannie Mae gets a new CEO, one **Jim Johnson**, who gets excited and starts using what is at least once called a **Tammany Hall** approach towards what he perceives as **'political enemies'**.

1993

William Clinton becomes President 1993 to 2001 Democratic

"There is nothing wrong in America that can't be fixed with what is right in America." **William Jefferson Clinton**

The Federal Reserve Bank of Boston got all 'active' and published "Closing the Gap: A Guide to Equal Opportunity Lending". Seems this turned out to be a guide for housing activist with recommendations like loosening up on those income thresholds. **One person I talked to likened this publication to 'The Anarchist Cookbook' but for financial collapse.**

> Czechoslovakia separates into Czech Republic (Bohemia) & Slovakia, gun battle erupts at Waco Texas between FBI & Branch Davidians (*men, women and children die in the resulting fire*), 86 killed by bomb attack in Calcutta, South Africa agrees to multi-racial elections, Paraguay holds its 1st presidential & parliamentary elections in 50 years, Guatemala president Jorge Serrano overthrown by army, US Court of Appeals rules congress must

save all E-Mail (*seems the court wants the evidence to hang around*) and Anti-Nazi riot breaks out in Welling in Kent, after police stop protesters approaching British National Party headquarters and Vatican recognizes Israel.

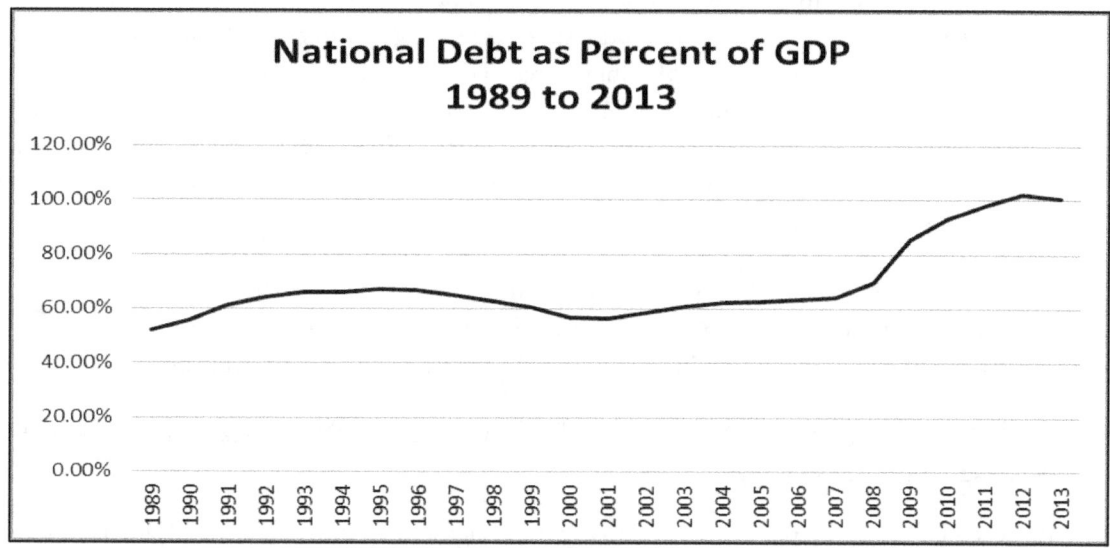

The **U.S. Commodities Futures Trading Commission** again keeps **swaps and derivatives free of regulation.** *You go Wendy Gramm.* This means nobody knows what they really are, who has what per se and how they might impact the financial health of the market place.

Wendy Gramm now leaves the *U.S. Commodities Futures Trading Commission* to take a seat on the board of **Enron on the audit committee.** *Talk about poetry in motion. I wonder if she ever did time in the big house for that mess.*

The potential of the existing problems were recognized as early as this year.

"……..the ongoing integration of financial industry activities makes it increasingly difficult to separate banking and securities operations meaningfully" …………….. "the separation of banking and securities functions is a proven, least-cost method of preventing the problems of one financial sector from spilling over into the other" Jane D'Arista and Tom Schlesinger. They also proposed uniform regulation of all banks. Alas it wasn't until the next year that Credit Default Swaps were developed.

1994

Subprime mortgages account for around 5% of mortgages originated this year, around **$40 billion. Freddie Mac** buys **$18.6 billion** of subprime loans. These are mostly rated as very good A to A-.

The first credit default swap

J.P. Morgan and Blythe Masters sell the first CDS, credit default swap, to the European Bank for Reconstruction and Development.

> Battles between army & rebellious Indians in South Mexico, 1 million Greeks attend (Never on a Sunday) Melina Mercouri's funeral, Aruba government of Oduber falls, 7,000 Tutsi's slaughtered in stadium of Kibuye Rwanda, Charles Kuralt, retires as CBS newsman (*On the Road*), Chunnel linking England & France officially opens, 1st parts of Comet Shoemaker-Levy hits Jupiter (*Flash: world does not end!*), military coup in Gambia, last British troops leave Hong Kong (*been there since Sept 1841*), Norway votes against joining European Union and Maltese Falcon auctioned for $398,590 (*I love that movie*).

The Home Owners Equity Protection Act added protections for borrowers, especially those using high cost/low equity loans, so they understand their situation and have three days to back-out. It also gave the Federal Reserve broad powers to regulate the home loan industry.

Federal Deposit Insurance Corp. v. Meyer (1994) same as O'Melveny and Myers v. Federal Deposit Insurance Corp. (1994).

The FDIC ended up as the receiver of an insolvent Savings and Loan. There were fraudulent real estate transactions that the law firm represented the Savings and Loan with. The FDIC sued in Federal District Court where the law said the Savings and Loan was alone responsible and as the FDIC was now in essence the S&L they couldn't bring action against the lawyers. The District Court said sounds good to me and you boys go have some more fun pillaging the poor ignorant stiffs.

The Court of Appeals reversed the decision saying there was federal common law rule that controlled the matter.

The Supreme Court said the California rule of decision, rather than a federal rule, governs petitioner's tort liability so go ahead and sue the twits.

NATIONS BANK OF NORTH CAROLINA, N.A. v VARIABLE ANNUITY LIFE INSURANCE CO.

Justice Ginsburg wrote the decision for a unanimous court.

Nations Bank of North Carolina and a subsidiary wanted to sell annuities so they went to the OCC to get permission for the subsidiary, which was a brokerage, to be the agent selling the annuities. The annuities would be either fixed or variable.

The OCC figures it is alright because annuities aren't insurance and the annuity business was incidental to the business of the bank anyway.

Variable Annuity Life Insurance Co. gets all up in the air about it because they sell annuities and files suit to stop Nations Bank

The District Court says the Comptroller of the Currency is right so go on ahead and sell the annuities.

The Appeals court says no way guys this is insurance and it ain't gonna fly.

The United States Supreme hears the case and says the OCC was correct so sell the dickens out of those annuities that are not insurance.

Riegle-Neal Interstate Banking and Branching Efficiency Act of 1994

This gets interesting as the Act allows banks to enjoy interstate mergers that were subject to Community Reinvestment Act (CRA) evaluations and other guidelines. CRA isn't that were a portion of lending had to be to minority and lower income groups. Let me get this right. Banks that are already combining with insurance and securities businesses and want to merge will be evaluated by the CRA. Yeah, that sounds about right.

It basically repeals the interstate provisions of the Bank Holding Company Act of. There seems to have been more than a couple of folks running around yelling doom about this move.

Federal Deposit Insurance Corporation v. Meyer

The 'thrift' Meyer worked at gets taken over by the FSLIC and he is summarily fired. Meyer feels he has been wronged and files suit.

The District Court says the FSLIC has to pay Meyer, the FSLIC appeals.

The Appellate Court says pay Meyer. The FSLIC takes it to the Supreme Court.

The Supreme Court finds as follows:

> His claim was properly brought against FSLIC "in its own name." (Meyer had the right to bring the case a to court)
>
> FSLIC's sue and be sued clause waives the agency's sovereign immunity for Meyer's constitutional tort claim. (the FSLIC could be sued)
>
> But there is no remedy available against the government agency. (but not for this)

The decision in this case was unanimous. The decision is interesting as it addresses some important issues such as the intent of congress and fairly easy to read.

O'Melveny and Myers v. Federal Deposit Insurance Corporation

The FDIC filed suit against O'Melveny and Myers in Federal District Court alleging state causes of action for professional negligence and breach of fiduciary duty. O'Melveny and Myers requested a summary judgment, alleging that knowledge of the fraudulent conduct of the Savings & Loan's officers must be imputed to the Savings & Loan, and hence to the FDIC, which, as receiver, 'stood in the Savings & Loan's shoes'.

The FDIC was estopped from pursuing its tort claims.

The Court of Appeals reversed the decision saying that actually a 'federal common-law rule' of decision controlled the matter.

The Supreme Court held the California, a state, rule of decision, rather than a federal rule, governs petitioner's tort liability. Besides there isn't any such common law rule, per se, addressing this case.

Aside to the case, apparently there were certain 'fraudulent real estate' syndications involved which was why the FDIC was so ticked.

Goldman Sachs & Company start an office Beijing and Jon Corzine becomes CEO and get in a little bit of trouble over using a Treasury account to cover their anterior posteriors in the Mexican bond market.

1995

New Community Reinvestment Act regulations delineate home-loan data by neighborhood, income, and race. As community groups can now collect 'brokers fees' when they generate loans they all excited and really start using that data to ensure equal opportunity and fairness.

Dot-com bubble starts and will collapse in 2000.

Fannie Mae & Freddie Mac are now able to get **affordable housing** credit for buying up subprime **mortgage backed securities.** These MBSs include **Adjustable Rate Mortgages, Interest Only and Balloon Payment mortgages**.

> Austria, Finland & Sweden act to join European Union, The Draupner wave in the North Sea in Norway is detected, confirming the existence of freak waves, a chemical fire in an apartment complex in Manila, Philippines, leads to the discovery of plans for Project Bojinka, a mass-terrorist attack, Ecuador & Peru involved in boundary fight, Federal judge allows lawsuit claiming US tobacco makers knew nicotine was addictive & manipulated its levels to keep customers hooked, bomb attack on train in Assam India, Hungarian Forint devalued 9%, poison Gas released in Tokyo subway 12 killed, 4,700 injured and Comet Hale-Bopp is discovered and becomes visible to the naked eye nearly a year late (*watched this with daughter, great fun*).

18 U.S.C. 1964(c)

"Any person injured in his business or property by reason of a violation of section 1962 of this chapter may sue therefor in any appropriate United States district court and shall recover threefold the damages he sustains and the cost of the suit, including a reasonable attorney's fee, except that no person may rely upon any conduct that would have been actionable as <u>fraud </u>in the purchase or sale of securities to establish a violation of section 1962. The exception contained in the preceding sentence does not apply to an action against any person that is criminally convicted in connection with the fraud, in which case the statute of limitations shall start to run on the date on which the conviction becomes final."

It used to be a person did not have to wait for a conviction and could proceed themselves in prosecution.

I wonder if this had anything to do with the way financial business was run from here on.

Truth in Lending Act a.k.a. **Screw the People Act** sponsored by Rep. Bill McCollum (D-Fla.). This bill totally destroyed existing regulations protecting people from crooked creditors.

Also consider that China, emerging economies and oil exporting nations have lots of money sitting around and were looking for places to put it. The housing market in the USA would rise and invite investors to try for profit. Better than leaving it lying around and inflation eating it up. Impact later

Newt Gingrich's Contract with America gets Congress to make it harder to sue security companies for fraudulent activities. *Was this to make doing business easier? No. It was to take accountability away from the buttheads! So what Americans was this contract with anyway?*

Again with trying to get rid of Glass-Steagall but it fails.

HUD publishes "National Homeownership Strategy: Partners in the American Dream," concerning affordable housing advocacy.

Oklahoma City Bombing

1996

"Our government has become too responsive to trivial or ephemeral concerns, often at the expense of more important concerns or an erosion of our liberty, and it has made policy priorities more dependent on where TV journalists happen to point their cameras.... As a nation we have lost our sense of tragedy, a recognition that bad things happen to good people. A nation that expects the government to prevent churches from burning, to control the price of bread or gasoline, to secure every job, and to find some villain for every dramatic accident, risks an even larger loss of life and liberty. **William A. Niskanen, Cato Policy Report**

President Clinton's **"National Homeownership Strategy: Partners in the American Dream"** Pioneered new strategies for lower income and minorities to purchase homes with aggressive goals such as ; Removing Barriers to Mortgage Financing for Starter Homes, Alternative Approaches to Home buying Transactions , Home Mortgage Loan-to-Value Flexibility, Subsidies to Reduce Down payment and Mortgage Costs, Flexible Mortgage Underwriting Criteria and Public-Private Leveraging for Affordable Home Financing.

"Third Rock from the Sun" premiers, Czech Republic applies for membership of the European Union, mortar attack on the US Embassy in Athens, Greece, humans can catch CJD (Mad Cow Disease), International Monetary Fund approves a $10.2 billion loan for Russia, Dutch/Italian Beppo-SAX launches from Cape Canaveral, the Montana Freemen surrender after an 81-day standoff with FBI, Khobar Towers bombing in Saudi Arabia kills 19 U.S. servicemen, Stone of Scone returned to Scotland (*about time*), Spain, an ETA bomb at an airport kills 35, Bomb explodes at Atlanta Olympic Park, 1 killed, 110 injured, Kennewick Man, the remains of a prehistoric man, is discovered near Kennewick, Washington, Afghanistan, the Taliban capture the capital city Kabul and United Nations Convention to Combat Desertification goes into force.

Chemical Bank of New York acquired Chase Manhattan Corporation but decided to use the Chase name.

Smiley v Citibank Simply stated: credit card companies can charge what they want on any type of fee they charge their customers.

Sub-prime mortgages are **9%** of originated loans.

August The Office of Thrift Supervision issues rules preempting almost all state laws regulating Savings & Loan credit activities.

HUD requires of Fannie Mae and Freddie Mac that at least 42% of the mortgages they purchase are issued to borrowers whose household income was below the median in their area.

December the **Federal Reserve Board** bank holding companies can now own **investment bank affiliates with up to 25%** of their business in securities underwriting.

Goldman Sachs was the main underwriter of the Yahoo IPO.

1997

Asian Financial Crisis

"… our whole monetary system is dishonest, as it is debt-based… We did not vote for it. It grew upon us gradually but markedly since 1971 when the commodity-based system was abandoned." **The Earl of Caithness**

Over $60 billion non-GSE, private label, **subprime mortgage backed securities** are marketed to investors.

Mortgage denial rate for conventional home purchases is 28%.

J.P. Morgan started bundling credit default swaps into BISTRO, the forerunner of Synthetic CDOs, and AIG provides credit protection for them.

The **Taxpayer Relief Act of 1997** increased the capital-gains exclusion to $500,000 (per couple) from $125,000.   More people start buying second homes and investment property. *I have to wonder what the hell they thought was going to happen what with Sub-prime going nuts and investor purchases so darn high the darn thing was bound to hit a wall.*

First Union Capital Markets (not a sub-prime lender) and Bear Stearns start selling the first **securitization of Community Reinvestment Act (CRA) loans** that are available to the public to buy. Freddie Mac guaranteed for timely interest and principal income.

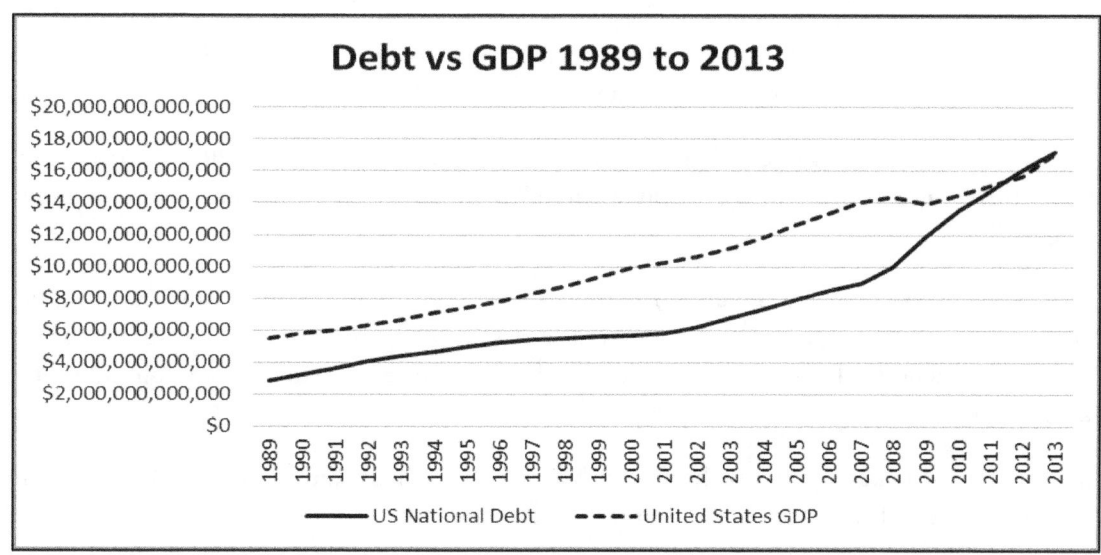

Republic of Zaïre officially joins the World Trade Organization, People's Republic of China announces it will spend $27.7 billion USD to fight erosion and pollution in the Yangtze and Yellow river valleys, Dow Corning provides $295 billion to settle breast implant suits, Boerge Ousland of Norway becomes the first person to cross Antarctica alone and unaided, 3 Swiss banks create $70 million Holocaust fund (*might have had something to do with all those secret accounts from the 1930s and 1940s*), scientists in Scotland announced they succeeded in cloning an adult mammal, producing a lamb named "Dolly", President Clinton bans federally funded human cloning research, Sandline affair, Thirty-nine bodies found in the Heaven's Gate cult suicides, Thalit massacre in Algeria, 69 year old Gordie Howe begins playing AHL game with Syracuse Crunch, **The Bank of England is given independence from political control, the most significant change in the bank's 300-year history,** military coup in Sierra Leone, 1st all female (20 British women) team reaches North Pole, Span scientists announce new human species in 780,000 year old fossil, Khmer Rouge leader Pol Pot orders the killing of his defense chief Son Sen and 11 of Sen's family members before Pol Pot flees his northern stronghold, Supreme Court strikes down Internet indecency law, 200-year-old USS Constitution sails under its own power, Acteal massacre and more Swedes died than were born in 1997, 1st time since 1809.

Atherton v. Federal Deposit Insurance Corp. point is it over rode Briggs v Spaulding of 1891.

From the decission

We conclude that the federal common-law standards enunciated in cases such as Briggs did not survive this Court's later decision in Erie R. Co. v. Tompkins. There is no federal common law that would create a general standard of care applicable to this case.

The decision allowed states to impose stricter standards of conduct on banks, their officers, and directors than those imposed by federal statutes.

The **Federal Reserve Board** eliminates many restrictions of **'Section 20'**, **the risks of underwriting had proven to be "manageable,"** and banks could acquire securities firms outright.

Sandy Weill, who heads up **Travelers Insurance**, tries organizing a merger with **J.P. Morgan**. But the deal falls through so Sandy goes out and buys Salomon Brothers investment bank. Salomon gets merged with Smith Barney (already owned by Travelers) and we get **Salomon Smith Barney.**

Bankers Trust (owned by Deutsche Bank) buys the investment bank Alexander Brown & Co. This is the first U.S. bank to acquire a securities organization.

1998

1998 to 2008 the amount of **Credit Default Obligations** outstanding increased about a hundred times to as much as $47,000,000,000,000.00. That's right **Forty-Seven Trillion Dollars**. _That is a poopy load of bucks going unregulated._

Frank Sinatra dies , Russia begins to circulate new rubles to stem inflation and promote confidence, the European Central Bank is established, Sidi-Hamed massacre takes place in Algeria, nineteen European nations agree to forbid human cloning, Boston Celtics retire Robert Parrish's #00, Rear Admiral Lillian E. Fishburne becomes the first female African American to be promoted to rear admiral, failed assassination attempt on Georgian President Eduard Shevardnadze, flight of RQ-4 Global Hawk, the unmanned aerial vehicle certified to file its own flight plans and fly regularly in U.S. civilian airspace, race riots break out in Jakarta, Indonesia, U.S. embassy bombings in Kenya and Tanzania and leaders of the Khmer Rouge apologize for the 1970s genocide in Cambodia that claimed over one million lives.

February brings a meeting between Sandy Weill head of Travelers Insurance and John Reed of Citicorp where they discuss the possibility of a merger despite it being illegal under Glass-Steagall. That makes a fellow go hum.

Meanwhile in **March First Union** snags up **The Money Store** that happens to the fifth largest subprime lender going. John Reed and Sandy Weill (herein after referred to as 'the boys') get together again and decide to make the deal.

Being prudent Weill runs around getting together with the Federal Reserve folks to see what they think of the idea as it stands and generally seems to get positive feedback. After this the boys make sure all the ducks are in order so the deal is cool with the recent rulings of the Federal Reserve Board and starting making their next move. Under current 'law' the deal is illegal as all get out unless Citicorp rids itself of some of the insurance parts of the business. No problem we'll tell everybody 'ok' and figure a way around it.

What's one of the best ways to get around something in the government? Lobby the caca out of it and bring lots of money! So that's exactly what they do. They contact the Federal Reserve, the Treasury Secretary and even the President as well as congressmen and senators.

April gets here with the boys all happy and they brief the President on the deal to be announced the next day. The next day the boys announce the merger, like the biggest ever $70 odd billion. This has some, but not that many, shaking their heads and going hum because this deal is still illegal under Glass-Steagall. Not to worry Sandy gets together a few million bucks to start campaigning to get rid of Glass-Steagall, after all it technically stands in the way of the like biggest deal ever. Anyway they still got five years after the deal closes to do away with the laws in their way or they're gonna have to break up the new company or just undo the whole deal (like that's gonna happen). Worthy of note is that had congress stuck their latest effort to kill Glass-Steagall on the shelf 'because they didn't have the votes or whatever.

Remember those folks who were shaking their heads and going hummm? Well they don't see this deal as maybe coming about and getting very expensive and the share price of both companies drop. This can't be making 'the boys' happy nor their boards of directors either. Maybe, or not.

The rush is on but the law can't be changed this session of congress because it might be too controversial and might muck up the elections. Ah beans say the boys.

May The House passes legislation by a vote of 214 to 213 that allows for the merging of banks, securities firms, and insurance companies into huge financial conglomerates.

Brooksley Born, over at the venerated **Commodity Futures Trading Commission**, gets up one day having '**Over the Counter' derivatives**, let's say those interesting little **credit default swaps**, on her mind. Seems she is all worried there might be a 'systemic risk' because they got no transparency and there seems to be no regulation of the little suckers. The 'good old boys', Levitt, Greenspan and others, tell dear Mz. Born to go play in another sandbox. Being a proper lady and of sound mind she tells one and all to 'Johnny Paycheck Song' and heads on down the road to saner surroundings. *Totally seriously I wish I could have seen the moment she quit.*

June arrives and what do you know Conseco buys GreenTree (*money grows on trees*) a major subprime money pit, ah I mean lender.

August and here comes that **Russian Ruble** thing again. Russia defaults on the bonds the government issued and everybody and his babushka run for cover straight to United States Treasury Bonds and drive the price to heaven or maybe some place else depending on how you perceive the effects.

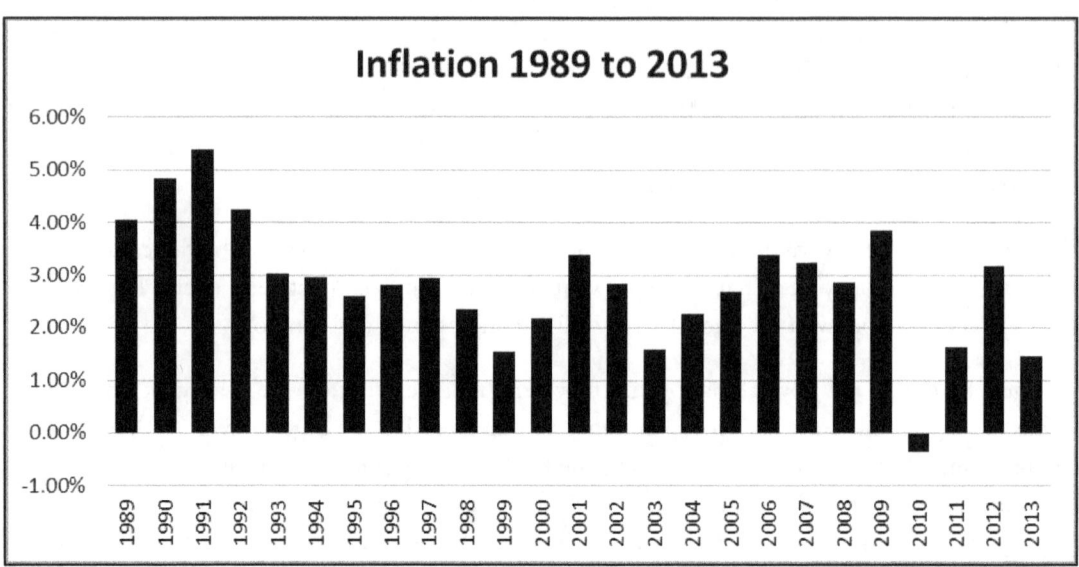

Here comes the 'moral hazard'

Long-Term Capital Management (LTCM), a hedge fund, is now all upside down and in order to get out from under it's going to have to sell, guess what, Treasury Bonds. This drastically reduces the number of happy faces in the neighborhood as it will create capital chaos and interest rates will go 'to the moon Alice, to the moon.'

The Federal Reserve decides to set the all-time, anybody that's ever worked as dip stick wouldn't do it, precedents ever and arranges to 'bail the sucker out' by rallying Wall Street banks to the rescue. All say sure enough except Bear Stearns who may have had really good reason. The Fed also cut rates and the markets were happy again. Not everyone was happy this bailout was done and feared large institutions would take more risks figuring Uncle Sam would come to the rescue thereby creating a **'moral hazard'**.

I guess the Federal Deposit Insurance Corporation Improvement Act of 1991 'Systemic risk' clause was working just fine.

Well maybe not so dip sticky, after all the sudden collapse could have started a domino effect and ruined lots more folks but *I am getting a little tired of hearing about bailing out people that make 100 times more than anybody I know. Besides, what is wrong with letting the mess fall and sort the mess out after?*

The **Federal Reserve Bank of New York's rescue of Long-Term Capital Management in 1998** seems to encourage large financial institutions to act with a sense of impunity as they think the Federal Government would bail them out because they were **'too big to be allowed to fail'**.

LTCM gets undone in 2000 going away forever.

September has the congress, yet again, not passing a new banking bill that would eliminate Glass-Steagall and the Bank Holding Company Act of 1956.

The Federal Reserve approves 'the boys' merger saying "the Board's approval is subject to the conditions that Travelers and the combined organization, Citigroup, Inc., take all actions necessary to conform the activities and investments of Travelers and all its subsidiaries to the requirements of the Bank Holding Company Act in a manner acceptable to the Board, including divestiture as necessary, within two years of consummation of the proposal and is subject to the condition that Travelers and Citigroup conform the activities of its companies to the requirements of the Glass-Steagall Act." Like that will ever happen!

October "Financial Services Modernization Act" plays dead ants in the Senate because of a lack of restrictions on Community Reinvestment Act-community type groups that have been reading all that information from the Federal Reserve Banks and making lots of money making sure loans are originated.

1997-98 elections, the **FIRE Sector (finance, insurance, and real estate industries)** puts out around $350 million on political donations and lobbying efforts.

The financial crises in Asia in 1997 and Russia in 1998 drove a lot of money into the US financial system. This likely contributed to the whole housing mess by causing a greater demand for investments that get filled with securitized mortgages which drives housing costs and prices higher than reasonable. Seriously, have you ever seen a bubble behave reasonably? I mean than what a bubble typically does which is float around on the currents of wind.

1999

Sub-prime mortgages amount to $160 billion, 13%, of loans originated.

Here is one to think long and hard about.

Washington Agreement on Gold is signed by the European Central Bank and several European National Banks stating that "gold will remain an important element of global monetary reserves". *This sure sounds to me like some folks are getting scared.*

Henry Paulson took over as **Senior Partner at Goldman Sachs**. Sachs goes public with 12% of the company. Paulson is now Chairman of the Board and CEO. Goldman Sachs also acquired Hull Trading Company, a market-making firm.

Chase gets Hambrecht & Quist for $1.35 billion.

> Jesse Ventura is sworn in as governor of Minnesota (*score one for the outsiders*), The Racak incident, Two Libyans suspected of bringing down Pan Am flight 103 in 1988 are handed over for eventual trial in the Netherlands, The World Trade Organization rules in favor of the United States in its long-running trade dispute with the European Union over bananas (*Yes we have no bananas we have no bananas today, that is a Lyric*), Columbine High School massacre, All My Children star Susan Lucci finally wins a Daytime Emmy after being nominated 19 times, the longest period of unsuccessful nominations in television history (*Finally*), The International Criminal Tribunal for the former Yugoslavia in The Hague, Netherlands indicts Slobodan Milošević and four others for war crimes and crimes against humanity committed in Kosovo, Olusegun Obasanjo takes office as President of Nigeria, the elected and civilian head of state in Nigeria after 16 years of military rule, Maurice Papon, an official in the Vichy France government during World War II, is jailed for crimes against humanity, Gunmen open fire in the Armenian Parliament, In Seattle, Washington, United States, protests against the WTO meeting by anti-globalization protesters, Portugal returns Macau to China, The Spanish Civil Guard intercepts a van loaded with 950 kg of explosives that ETA intended to use to blow up Torre Picasso in Madrid and the Spanish Civil Guard finds near Calatayud (Zaragoza) another van loaded by ETA with 750 kg of explosives.

July must have been hot in North Carolina because the General Assembly gets all upset and says screw deregulation we want this predatory lending to stop and they pass a law. *Go team! But the rating agencies say if they don't settle down they won't rate their paper, bonds et al, and that would really screw North Carolina. I think this happened with some other states also.*

September Fannie Mae eases up on the credit requirements. *Ghee Whiz, I wonder why? NOT!*

October Gramm-Leach-Bliley Financial Services Modernization Act is passed Act or as I like to say "let's sell the morons out and get rich act, and Glass-Steagall and the 1956 Bank Holding Company Act are basically dead and gone. Funny thing though. That Treasury Secretary who was in favor of the law and the Citi/Travelers merger quits his post and goes to work for Sandy Weill at Citi. *If that don't smell like a camels rump I don't know what does.*

Looks like decades of effort by the banking industry had finally paid off, *'paid off' does have a double meaning here in case you missed it*, and those messy little laws are gone and it's party time. Hundreds of millions of dollars went into repealing Glass-Steagall. Lobbyists got to put their kinds in good colleges, congresspersons got great donations to their political campaigns and regulators got great jobs with private companies when they left government work.

In Gramm-Leach-Bliley Financial Services Modernization Act the Community Reinvestment Act evaluation requirements are preserved.

The next day the boys have a press conference congratulating everybody, some by name and President Clinton signs it into law.

Some key players are Thomas J. Bliley, Jr., Jim Leach, Chuck Schumer, Phil Gramm and Chris Dodd.

Unlike Europe and Japan financial holding companies are not allowed to own non-financial corporations. So 'private equity firms' use a "workaround" "loophole kind of thing" to avoid those nasty regulators.

$300 million of lobbying weds the risk-taking culture of investment banking and the conservative commercial banking culture. I wonder which philosophy wins out. *Hint; bankers income depends on action and deals and make things happen or they don't make the big bucks.*

October The Federal Reserve made an emergency rate cut.

2000

Financial crisis in Argentina

HUD set a goal for Fannie Mae and Freddie Mac that at least 42% of the mortgages they purchase are issued to borrowers whose household income was below the median in their area. This target was increased to 50%.

Household debt is over $7 trillion.

Lehman Brothers gets their silly asses convicted of **'aiding and abetting'** in the fraud of Famco, a bankrupt sub-prime lender.

> German extortionist Klaus-Peter Sabotta is jailed for life for attempted murder and extortion, last original "Peanuts" comic strip appears in newspapers one day after Charles M Schulz dies, Metallica drummer Lars Ulrich files a lawsuit against P2P sharing phenomenon Napster, conjunction of Sun, Mercury, Venus, Mars, Jupiter, Saturn & Moon *(and the world kept on rotating)*, leaders of Salt Lake City's bid to win the 2002 Winter Olympics are indicted by a federal grand jury for bribery, fraud, and racketeering, argon fluorohydride, the first argon compound ever known, is discovered at the University of Helsinki by Finnish scientists, anti-globalization protests in Prague, USS Cole is badly damaged in Aden, Yemen, by two suicide bombers, killing 17 crew members and wounding at least 39, Laurent Gbagbo takes over as president of Côte d'Ivoire, Philippine House Speaker Manuel B. Villar, Jr. passes the articles of impeachment against Philippine President Joseph Estrada and U.S. retail giant Montgomery Ward announces it is going out of business after 128 years.

April Chase Manhattan Bank **pays $7.7 billion Robert Fleming & Co.** in the United Kingdom.

Chase/Chemical Bank of New York merges with JP Morgan & Company and become JP Morgan Chase & Company.

Off-balance-sheet vehicles, derivatives and the 'shadow banking system' was no more than a way to find a way to avoid regulation.

May the Fed Interest Rate was 6.5%. By January 3, 2001 it was 1% and stayed there. *No darn wonder things went thru the roof.*

June Treasury and HUD urge Fed to investigate subprime units of major banks. No Fed action follows.

The bursting of the First Subprime Bubble

First Union closes The Money Store, takes $2.8 billion write-down. Didn't they just buy the darn thing in 1998? Didn't a bunch of other guys get bit in this stage of the sub-prime mess? Yes! So why the devil are they still pushing the subprime mess down our throats? I'll bet money and power are involved.

December Congress heads for Christmas recess and Sen. Gramm attaches 262-page amendment to an omnibus appropriations bill. **Commodity Futures Modernization Act** will deregulate derivatives trading, give rise to Enron debacle, and opened the door to an explosion in new, unregulated securities. This act makes bucket shops legal again after they were made illegal after the 1907 financial crisis. *Ok, alright let's make sure those unregulated investment vehicles go totally unregulated by anybody and everybody that might have even the greatest possible interest in making sure they are sound and get totally out of control!!!!!!*

Seems some folks by the names of Rainer, Greenspan, Levitt and Summers had a hand in getting this Act structured as it was. There are few million people that would like to thank you for your diligence, deep concern and forethought in making sure the economy is on a sound footing. We are sure that every darn penny you earned in the performance of your duties will be repaid to us with interest, MOTHERS!

December The **American Homeownership and Economic Opportunity Act** makes it harder for consumers to get out of lender-required insurance. National Association of Realtors lobbies hard for it, spending $9 million, plus $4 million in contributions. *Could this be first indicator that something is wrong???? Added income for the lender or a feeling that things could and would head south so grab some more up front and forget about tomorrow.*

Wharf Holdings Ltd. v. United Int'l Holdings, Inc. upheld an 'oral contract' to purchase 'securities'.

"We need a spirit of community, a sense that we are all in this together. If we have no sense of community, the American dream will wither." **William Jefferson Clinton, Really!**

Trying to overcome the early 2000s recession **the Federal Reserve** lowers Federal the funds rate several times, from **6.5% to 1.75%** over the course of several months.

Goldman Sachs buys Spear, Leeds, & Kellogg for $6.3 billion.

George W. Bush becomes President 2001 to 2009

"Recognizing and confronting our history is important. Transcending our history is essential. We are not limited by what we have done, or what we have left undone. We are limited only by what we are willing to do." **George W Bush**

A Home without Equity is just a Rental with Debt by **John Posner** comes out and practically nobody pays any attention.

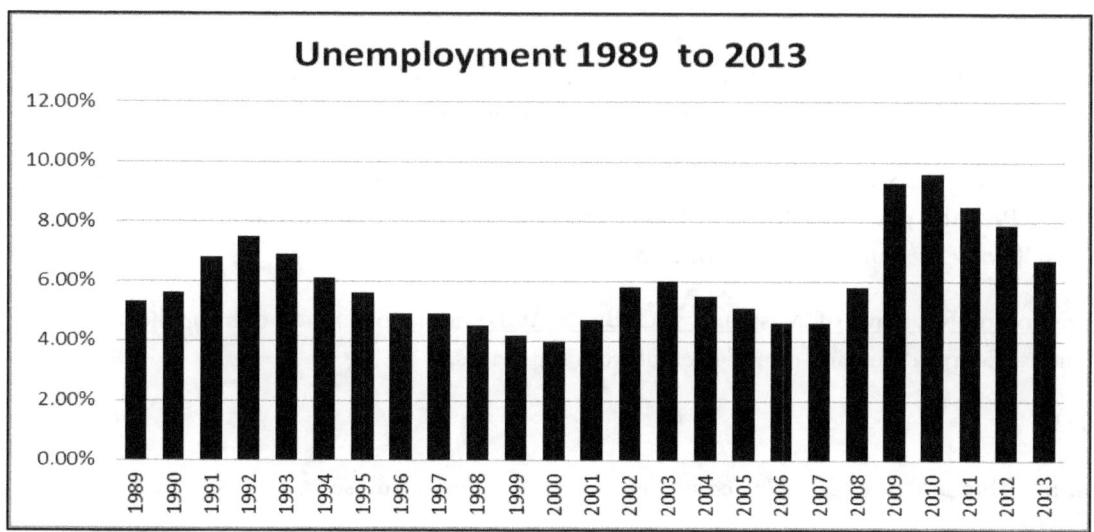

Wikipedia, goes online, draft of the complete Human Genome is published in Nature, FBI agent Robert Hanssen is arrested for spying for the Soviet Union. He was ultimately convicted and sentenced to life in prison (*guess in ain't over*), French Taubira law officially recognizes the Atlantic slave trade and slavery as crimes against humanity (*I just don't know what to say about this*), China, Russia, Kazakhstan, Kyrgyzstan, Tajikistan and Uzbekistan form the Shanghai Cooperation Organization, US President George W. Bush announces his support for federal funding of limited research on embryonic stem cells, **September 11 - Terrorists hijack two passenger planes crashing them into New York's World Trade Towers causing the collapse of both & death of 2,752 people - Terrorists hijack a passenger plane and crash it into the Pentagon causing the death of 125 people - Attempt by passengers and crew of United Airlines Flight 93 to retake control of their hijacked plane from terrorists causes plane to crash in Pennsylvania field killing all 64 people onboard,** Ansett Australia, Australia's commercial interstate airline, collapses due to increased strain on the international airline industry leaving 10,000 people unemployed, mailing of anthrax letters from Trenton, New Jersey in the 2001 anthrax attacks, the People's Republic of China joins the World Trade Organization and

Argentine economic crisis: December 2001 riots - Riots erupt in Buenos Aires after Domingo Cavallo's corralito measures restrict the withdrawal of cash from bank deposits.

The Federal Reserve's **Funds rate hits about 1% and lingers** *This was below the inflation rate. Seems kinds odd they'd do that.*

March The FTC sues Citigroup and its subsidiary Associates, the nation's 2nd-largest subprime originator, charging "systematic abusive lending practices" involving 2 million borrowers; 18 months later Citigroup settles for a piddley assed $215 million. Yes it was!!!!!!!!!!!!!!!!!!!!!

April Alan Greenspan signals concern with "abusive lending practices that target vulnerable segments of the population and can result in unaffordable payments, equity stripping, and foreclosure." *Maybe he did pay some attention.*

July 'Predatory' is really a high-profile word with no definition," Ameriquest chairman Stephen W. Prough tells Congress, urging rollbacks of subprime mortgage regulations.

Enron fraud discovered. Ley gets 45 years, Jeffery Schilling gets 24 years, Arthur Andersen loses CPA Lic., goes 'KAPUT', 28,000 people lose their jobs and investors $11 billion. *To think Wendy was on the audit committee.*

<u>Director of Revenue of Missouri v CoBank ACB</u> via a unanimous decision held that the National Cooperative Bank is 'not' exempt from state taxes.

2002

Fannie Mae and Freddie *Mac* combined buy **$38 billion** of those very highly rated sub-prime mortgages.

Home loans to higher-risk borrowers increases. Perhaps to fulfill all kinds of demands

Mortgage denial rate for conventional home purchases is 14%. (very low)

Houses are appreciating 10% or more a year in California, Florida, and lots of the Northeastern states.

> *Perhaps that CRA was there was used by some to influence the decisions of others. I am coming to believe the modifications to CRA and the timing thereof is germane to the entirety of the situation. I believe the CRA was used in a back-handed way by some regulators to encourage subprime loans and the use of alternative mortgages was not restricted to in any way to subprime markets but was aggressively introduced into investment and vacation home markets.*

Paul O'Neill (Secretary of the Treasury) gets fired by President Bush. Might have had something to do with telling the Administration higher taxes were needed and half a Billion dollar deficits were on the way. *Dead Messenger!*

President Bush presents the **"Blueprint for the American Dream".** *Since nobody seems too interested in fixing it let's take that **"Partners in the American Dream"** give it a **Blueprint** and go out* *and get some votes too.   We'll go after five and a half million minority voters by making tax credits available, use some subsidies and we can give Fannie Mae some bucks to create a Neighbor Works America with the help of all those religious voters. Yep, that ought to do it. They got their CRA and I got this.*

"And so, therefore, I've called .. yesterday, I called upon the private sector to help us and help the home buyers. We need more capital in the private markets for first-time, low-income buyers. And I'm proud to report that Fannie Mae has heard the call and, as I understand, it's about $440 billion over a period of time. They've used their influence to create that much capital available for the type of home buyer we're talking about here. It's in their charter; it now needs to be implemented. Freddie Mac is interested in helping. I appreciate both of those agencies providing the underpinnings of good capital.

"People take a look at the down payment; they say that's too high, I'm not buying. They may have the desire to buy, but they don't have the wherewithal to handle the down payment. We can deal with that. And so I've asked Congress to fully fund an American Dream down payment fund which will help a low-income family to qualify to buy, to buy." **[President Bush, June 18, 2002]**

> Euro banknotes and coins become legal tender in twelve of the European Union's member states,   Mount Nyiragongo erupts in the Democratic Republic of the Congo, displacing an estimated 400,000 people, Canadian Dollar sets all-time low against the US Dollar (US$0.6179), US Secretary of Energy makes the decision that Yucca Mountain is suitable to be the United States' nuclear waste repository, U.S. invasion of Afghanistan, attempted coup d'état in Venezuela against President Hugo Chávez and a near-Earth asteroid estimated at 10 meters diameter explodes over the Mediterranean Sea between Greece and Libya.

December Chase gets hit with fines of $80 million because it **deceived investors with biased research**. They also cannot have any allocation of IPO shares. *I'll bet that hurt.*

"The Congress has historically played covert communal politics in order to create what in India we call vote banks where you pit one community against another and so on in order to secure votes." **Arundhati Roy**

2003

New York Times Sept. 11 "The Bush administration today recommended the most significant regulatory overhaul in the housing finance industry since the savings and loan crisis a decade ago."

Warren Buffet calls CDS (Credit Default Swaps) "weapons of mass destruction". *Wow, from the 'Oracle' himself.*

> *CDSs are a derivative in which Party A pays Party B what is essentially an insurance premium, in exchange for payment should Party C default on its obligations. Party A buys a MBS (Mortgage Backed Security) from Party C who may or may not have done their due diligence on the product.*

219

The use of synthetic products to me is nothing more than a means of satisfying a gambling compulsion. Synthetics are nothing more than side bets backed by thin air and I consider them abominable.

"These two entities — Fannie Mae and Freddie Mac — are not facing any kind of financial crisis," said **Rep. Barney Frank**, *then ranking Democrat on the Financial Services Committee. "The more people exaggerate these problems, the more pressure there is on these companies, the less we will see in terms of affordable housing.",*

Chase gets wacked for **$160 million** settlement for claims against it by the **Securities and Exchange** Commission and the **Manhattan District Attorney's** office.

The Federal Reserve Chairman, **Alan Greenspan**, lowers the Federal Reserve's key interest rate **to 1%**. *Maybe he wasn't paying attention after all.*

At the **Jackson Hole Economic Symposium** a couple of folks from the **Bank of International Settlements** state concerns about issues the **rating agencies and collateralized debt obligations**. *Seems they were not taken to heart or wallet.*

Bush's administration starts making noise about getting **Fannie and Freddie** to be supervised under **new agency** in the Department of the Treasury because they see potential problems. Congress says, **"Don't think so fellas."**

Sub-prime mortgages are over $330 billion.

World Com fraud comes to light. Bernard Ebbers gets 25 years.

Federal Reserve is figuring the movement of higher risk loans to the securitization process and package and sell off the loans is all that is needed instead of exercising its regulatory powers. This is the dumbest freaking thing ever done – move the risk to insurance, like they have the real financial ability to take this kind of hit. Their ability to sustain losses is predicated on historical percentages built in to their business plans.

September 10th the **House Financial Services Committee** had a hearing to look at **'safety and soundness'** issues of the GSEs and to consider a report from the **Office of Federal Housing Enterprise Oversight** (OFHEO) that said there were accounting problems at Fannie and Freddie.

Nothing came of it other than a few of the Committee members getting a riled at the Office of Federal Housing Enterprise Oversight group. *I wonder if these messengers got shot too.*

2004

"Fannie, Freddie to Suffer under New Rule, Frank Says," from the Bloomberg issue of June 17, 2004

January Federal Office of the Comptroller of the Currency issues final rule to preempt states from applying most of their credit laws to national banks and their subsidiaries. *What happened to the 'Republic' idea?*

Early in 2004 the Financial Times reported that "financial supermarkets" were failing all over the world, show that diversification and larger size didn't absolutely increase the ability to generate profits..

Federal Reserve Board Chairman Alan Greenspan testified to Congress that commercial bank consolidation had "slowed sharply in the past five years."

The **Federal Bureau of Investigation** warned of an "epidemic" in mortgage fraud, an important credit risk of nonprime mortgage lending, which might become "a problem that could have as much impact as the Savings and Loan crisis".

April Flash: the SEC ruled that investment banks, the big five on Wall Street, may essentially determine their own net capital. **WT_O!**

The SEC allows Goldman Sachs, Merrill Lynch, Lehman Brothers, Bear Stearns and Morgan Stanley to determine their own capital reserve percentages. They go straight to the friggin' moon with leverages from 20 or 40 to 1. Let us put this in perspective. These are the best of the best and they mortgage not only the farm but the manure that is still in a darn cow that hasn't even been born yet. Incidentally these are the banks that went belly up in 2008 costing us.......who knows yet. Do you smell some camel poop?

Ameriquest employees give total of $200,000 to Bush campaign; founder Roland Arnall and wife Dawn give more than $5 million to pro-Bush PACS. Arnall is later appointed ambassador to Netherlands. *That must be a great posting!*

Large financial institutions are borrowing to buy MBS's believing the housing market and the economy in general will continue to rise. Apparently they don't understand bubbles.

Homeownership in the United States reaches an all-time high of slightly over 69 %.

Following the example of Countrywide Financial leads the mortgage lenders of the country to the precipice with automated loan approvals. Get that, no underwriting or review, just get the money out the door and get the fees and sell of the darn loan so we can do it again and get more fees. **Shortly thereafter mortgage fraud increases, I'd bet. DUH!**

HUD raises the bar for Fannie Mae and Freddie Mac affordable-housing goals to go from 50% to 56% by 2008

JPMorgan Chase and Bank One Corp. merge. **Jamie Dimon** becomes COO and later CEO.

2005

FHA Commissioner Montgomery brings subprime concerns to the attention of the Bush administration.

Home purchases, 28% for investment and 12% vacation homes.

Apparently one **Mr. Greg Lippman of Deutsche** Bank goes to management and tells them the CDO thing is just a **'ponzi scheme'** and I want to make some bets against it. Management says sure enough you go ahead and put **$5 billion on the 'down side'** but don't tell anybody else about this 'cause we gonna still sell mortgage securities to any investors we can find.

The **Securities and Exchange Commission** stops investigating **Bear Stearns** for the way their doing the "pricing, valuation, and analysis" of **mortgage-backed collateralized debt obligations.** *Hum!*

Over at the **Office of the Comptroller of the Currency and the Federal Deposit Insurance Corporation a Mr. Robert Schiller** starts telling folks **'hey look at this bubble all surrounding these houses'.** Recalling the blank faces, Mr. Robert Schiller then decides maybe the world ought to know and puts the information along with the threat of a world encompassing recession in his 2nd edition of, I love this title, Irrational Exuberance.

Federal Reserve Governor Edward Gramlich says hey there might be a bubble here with what those mortgage brokers not having any incentive to be honest and careful

The **Bank of International Settlements** says hey folks these rating agencies are getting paid by the guys putting out these very popular structured financial products, think 'conflict of interest'. *Glad to see they have mastered the obvious.*

Over at the **Office of Thrift Supervision** new rules come a long allowing savings and loans with **over $1 billion in assets** to meet their **CRA obligations** without even having to invest in local communities.

Lehman Brothers starts getting all afternoon soap operaish when some folks start figuring out the mortgage market might be a real bad idea soon. So what happens? Long story short, they short the market and a Mike Gelband, his pals and Dr. Madelyn Antoncic get shown the door for being the messengers of doom.

Hedge funds get all happy when the International Swaps and Derivatives Association make the manner of creating credit default swaps against ABS CDOs way easier. *This sounds like a de-reg. to me or perhaps not. Maybe I just don't have enough education.*

Jackson Hole again Mr. Raghuram Rajan presents a paper called **"Has Financial Development Made the World Riskier?"** *Near as I can tell he thinks 'credit default swaps probably have encouraged greater risk than the financial industry believes or can bear and after the presentation they still don't believe it.*

The Mortgage Insurance Companies of America are starting to sweat because they try to warn the Federal Reserve about 'risky lending practices' going on.

Chase paid $2.2 billion to settle with Enron investors.

JPMorgan Chase screwed the pooch when it rejected an offer from World Com investors of about $1.3 billion and ended up getting stuck with a $2 billion hit for its role in underwriting WorldCom bonds.

2006

Sub-prime mortgages amount to $600 billion 20% of generated mortgages for the year.

Home purchases; 22% for investments and 14% for vacation homes.

In the six months from October 2005 to March 31 2006 the nationwide median home price drops over 3%.

Commerzbank stops investing in sub-primes mortgages.

AIG begins to get cautious and stops covering Credit Default Obligations but MBIA, AMBAC and other of the Monolines continue.

Ameriquest goes to WEB based mortgages and fires a bunch of people.

Fannie Mae decides against a benchmark debt offering. *Seems nobody is interested.*

Merit Financial Inc. closes up shop and files for bankruptcy as sales crash.

Paulson leaves Goldman Sachs to become **United States Treasury Secretary.**

Merrill Lynch follows **Lehman Brothers** to the gallows as they get rid of some folks who think the CDO mortgage market might not be so keen right now. Here is a real kick in the teeth. Some other folks in Merrill Lynch know CDO sales are off but they devise a scheme to keep getting their bonuses and incidentally not get fired like the messengers of doom did. Lo and behold a Merrill company within a Merrill company starts buy CDOs. Resulting in, I don't know but it has to have been a mess.

Allegedly Magnetar Capital started creating CDOs designed to fail and then bet against them to a degree where they would make greater profits if they failed. It is further felt that this process extended the run to a crisis point and made it all worse. These boys say they were just covering their butts. *I can see covering your but to the extent of potential losses but not to a level of extreme profits. That just plain sounds like a bullroar set up to me.*

The Home Construction Index drops in a year over 40%. *Now there is a clue!*

A Nouriel Roubini tells the International Monetary Fund the good old US of A is heading for a big housing bust and a whole lot more.

J.P. Morgan CEO Jamie Dimon decides to **cut the company's exposure to subprime mortgages**.

Goldman-Sachs may have followed suit.

Foreclosures reach epidemic proportions as those with **upside down home loans** start to walk away from the sucking sound.

JPMorgan Chase buys Collegiate Funding Services for $663 million.

JPMorgan Chase buys part of the **Bank of New York Co.** getting access to 338 branches with 700,000 customers covering Connecticut, New York and New Jersey. *Looks like Mr. Dimon is a pretty canny fellow.*

2007

Another Great Recession gets started.

According to the Financial Crisis Inquiry Commission report of Jan 2011 the Financial Sector held $36 trillion in debt and the US GDP is about $14 trillion, 2.57 times GDP.

40% of all subprime loans resulted from automated underwriting. *You don't suppose anybody would ever lie to a machine?*

Sub-prime mortgages are over $1 trillion.

Home sales and prices are falling with foreclosures increasing at an alarming rate. Interest rates climb further threatening the housing industry and bring pressure on the ARMs, interest only and balloon mortgages.

Lehman Brothers leaps further into the real estate market sealing their fate. *This one really makes me wonder. The information is out there that this is a time for caution yet the company basically goes all in.*

January

Ownit Mortgage Solutions files for Chapter 11.

American Freedom Mortgage files for Chapter 7.

February

Mortgage Lenders Network USA, a big subprime lender files for Chapter 11.

HSBC announces that bad debt provisions for 2006 would be cost over $20 billion and fires its head of United States mortgage business

Alan Greenspan, now former Federal Reserve Chairman says things don't look great and the market goes bonkers. Dow Jones off over 400 points the next day.

March

Bernanke says Fannie Mae and Freddie Mac are source of systemic risk and there might be a need for legislation to prevent a financial crisis. *Oops there Ben it is already too darn late.*

New Century Financial, the biggest subprime lender, files for chapter 11.

April

Freddie Mac gets spanked by the **Federal Election Commission** for illegal Campaign contributions with lots of it going to House Committee on Financial Services whose members who are supposed to 'oversee' Freddie. The fine is nearly $4 million, *a pittance. What happened to the people on the committee?*

"Shorts", proprietary bank traders and hedge funds are making money hand over fist all day long as they drive down **the over leveraged banks**.

June

Bear Stearns stops redemptions two of its hedge funds.

Merrill Lynch grabs $800 million in assets from Bear Stearns. *Sharks do eat sharks.*

"There are strong reasons for believing that banks left to their own devices would maintain less capital -- not more -- than would be prudent. The fact is, banks do benefit from implicit and explicit government safety nets...In short, regulators can't leave capital decisions totally to the banks." Sheila Bair, FDIC Chair

July

The Dow Jones Industrial Average closes above 14,000 for the first time ever. *Why I just can't imagine.*

August:

Internationally subprime mortgage backed securities start dragging down 'credit' as the losses are starting to be realized.

American Home Mortgage Investment Corporation (AHMI) files Chapter 11.

BNP Paribas, French, suspends three subprime mortgage investment funds.

Central Banks all over the world start dumping billions in to banking markets to provide liquidity and prop up the system.

Sentinel Management Group files for Chapter 11.

The **Federal Reserve** cuts the discount rate by half a percent.

Ameriquest does the GOB thing.

'One more time with feeling!' Fannie Mae skips another benchmark debt offering.

Non-farm payrolls drop by 4000 for the month.

September

As the worm turns the Economic Symposium in Jackson Hole gets nasty as folks criticize The Federal Reserve for not using regulation and better use of control via interest rates. Alan Greenspan gets raked over the coals for those super low rate policies for inciting the 'housing bubble'. There are warnings of huge reductions in home values

The **Libor** rate jumps to levels not seen since 1998. *I used to watch this one a lot.*

The Federal Reserve drops $31 billion into temporary reserves, 14 day loans, and drops interest rates half a point.

Citibank borrows $3.375 billion and foreign banks borrow over $1.5 billion via the Fed discount window.

Jim Cramer, on The Today Show, tells folks "don't you dare buy a home—you'll lose money." The Real Estate people can't be happy about that.

NetBank goes bankrupt.

UBS, Switzerland, announces a third quarter loss of $690 million, that's US dollars.

Merrill Lynch announces a $5.5 billion loss. Later in the month Merrill Lynch says OOPS that was $8.4 billion down the crudder.

Standard & Poor's says that's "startling". I do believe a cranial rectal inversion has occurred.

Poor Stan O'Neal gets fired by the **Merrill Lynch** board because he tried to sell the company. Merrill Lynch ends up going for lower than a bargain basement price the next year. *I wonder if this was 'startling' too.*

Hope Now Alliance gets going with the Federal government and private industry trying to help out some of those folks caught in the sub-prime mess.

Meanwhile **Alan Greenspan** is grasping the obvious when he is quoted as saying, "we had a bubble in housing" and there could be "large double digit declines", referring to values of homes.

The **"super fund"** to pick up those subprime MBSs that are going south is announced. This super fund is $100 billion, *doesn't seem so super.*

Treasury Secretary Hank Paulson says "the housing decline is still unfolding and I view it as the most significant risk to our economy. … The longer housing prices remain stagnant or fall, the greater the penalty to our future economic growth." So why are you so surprised the darn bubble bursts, didn't read any of the first part of this book in your economic education or maybe you figured you could re-invent a couple of hundred years of economic history.

The **Federal Reserve** lowers the federal funds rate by 25 basis points to 4.5% as Ben Bernanke expresses concern over the housing bubble.

November

The Federal Reserve dumps $41billion to boost the money supply and banks can have cash to borrow at a low rate.

Fannie Mae says oh my lord we just lost $1.4 billion last quarter. Then **Freddie Mac** says oh that ain't nothing we lost $2 billion. The stocks start "down to the bottom of the sea."

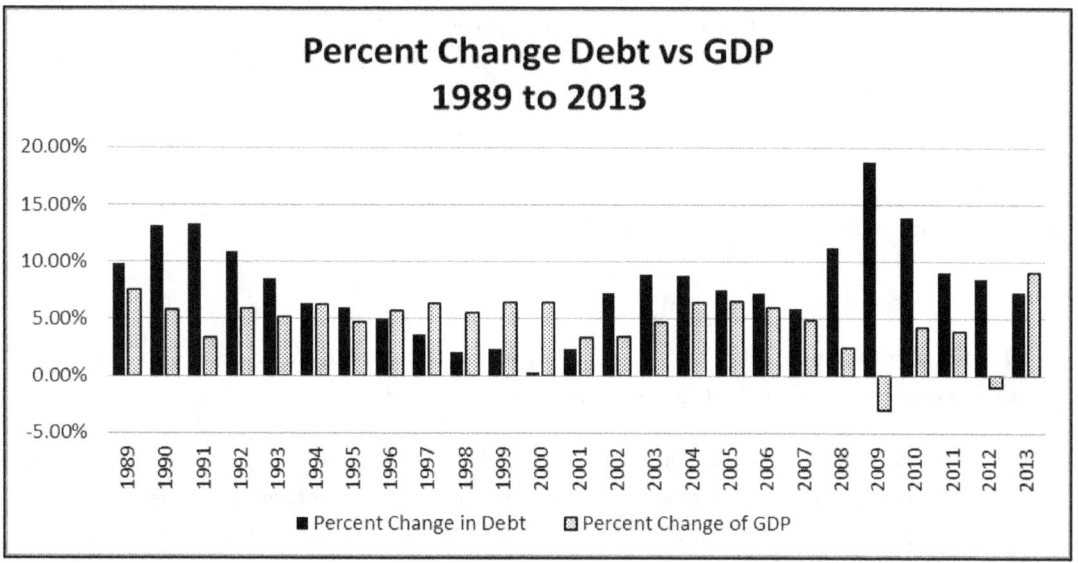

December

President Bush asked for legislation to reform Government Sponsored Enterprises (GSEs) that's Fannie and Freddie, adjust the tax code to help people refinance and support mortgage counseling.

Super Fund goes kaput as banks decide buying crap doesn't make sense.

Goldman Sachs opens a full-service broker-dealer operation in Brazil.

2008

Household debt is over $14 trillion or over 134% of disposable personal income.

Remember when AIG stopped insuring the Credit Default Obligations and the 'monoline' insurance companies like AMBAC and MBIA et al kept at it? Those CDO tranches started to fall like sailors playing 'dead ants' in a Singapore bar. B*een there, done that*. This isn't even the best of it. Those Monolines are mostly in the business of "municipal bond insurance", you know, like your city and mine. Here's the rub, if they don't have an AAA rating they are all upside down and FUBARed. The credit rating agencies are starting to sweat because all those 'great ratings' they had been handing out to the hand that feeds them are starting to smell like Granny's old wooden

227

teeth, *maybe had to be there*, and they reckon there will be some scalp hunting if this keeps going the way it looks like it will go, which is south, and I don't mean Miami with Jimmy Buffett. So they, the ratings agencies, cut the Monolines ratings and the FUBAR thing happens.

They are now all gone, say bye-bye.

January

Depression medication sales soar as the **National Association of Realtors** announces 2007 experienced the biggest decline in existing home sales in 25 years and the kicker is "the first price decline maybe since the "Great Depression."

February

No buying action for auction rate securities.

March

The **FBI** starts arresting people all over the place for mortgage fraud, from sellers to buyers and everybody in between. *Seems the FBI has been paying attention all along.*

Bear Stearns was propped up by the Fed even as their shares were falling like bowling pins. Then **JPMorgan Chase** picks up Bear Stearns, is acquired for $2 a share in a deal backed by the Federal Reserve as they agree to cover up to $30 Billion of possible losses of Bear Stearns' assets acquired in the deal.

Through a whole bunch of deals over the next couple of months the government, largely via Fannie Mae and Freddie Mac; end up guaranteeing over $700 billion in subprime mortgages. Meantime during all this Fannie and Freddie start a couple of programs to encourage people to stay in their homes, Home Stay and Home Possible respectively.

May

Remember UBS the Swiss bank that had a $690 million dollar loss a little while back, well they are cutting loose over 5000 employees.

June

Christopher Dodd, chairman of the Senate Banking Committee, steps in a cow pie as he supports bailout bill that would help subprime mortgage lenders, **Countrywide Bank** being one of them. It might not have so bad if he hadn't received perks from Countrywide like campaign donations, which wouldn't be so bad except he also got 'special friend' consideration on his mortgage. Additionally **Jim Johnson**, head of Fannie Mae and **Kent Conrad**, Chairman of the Senate Finance Committee also got special consideration on their mortgages. *I don't believe any of these guys got the opportunity to make new 'special friends' in the 'big house'.*

The total over-the-counter derivatives notional value is around $680 trillion about $40 trillion are CDS. At this point it might be interesting to note that all of the refined gold in the whole world comes to under $30 trillion at market value.

July

Indymac Bank goes into receivership under the FDIC.

Describing the condition and future of Fannie and Freddie **Barney Frank** says 'solid'.

Treasury Secretary Henry Paulson asked Congress for $25 billion to prop up **Fannie and Freddie**. He gets it, but what is $25 billion compared to the $5 trillion plus on their books. They continue to tank.

The **Housing and Economic Recovery Act of 2008** authorized the Federal Housing Administration to guarantee up to $300 billion in new 30-year fixed rate mortgages for subprime borrowers. The catch is the lenders have to make these new loans at 90% of currently appraised value. *Like 90% is enough for the borrower and I doubt many lenders saw this as an opportunity.*

September

Fannie Mae and Freddie Mac are essentially nationalized.

Bank of America kinda gets talked into picking up Merrill Lynch right in the middle of everything falling apart

Lehman Brothers files for bankruptcy protection. Kaput!

Moody's and Standard and Poor's downgrade AIG. *Big heads up here as the insurance company looks to be in trouble. Actually they are 'sucking eggs'.* That doesn't top the Federal Reserve from throwing them $85 billion to keep them from bankruptcy.

"If we don't do this, we may not have an economy on Monday." Treasury Secretary Henry Paulson and Federal Reserve Chairman Ben Bernanke meet with legislators to propose a $700 billion emergency bailout.

The Federal Bureau of Investigation discloses that it had been investigating a number of corporate lenders for fraud including **Fannie Mae and Freddie Mac, AIG and Lehman Brothers**.

Washington Mutual is seized by the Federal Deposit Insurance Corporation. **JP Morgan Chase** gets its assets for under $2 billion.

The **United States Treasury** announces changes to the tax law that allow a bank to write off all of the acquired banks losses.

October

The Emergency Economic Stabilization Act, creating Troubled Assets Relief Program (TARP) with $700 billion to purchase failing bank assets.

Wells Fargo acquires Wachovia.

Beginning October 6th the stock market has its worst week in 75 years as the **Federal Reserve** announces it will provide $900 billion in short-term cash loans to troubled banks and gets ready to lend over $1 trillion to companies not in the financial industry.

Central banks everywhere are cutting interest rates.

To get money from the EESA funds banks have to give the government equity stakes in their companies and cut executive compensation. The big 5 on Wall Street and a number of others agree.

November

The **Federal Reserve** loans over $50 billion to Dexia Credit of Belgium and German Irish Bank Depfa?!

The **Federal Reserve** makes available makes available $800 billion more.

The **Bank for International Settlements** (BIS) puts out a paper telling banks how to value their assets.

"Investment banking has, in recent years, resembled a casino, and the massive scale of gambling losses has dragged down traditional business and retail lending activities as banks try to rebuild their balance sheets. This was one aspect of modern financial liberalization that had dire consequences." **Vince Cable**

That was one big BOOM and the darn BUST is taking YEARS and YEARS.

"The issue which has swept down the centuries and which will have to be fought sooner or later is the people versus the banks". **Lord Acton**

Aftermath

2009

Barak Obama becomes President 2009 to 2017 Democratic

Governments and central banks came to the rescue with enormous fiscal aid to save the world's economies, trillions and trillions.

November **JPMorgan Chase & Co**. agreed to a $722 million settlement with the Securities and Exchange Commission ending a probe into sales of derivatives to Alabama's Jefferson County had brought Jefferson County near bankruptcy. This coming shortly after Birmingham, Alabama Mayor Larry Langford was convicted on multiple counts of bribery and money laundering related to the bond swaps for Jefferson County.

Goldman Sachs is now about two thirds owned by pension funds and other banks.

"Economics is extremely useful as a form of employment for economists." **John Kenneth Galbraith**

2010

Dodd–Frank Wall Street Reform and Consumer Protection Act

A broad summary can be found at,
070110_Dodd_Frank_Wallstreet_Reform_comprehensive_sum…

A more comprehensive summary can be found at Wikipedia. Dodd–Frank Wall Street Reform and Consumer Protection Act

Here was an opportunity missed. Instead of enacting plain and simple legislation to stop the abuses that got us in to this mess Congress compromised until the meat was gone and now lobbyists are daily trying to tear apart what little effect it could have had.

"For small community banks and credit unions, like those in Central and Northern Wisconsin, the hundreds of new rules will require an estimated 2,260,631 labor hours just for compliance. Those are hours that your local bank or credit union will spend dealing with some Washington bureaucrat instead of focusing on the needs of customers like you." **Sean Duffy**

Some believe it went too far while others think it did not go far enough.

"I mean, Dodd-Frank is strangling small community banks. It doesn't make any difference what the interest rate is. They're not - they're not going to loan the money because they can't make any money for one thing plus the cost of compliance." **Rick Perry**

"Taxpayers have put more than $24 trillion on the line to resuscitate Wall Street after the economic meltdown of last year. With the help of this massive taxpayer support, the nation's largest banks are posting record profits." **Maria Cantwell**

Mozilo paid $67.5 million to the Securities and Exchange Commission on charges of insider trading, misleading investors and disclosure violations.

The Securities and Exchange Commission sued **Goldman Sachs** for fraud as they apparently failed to disclose to investors that Goldman was betting against the "Abacus" mortgage-backed CDO it was selling.

A process called "robo-signing" of the legal documents brings about a foreclosure crisis. This should have brought major jail time.

J.P. Morgan Securities gets fined a record £33.32 million by the UK Financial Services Authority (FSA) for failing to protect around £5.5 billion of clients' money.

2011

Raj Rajaratnam of the **Galleon Group** hedge fund is convicted of conspiracy to commit fraud and securities fraud while making $50 million illegally and is convicted receiving 11 years in the pen.

MF Global files for bankruptcy **and CEO and Chairman Jon Corzine**, a former governor, senator and CEO of Goldman Sachs, whines about his intent in testimony before Congress.

UBS, a Swiss bank, had a rogue trader making over $2 billion in so called unauthorized transactions of a nature constituting malfeasance by one Kweku Adoboli.

Meanwhile in Canada the Sino-Forest Corporation, Mega Brands Incorporated and Portus Alternative Asset Management Incorporated were all under investigation.

FB I

Category	Indictments	Convictions
Corporate Fraud	242	241
Securities and Commodities Fraud	520	394
Healthcare Fraud	1676	736
Mortgage Fraud	over 210 cases pending	

Fewer Americans own homes than in 1998.

"the crisis was avoidable and was caused by: Widespread failures in financial regulation, including the Federal Reserve's failure to stem the tide of toxic mortgages; Dramatic breakdowns in corporate governance including too many financial firms acting recklessly and taking on too much risk; An explosive mix of excessive borrowing and risk by households and Wall Street that put the financial system on a collision course with crisis; Key policy makers ill prepared for the crisis, lacking a full understanding of the financial system they oversaw; and systemic breaches in accountability and ethics at all levels." **The U.S. Financial Crisis Inquiry Commission conclusion**

The US Senate Permanent Committee on Investigations releases the **Levin-Coburn** report, "Wall Street and the Financial Crisis: Anatomy of a Financial Collapse". It presents new details about the activities of Goldman Sachs, Deutsche Bank, Moody's, and other companies preceding the financial crisis. Eliot Spitzer says that if the Attorney General cannot bring a case against Goldman Sachs, after the revelations of the Levin-Coburn report, then he should resign.

After reading the Levin-Coburn report I have to agree with Mr. Spitzer and hope we see some very hefty fines and long jail time.

JPMorgan Chase admitted violating of the Service Members Civil Relief Act by overcharging interest to military personnel and foreclosing on active duty personnel. The bank seems to have stepped up to correct it errors appropriately.

2012

Flash: 25% of the big United States banks **likely unable to survive another recession**.

JPMorgan Chase experiences multibillion-dollar trading losses by Bruno Michel Iksil. *The 'big dog' got bit by a whale.*

Libor Scandal – It rather looks like the London Interbank Offered Rate was manipulated to provide funds for banks like Barclays and the Royal Bank of Scotland to the tune of around $6 billion. This was naturally to the detriment of others like clients in the United States.

"Much of what Germany and France have done in the rescue of Greece has also helped German and French banks, who for a long time were major creditors for Greece and Greek banks." **Mario Monti**

The **Facebook IPO** screws the pooch and small investors as income estimates are cut and nobody tells the little guy.

The **Euro Debt Crisis** is well underway with Greece 'seeming' to be bailed out as recession grows in Europe.

Knight Capital has a software glitch that's cost them a bundle.

Chinas' economy slows probably more than is being stated by their government.

Stanford 'Certificates of Deposit' Ponzi scheme sentence of 110 years.

Jerome Kerviel, a **rogue** junior trader at **Societe Generale**, a French bank, gets 5 years after costing the bank up to 4.9 billion Euros in 2006 to 2008.

Financial lobbyists assault Congress sponsoring bills that would gut Dodd-Frank by making foreign affiliates of US firms exempt from Dodd-Frank restrictions and regulations.

As of close of business 2012 the top ten U.S. banks by assets are…

1 JP Morgan Chase		6	Morgan Stanley
2 Bank of America		7	U.S. Bancorp
3 Citigroup		8	Bank of NY Mellon
4 Wells Fargo		9	HSBC North American Holdings
5 Goldman Sachs		10	Capital One Financial

2013

Standard & Poor's lawsuit alleges they mislead investors and might pursue $5 billion in damages. That is not enough.

HSBC is too big to Jail – you gotta look this one up.

"Institutions develop because people put a lot of trust in them, they meet real needs, they represent important aspirations, whether it's monasteries, media, or banks, people begin by trusting these institutions, and gradually the suspicion develops that actually they're working for themselves, not for the community." **Rowan Williams**

Financial lobbyists are at it again focusing their attack on Title VII, derivatives.

H.R. 992   "Swaps Regulatory Improvement Act" Repeals the non-bailout of swaps related   activities and entities.

H.R. 1062   "SEC Regulatory Accountability Act" Requires cost-benefit analysis of any new rule be it can be adopted.

H.R. 1256   "Swap Jurisdiction Certainty Act" Allows US companies with foreign offices exemption from US regulations concerning derivatives swaps if traded in that foreign office and if the Securities and Exchange Commission and the CFTC determine that the rules of that country are broadly equivalent to US rules.

Fortune Magazine – The Gray Art of Insider Trading and what the SAC Capital Case tells us about this murky world by Roger Parloff.

"I have never seen more Senators express discontent with their jobs....I think the major cause is that, deep down in our hearts, we have been accomplices in doing something terrible and unforgivable to our wonderful country. Deep down in our heart, we know that we have given our children a legacy of bankruptcy. We have defrauded our country to get ourselves elected." — John Danforth (R-Mo)

So why didn't they actually put the banks in their place and protect the nation and each individual?

I like quotes so here are some more....

"Don't reward bad behavior. It is one of the first rules of parenting. During the financial cataclysm of 2008, we said it differently. When we bailed out banks that had created their own misfortune, we called it a 'moral hazard,' because the bailout absolved the bank's bad acts and created an incentive for it to make the same bad loans again." **Eliot Spitzer**

"We need to think deeply about whether we can sustain banks that are not only too big to fail, but potentially too big to bail." **George Osborne**

"On banks, I make no apology for attacking spivs and gamblers who did more harm to the British economy than Bob Crow could achieve in his wildest Trotskyite fantasies, while paying themselves outrageous bonuses underwritten by the taxpayer. There is much public anger about banks and it is well deserved." **Vince Cable**

"I am afraid that the ordinary citizen will not like to be told that the banks can and do create and destroy money. And they who control the credit of a nation direct the policy of governments, and hold in the hollow of their hands the destiny of the people." **Richard McKenna**

The Affordable Care Act divides the country. Apparently some believe being lied to yet again makes' the proposition null and void while others feel, so what, if that's what it takes.

Pondering Points

They sure have stuck it to us!

Balderdash & Poppycock!

Skipping merrily hand in hand down the primrose path on our way to perdition we did this to ourselves, each and every one of us with dogged determination had a hand in the financial debacle we endure now and will likely endure again. Whether those hands actively supported or were involved directly in creating and encouraging this crisis or whether those hands merely jumped on the wagon by making foolish/greedy decisions or whether those hands simply did not see or care what was happening and happily went about their own pursuits all hands contributed to this mess.

The past few decades we have struggled to cure ailments of poverty, healthcare and welfare. We have experienced fervent discourse concerning guns in private hands, the position of religion in our society and to define what is adequate and proper education for our children. All the while personal and public debt has buried government and persons with a burden to liberty the founders foresaw as a threat to this Republic greater than armies. Despite these warnings we rushed to garb ourselves in chains of debt in the name of what, seemingly good intentions or maybe not so much. Look at the 'interest on the debt chart' in the back of the book; then look in a mirror and tell yourself this is sustainable and this wasn't a mass insanity. As we sought to resolve issues before the Republic we failed to learn from history and freed the financial institutions from regulation to lead us to ruin again. Enough! Be gone damn sprite!

Was there greed involved? Were there feelings of helplessness? Was there apathy? Was there corruption? Was there criminal activity? Were we busy with our lives? Likely all the aforementioned and more fostered this collapse. Perhaps the distractions of factionalism focused our attention on issues manufactured. Perhaps deregulation of the financial institutions was served up as a benefit when in reality it was for political profit. Surely all this and more contributed to the collapse. Maybe the 'Revolving Door' between government and Wall Street was the primary culprit. Maybe, just maybe, it was us. Maybe we just failed to deserve financial stability in this Republic because we didn't dedicate ourselves to deserving the opportunity to govern ourselves. It looks to me that every move to deregulate or avoid regulation was touted with Balderdash & Poppycock that told us it would benefit us and our economy.

About now you may be thinking some are more culpable than others. True enough that some were more actively involved than others and those same persons should have known better. The members of the Treasury, the Comptroller of the Currency, The Federal Reserve Board, bankers of all manner, the ratings agencies, insurance agencies, members of congress and Presidents all should have known better and seen this coming a long way off or maybe the system in place blinded them. But it appears they didn't see it until it was likely too late to have stopped an eventual collapse of some kind. More than likely they were all too caught up in the Balderdash & Poppycock to brace the issues and trust the American people with accurate information.

Equally the American people were all too accepting of the Balderdash & Poppycock being presented to us. We just weren't involved and engaged enough to see what was coming in time to avert the worst. Even now there are entirely too many folks sitting on the sidelines and scratching their heads. The technology of today, where a person can get on the internet and access the laws on the books or the laws being considered, the financial statements of large businesses or any of hundreds of documents leaves no room for any excuse not to know what is about or what may be happening.

When some started asking questions the stage had been set and damage was going to be done. So why wasn't something done earlier? Some folks did indicate there might be a problem developing but were shushed or ignored as 'doomsayers'. Factionalism, also known as political finger pointing certainly had a role here too. Factionalism is perhaps the greatest danger to the Republic according to Alexander Hamilton. Factionalism also limits the issues or questions we consider each election because the two primary factions are just trying to limit what we consider as we go to the polls so they can control the arena of ideas to their benefit. Those in or seeking power were entirely too interested in taking political advantage of the situation or muddying the waters so their fault could not be seen. Denial may have played a part or ignorance by choice could have played a small part.

The pursuit of power by the factions surely created and sustained a fog of political issues, denying realities, designed to sustain power by appealing to various portions of the population. In the course of the struggle over the last four decades or so we have moved to acme of choice between central and totalitarian government, unrestrained free market capitalism, neither of which I find appealing. The choices presented had little or nothing to do with long term sustainable benefit.

Democracy, liberty, freedom, financial security and anything else we fancy as rights is not for the faint of heart, the lackadaisical, weak spirited, lazy, cowardly, timid, too busy, ignorant or any of dozens of other adjectives. These rights require active knowledgeable participation sometimes to the point of 'demanding' attention and satisfactory answers. The effort is not easy. The effort is difficult and time consuming. The effort is also a never ending endeavor. No one living now will see a complete and satisfactory conclusion to their efforts. Rights are not given they are defended.

The political/economic environment is such that the largest financial institutions and multinational corporations have become the latest Barons of the world, effectively royalty without borders. They seemingly are above the laws of states and nations because the mere threat of any of them failing or deserting an area brings such a morbid fear of economic collapse and the accompanying suffering few uncorrupted officials dare try bringing them in to line or to prosecute the heads of these institutions.

Maybe the collapse threat is a myth. After all any institution could be sold off as any bankrupt entity could with many adequately financed sharks circling for the tidbits. What would the downside be? Surely it would have a 'chilling effect' on the activities of other banks. The implied threat is they take their money and go play someplace else. But where else can they go? Maybe they really can't.

Russia is out simply because the political elements, governmental and non-governmental would simply eat them and spit them out any time it would suit the Russians, after all they have defaulted on their financial obligations twice before and are still functioning. China is out simply because China is a game all by itself with adequate history of absorbing or consuming anything doesn't suit their goals. Africa is out simply because the factions are so deeply rooted all they could finance is war without winners and that won't provide a stable or reliable return on investment. South America perhaps has some prospects right up until time some government introduces them to the convenience of a firing squad which they have done from time to time. South East Asia is another possibility, good luck with that. Western Asia has lots of resources but has no stability what with borderless religious activities and conflicts. Europe has a history all its' own and currently has few prospects of a booming economy without stable trade relations, beside Russia still wants to eat Europe. The fact is the world is not nearly stable enough for the banks to simply decide to not play well with others when put to the question. The one historical out for banks is financing war in general or lately drugs. Hum?

May of 2014 the Justice Department is discussing the impact of criminal charges against Credit Suisse and BNP Paribas on the stability of the economy. In other words they are weighing the dangers of allowing criminals to be prosecuted against the dangers of allowing criminals to keep being criminals. This is a no brainer to me. Throw them in the stocks!

Dodd-Frank in reality does nothing to truly guarantee the public's safety from the risk from excesses of the largest financial institutions. As of this writing the reserve requirements of Dodd-Frank have not been met and extensions are being requested by financial institutions. When the collapse came there was already in place systems to deal with Fannie and Freddy yet those systems were not used, just why I still do not know. The point is when the stuff hit the fan the persons in place to protect the economy at the time chose different methods and one Congress is unable to force a later Congress to act in a certain way. Hence the never ending battle or as a far better mind than any I have ever met put it, "The price of liberty is eternal vigilance."

So what does the financial industry have to do with liberty? The answer is everything in our economy. Part of the issue is whose money is it anyway? The money I refer to is ours that we have in savings, public retirement funds, 401K's and any number of investment vehicles we as individuals place for investment or retirement savings. Also in a sense the money issued via the Federal Reserve is ours as our government guarantees the loans made to put it in circulation. In the end all liabilities are ours on our shoulders yet the financial institutions behave as though they have no responsibility to us and the pieces of our lives our money represents. Judging by the number cases against financial institutions we see I wonder why some have not been treated as 'criminal enterprises'.

Some Whys

Why aren't there more folks from the financial industry in jail?

Why are we allowing the 'Revolving Door' to continue?

Why do we allow the financial industry to make such large donations to political candidates?

Why do we swallow all the Balderdash & Poppycock the politicians and bankers toss our way?

Why does the media feed us Balderdash & Poppycock and incomplete reporting?

Why are the financial institutions still in non-banking businesses like aluminum?

This chronology was meant to provide some perspective and many places to start looking should you decide you or your progeny are worth the effort. This chronology was never meant to provide solutions or answers because if you don't put it together yourself you just won't really get it and my answers probably won't be your answers. The project was done by me for me. It is published because a few who read parts of it kept saying I should.

Whatever else you gain from this will be done by you and for you. That is not to say it cannot be done by people sharing in the efforts and then sharing with others. That is actually a good idea. A primary point I will articulate is look out for the Balderdash & Poppycock that distracts from the real and material questions. Challenge your own point of view to ensure its' validity.

Dodd-Frank has not and will not do enough to reign in the financial institutions. Those institutions need to be rendered until none is too big to be allowed to fail or jail. The commercial and investment banking need to be separated again.

The Brown-Vitter bill seems to add a level of safety to our money and our economy but not enough.

Rules concerning financial institutions and politicians

Rule 1   If 'they' are doing it behind closed doors (without transparency and regulation) we are getting screwed. We might be getting screwed anyway.

Rule 2   Bubbles burst, always!

Rule 3   Any time somebody tells you 'You're not capable of understanding something' you're getting screwed.

Rule 4   If you don't understand an explanation somebody is giving you, they probably don't either or they don't want you to understand.

Rule 5   If it can't be explained in 50 words or less it's all Balderdash & Poppycock.

Rule 6   The best people for elected office are the ones who don't want the job. It means they are sensible.

Rule 7   Free lunches are the most expensive.

Rule 8   Talking heads are just employees being told what to say. The question is who's pulling the strings and why.

Rule 9   Unintended and unanticipated consequences are the worst.

Rule 10 Just when you think everything is fine disaster is just around the corner.

Rule 11 Races never run are never won.

What is need to make the banks responsible

- Separate commercial and investment banking.
- No bank or financial entity can hold in any form more than three percent of the Gross Domestic Product for a period of two consecutive years.
- Enact a national usury law where no financial vehicle can charge interest more than six percent above prime.
- When a financial institution of any kind is convicted of any type of crime or any type of violation of financial activities laws or regulations or pleads to any of the above that institution and any and all of its affiliates or holdings are forbidden from participating in that activity for a period of twenty years.
- Mandatory prison time for any of the above stated that cause greater than $1 million in loss or damages to any business entity or $10 thousand to any individual and full restitution to the damaged person or entity and forfeiture of personal or business income from said activity.
- Require prison time for all convictions and plead cases of the above.
- Restrict all forms of insuring or swaps to 10 percent of the established value of the transaction.
- Halt tranching.
- Place the Comptroller of the Currency and the Treasury Secretary back on the Federal Reserve Board.
- Require a complete audit of the Federal Reserve.
- Require that any Regulator or employee of any industry of any regulatory industry may not work for, consult for, lobby for or represent that industry or any related industry for period of twenty years after leaving their post.
- Restrict campaign contributions from any form of financial institution and its employees to $50 thousand in total annually.
- When a politician leaves office they be required to completely divest of all monies remaining as campaign funds to the national campaign fund we have the option of checking on our tax forms.
- Restrict the use of private transportation, housing or anything else including money or investment value funds or commodities that could be a gratuity to zero by public officials.
- Completely close all offshore tax advantages and a 50% tax on any money in offshore banks.

As an aside, the 22,000 US citizens that were part of the Credit Suisse program of hiding money ought to be losing that money and doing jail time.

A couple more pondering points

This is a never ending story as each generation must learn anew the ways of the world and the nature of mankind. The relationship between the financial institutions and the people as an issue before this Republic will not be settled in our or our children's lifetimes and likely not for a very long time after that. After all we cannot agree on where we've been, hardly understand where we are now and have no understanding of where we're going. Seems like a concerted effort and flattening the peaks and valleys of the boom and bust cycle is a good thought to hold close.

If you think Dodd-Frank is the fix read this again. One congress cannot limit the next congress and the world changes each moment and you know the financial institutions will do everything they can when they can to find new ways to make money legally or illegally.

Why do the financial institutions need new ways to make money?

All of the rest of the issues before the Republic should not be barriers to folks working towards a common goal such as this. If financial insecurity is not mitigated it will just exacerbate the other issues we need to address as a people and divide us further.

So what do we do you ask?

I don't know about you but I'm going to see how many politicians I can drive up a stump.

If you are not screaming in terror...

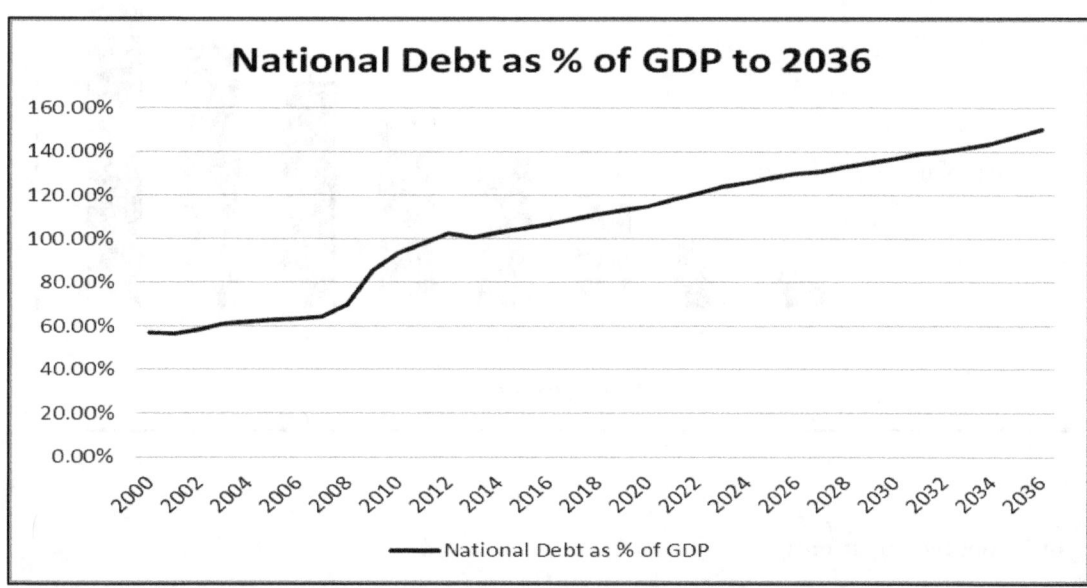

Sometime around 2036 National Debt will be about 150% of GDP or more.

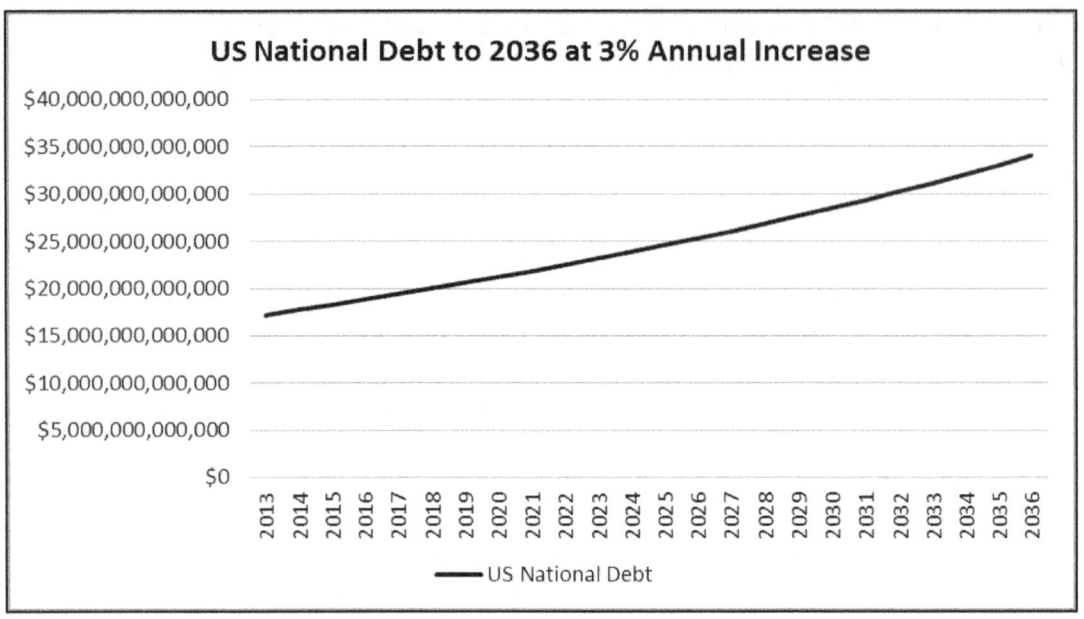

"… The modern theory of the perpetuation of debt has drenched the earth with blood, and crushed its inhabitants under burdens ever accumulating." **Thomas Jefferson**

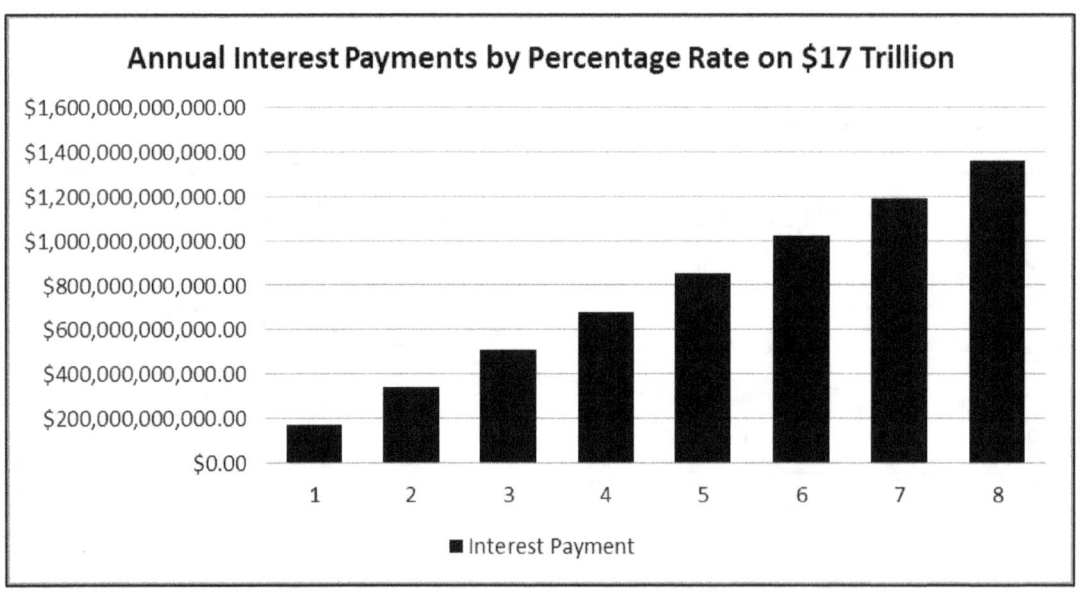

…you're not paying attention.

Challenge and question everything.

What is the American Vision or Identity?

Considering democracy has only been going on for a little under 250 years the country has come far, not far enough, but the people have done better than many had expected back then.

In pursuit of adequately adjusting the financial systems to serve and secure the people terms such as Demon-Krate or Rip-off-liKan (the Ks stand for Kafka), conservative or liberal and the associated prejudices will not serve well.

The entire financial system reminds me of the old saying about the local crap game. "Sure it's crooked but it's the only game into."

This could go on and on becoming a convoluted quagmire and enough is enough so good-bye, good luck, good hunting, good etc. etc., point made, adios.

Best Regards

Mike

Email at balderdashandpoppycock@gmail.com

www.facebook.com/balderdash&poppycock   discussion board available

P.S. I tried to find some happy quotes about banks, didn't find any.

Resources

ABC, Bureau of Economic Analysis, Bureau of Labor & Statistics, Business Week, CBS, Census Bureau, CNN, CNN Money, Commerce Department, Congressional Budget Office, Cornell Law, Denver Post, Department of Commerce, Fannie Mae, Federal Bureau of Investigation, Federal Bureau of Land Management, Federal Deposit Insurance Corporation, Federal Reserve, Forbes, Freddie Mac, Fox News, General Accounting Office, History Orb, United States House of Representatives (US), Huffington Post, Inflation Rate dot com, International Monetary Fund, Justica, LA Times, Library of Congress, London Times, Lone Star College – Kingwood, Men to Match My Mountains, Money Magazine, MSNBC, NBC, New York Journal, New York Times, Office of the Comptroller of the Currency, Office of Management and Budget, Open Jurist, Oyez, Ralph Nader, Reuters, Rolling Stone, Security and Exchange Commission, United States Senate, Silver Commission of 1876, Congressional, Sound Money, Supreme Court of the United States, The Library of Congress, The Street, The Wall Street Journal, United States Treasury, White House, Wikipedia, World Bank and hundreds of blogs and other sites that gave me direction and stimulated ideas.